D1036796

NATURAL LIFE

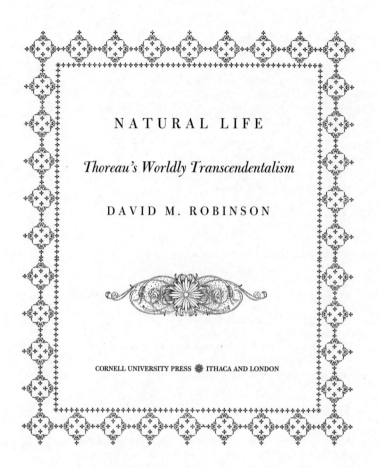

NATURAL LIFE

Thoreau's Worldly Transcendentalism

DAVID M. ROBINSON

CORNELL UNIVERSITY PRESS ❈ ITHACA AND LONDON

Copyright © 2004 by Cornell University

All rights reserved. Except for brief quotations in a review, this book, or
parts thereof, must not be reproduced in any form without permission in
writing from the publisher. For information, address Cornell University
Press, Sage House, 512 East State Street, Ithaca, New York 14850.

First published 2004 by Cornell University Press

Printed in the United States of America

Design by Scott Levine

Library of Congress Cataloging-in-Publication Data

Robinson, David, 1947-
Natural life: Thoreau's worldly trancendentalism / David M. Robinson.
    p. cm.
  Includes bibliographical references and index.
  ISBN 0-8014-4313-X (cloth: alk. paper)
  1. Thoreau, Henry David, 1817-1862—Knowledge—Natural history.
2. Transcendentalism in literature. 3. Transcendentalism (New England)
4. Natural history—New England. 5. Nature in literature. I. Title.
  PS3057.N3R63 2004
  818'.309—dc22

                                                    2004010398

Cornell University Press strives to use environmentally responsible suppli-
ers and materials to the fullest extent possible in the publishing of its
books. Such materials include vegetable-based, low-VOC inks and acid-
free papers that are recycled, totally chlorine-free, or partly composed of
nonwood fibers. For further information, visit our website at www.cor-
nellpress.cornell.edu.

Cloth printing   10 9 8 7 6 5 4 3 2 1

For Gwendolyn, Elena, and Paul
And Eli!

CONTENTS

Acknowledgments
xi

Abbreviations
xiii

INTRODUCTION
I

CHAPTER ONE: AN ORIGINAL RELATION TO THE UNIVERSE
9

CHAPTER TWO: THE SCRIPTURE OF ALL NATIONS
29

CHAPTER THREE: NO HIGHER HEAVEN
48

CHAPTER FOUR: DEVOUR YOURSELF ALIVE
77

CHAPTER FIVE: LIVING POETRY
100

CHAPTER SIX: THE ACTUAL WORLD
125

CHAPTER SEVEN: LIFE WITH PRINCIPLE
148

CHAPTER EIGHT: LEAF, FRUIT, SEED: NATURE'S GREAT CIRCLE
176

Epilogue
202

Notes
205

Bibliography
221

Index
231

Dwell as near as possible to the channel in which your life flows.

THOREAU

JOURNAL, MARCH 12, 1853

ACKNOWLEDGMENTS

A century and a half after the publication of *Walden*, Thoreau's message and example are growing in value and consequence. The course of modern life, with its increasing hurry, complexity, and pervasive insecurity, has given an ever-renewing potency to Thoreau's message of simplicity, complete alertness, and determined principle.

This book has evolved through years of reading, discussing, and teaching the works of Thoreau and his Transcendentalist colleagues, and it owes much to many students, fellow teachers, and Thoreau enthusiasts. I am grateful to Dennis Martin, with whom I first read and taught *Walden* at the University of Wisconsin, and to the late Walter Harding, whose address to the Pacific Northwest American Studies Association and subsequent visit to Oregon State University in the late 1970s deepened my engagement with Thoreau's rich literary and ethical achievement. The exuberance and generosity of his approach to scholarship made a deep impression on me. Several Transcendental colleagues—Lawrence Buell, Philip F. Gura, Joel Myerson, and Robert D. Richardson Jr.—have provided me with scholarly examples and invaluable collegial support. And I cannot fail to mention my kindly taskmasters, David J. Nordloh and Gary Scharnhorst, who have allowed me the chance to try to read almost everything Thoreauvian over the past decade for *American Literary Scholarship*.

My colleague Michael Oriard read an early draft of this manuscript and provided important help, and I have also received valuable suggestions on parts of the work, at various stages, from Richard J. Schneider, Wesley T. Mott, Robert Burkholder, and Lawrence Buell, each of whom I thank. I am grateful to the Thoreau Society and to its officers, Sandra Harbert Petrulionis and Laura Dassow Walls, for opportunities to air parts of the work in progress at meetings of the American Literature Association and the Modern Language Association, and to Barry Andrews, who has deepened my recognition that Emerson and Thoreau continue to be living voices. The English Department at Oregon State University and its chair, Robert Schwartz, have been a constant source of crucial support, and I owe particular thanks to the Center for the Humanities at Oregon State University, where much of the work was drafted during a fellowship year in 1999–2000. And always, the love and support of my wife, Gwendolyn, and my children, Elena and Paul, has sustained me.

I am grateful to the following publishers for permission to reprint in revised form earlier versions of parts of this work: "'Unchronicled Nations': Agrarian Purpose and Thoreau's Ecological Knowing," *Nineteenth-Century Literature* 48 (1993):326–40, © 1993 by the Regents of the University of California. Reprinted by permission of the University of California Press. "Thoreau's 'Ktaadn' and the Quest for Experience," in *Emersonian Circles*, ed. Robert Burkholder and Wesley T. Mott (Rochester: University of Rochester Press, 1997), 207–23. Reprinted by permission of the University of Rochester Press. "The Written World: Place and History in Thoreau's 'A Walk to Wachusett,'" in *Thoreau's Sense of Place: Essays in American Environmental Writing*, ed. Richard J. Schneider (Iowa City: University of Iowa Press, 2000), 83–92. Reprinted by permission of the University of Iowa Press.

D. M. R.

Corvallis, Oregon

ABBREVIATIONS

The following abbreviations are used for parenthetical documentation in the text.

CEP Thoreau, Henry David. *Collected Essays and Poems*. Ed. Elizabeth Hall Witherell. New York: Library of America, 2001.

Corr Thoreau, Henry David. *Correspondence*. Ed. Walter Harding and Carl Bode. New York: New York University Press, 1958.

CW Emerson, Ralph Waldo. *The Collected Works of Ralph Waldo Emerson*. Ed. Alfred R. Ferguson et al. 6 vols. to date. Cambridge: Harvard University Press, 1971–.

EEM Thoreau, Henry David. *Early Essays and Miscellanies*. Ed. Joseph J. Moldenhauer and Edwin Moser, with Alexander C. Kern. Princeton: Princeton University Press, 1975.

ELet Emerson, Ralph Waldo. *The Letters of Ralph Waldo Emerson*. Ed. Ralph L. Rusk (vols. 1–6) and Eleanor Tilton (vols. 7–10). New York: Columbia University Press, 1939–95.

FS   Thoreau, Henry David. *Faith in a Seed: "The Dispersion of Seeds" and Other Late Natural History Writings*. Ed. Bradley P. Dean. Washington, D.C.: Island Press, 1993.

J   Thoreau, Henry David. *The Journal of Henry D. Thoreau*. Ed. Bradford Torrey and Francis H. Allen. 14 vols. Boston: Houghton Mifflin, 1906.

JMN   Emerson, Ralph Waldo. *The Journals and Miscellaneous Notebooks of Ralph Waldo Emerson*. Ed. William H. Gilman, Ralph H. Orth et al. 16 vols. Cambridge: Harvard University Press, 1960–82.

JP   Thoreau, Henry David. *Journal*. Ed. John C. Broderick, Robert Sattelmeyer, Elizabeth Hall Witherell et al. 7 vols. to date. Princeton: Princeton University Press, 1981–.

MW   Thoreau, Henry David. *The Maine Woods*. Ed. Joseph J. Moldenhauer. Princeton: Princeton University Press, 1972.

RP   Thoreau, Henry David. *Reform Papers*. Ed. Wendell Glick. Princeton: Princeton University Press, 1978.

Trans   Myerson, Joel. Ed. *Transcendentalism: A Reader*. New York: Oxford University Press, 2000.

Wa   Thoreau, Henry David. *Walden*. Ed. J. Lyndon Shanley. Princeton: Princeton University Press, 1971.

WE   Emerson, Ralph Waldo. *The Complete Works of Ralph Waldo Emerson*. Ed. Edward Waldo Emerson [Centenary Edition]. 12 vols. Boston: Houghton Mifflin, 1903–4.

Week   Thoreau, Henry David. *A Week on the Concord and Merrimack Rivers*. Ed. Carl Hovde et al. Princeton: Princeton University Press, 1980.

WF   Thoreau, Henry David. *Wild Fruits: Thoreau's Rediscovered Last Manuscript*. Ed. Bradley P. Dean. New York: W. W. Norton, 2000.

NATURAL LIFE

Introduction

Returning on the Concord River from a week's boating trip with his brother John, his impending reentry into society much on his mind, Henry David Thoreau lamented the artificial and disjointed life that he must again face: "Men nowhere, east or west, live yet a *natural* life, round which the vine clings, and which the elm willingly shadows. Man would desecrate it by his touch, and so the beauty of the world remains veiled to him. He needs not only to be spiritualized, but *naturalized*, on the soil of the earth" (Week 379). As we find the passage in the last chapter of *A Week on the Concord and Merrimack Rivers*, Thoreau's lament intimates his melancholy realization that his brief sojourn on the river with his brother is coming to a close, and voices the observation that surfaces so persistently throughout this book, and all Thoreau's writings: men and women lead lives against the current of nature, unfulfilling lives that align them against their own deepest needs and instincts. His yearning for a "natural life" carries an implicit resolution, a new determination to bring the life of the river home with him. It is as if he returns to Concord to begin his life anew.

The resolution to live a natural life which Thoreau attributes to the remembered self of his river narrative actually reflects the much-changed man who has reconstructed the journey as an act of determined authorship and personal myth making. Some two years after their return, John Thoreau died, in agony, from a tetanus-infected cut, while Henry Thoreau watched helplessly to the end, and then came near death himself from severe psychosomatic symptoms of his brother's disease. One of the most arresting and complex incidents in Thoreau's life, the case of "sympathetic" lockjaw that shocked and terrified his family and friends in 1842, was a dramatic revelation of the depth of his love for his brother, and a sign of the emotional trauma of so closely witnessing John's brutal death. It also seems to have been a self-imposed punishment for the sin of surviving while one more worthy to live was taken.

By the time Thoreau had recovered fully enough to memorialize his cherished week with John some six years later, he had moved to Walden Pond and initiated the experiment in solitude that became the emotional and creative watershed of his life. This trial of returning to life's fundamentals, perhaps the first significant act of complete self-direction in Thoreau's life, required a transforming confidence and an orientation to activism that altered his self-conception and his patterns of behavior and social interaction. It was not Thoreau's return to Concord after the 1839 boating trip but this subsequent withdrawal to Walden that initiated what seemed to be a new, "natural" life for him. Life by the pond, his own and that of the animals and plants around him, gave him the ability to reenact imaginatively that moment of return as a moment of redemption. Thoreau was now building the life that, in the aftermath of John's death, he had believed himself unworthy to live.

Although John's death was certainly the primary emotional crisis of Thoreau's life, it also deepened another crisis that simmered throughout his early and middle twenties—what we might call a crisis of vocation. Thoreau is a modern cultural hero in part because of his trenchant and courageous critique of the bondage of tedious and deadening work in the modern world. His own prolonged struggle to find a fulfilling vocation underlies that critique. Teaching had been his initial vocational path. Thoreau's first experiment in teaching ended in his resignation because of a conflict over his classroom discipline and his reluctance to administer corporal punishment. But for several years after that incident, he and John were successful partners in their own private school, an undertaking that produced an income and kept them together in a satisfying communal enterprise. Their 1839 boating trip had been a shared vacation from their schoolmastering duties. John's delicate health, however, forced him to give up teaching in the spring of 1841, and Henry was unwilling to carry on with the school alone. The ending of this shared enterprise left Thoreau rudderless, for John had in many ways been a source of stability and guidance for him. John's sudden and unexpected death a year later dramatically emphasized Thoreau's lack of a secure sense of vocation and purpose.

Left only with sincere but somewhat vague literary ambitions, Thoreau gravitated increasingly toward Ralph Waldo Emerson in the early 1840s, finding in the Emerson household solace, friendship, mentoring, room and board, and encouragement for his literary growth. He developed a strong relationship with Emerson in which he played a complex role as friend, critic, pupil, secretary, gardener, and family handyman. His close work with Emerson on the *Dial* was particularly important; the short but influential life of that journal (1840–44) offers one of the best handles on the movement of new ideas that had come to be known as Transcendentalism. Working with Emerson and the network of *Dial* authors put Thoreau in contact with the freshest thinking in America at that moment.

But there was a persistent quality of apprenticeship in Thoreau's relationship with Emerson. Intellectual nurturing, professional encouragement, and stable emotional support were exactly what Thoreau needed in the early 1840s, especially in the immediate aftermath of John's death, but apprentice was not a role that he could comfortably play forever. His unsuccessful stint in 1843 as a tutor for the children of Emerson's brother William in New York was a first move toward independence, an experiment that suggests that both Thoreau and Emerson understood the ultimate necessity of Thoreau's taking an independent path. It would be Emerson again who provided the means for Thoreau's breaking away, by purchasing the land near Walden Pond that Thoreau used for his experiment in simplicity and self-reliant living.

Life at Walden offered Thoreau at least a provisional solution to his vocational dilemma, and the important opportunity to do concentrated literary work. Although his initial literary product was *A Week* (1848), his fame would eventually rest on a quite different work, his account of his life at the pond itself, which would not be completed until 1854, seven years after he abandoned his Walden Pond cabin and returned to Concord.

It is important to recognize the pivotal importance not only of the two years at Walden that Thoreau himself made famous, but also of the seven years that followed, in which he completed his masterwork and determined a new focus and direction for his life. There is no doubt that the two years of concentrated reading, writing, and nature study at the pond had an enormous and positive impact, beginning his transformation from an aspiring but unfocused literary hopeful into an artist with a compelling message. But

Thoreau wrote *Walden* in large part in retrospect, filtering his experience through the somewhat different conditions of the life he was building in Concord. If his Walden sojourn, a withdrawal from society into nature and meditative solitude, represented the beginning of his experiment with a "natural life," in the years that followed he both expanded the meaning of that concept and refined its adaptability and practice. Those years gave us not just *Walden* but the beginnings of a series of intellectual projects of profound significance. If we know only the Thoreau of *Walden*, we have missed an enormously important part of his life, accomplishment, and vision.

Thoreau was already a lover of the outdoors and a skilled woodsman, fisherman, hiker, gardener, and nature observer when he moved to the pond, and his experience there seems to have further kindled his desire to bring human life into a more harmonious accord with nature. He left the pond to return to Concord, but he returned permanently changed. *Walden* is filled with testimony to his observations of nature, and also records those extremely significant moments when Thoreau seemed to lose his separation and detachment as an observer, melting into the scene around him. Two other immersions in the natural world also had an enormous impact on him, and they help us understand the impact of the Walden experiment and the significance of the years following it. The first of these occurred in the summer of 1846, during his Walden stay, when he undertook an excursion into the Maine forest and hiked up its highest peak, Mount Ktaadn. This journey generated one of his most profound discussions of the spiritual impact of the deep wilderness. In coming finally into real "contact" with "the *actual* world" (MW 71) on his descent from Ktaadn, Thoreau also indicated the larger direction in which his accumulating natural experiences were beginning to take him. Such moments of extreme sensory stimulation which placed him bodily within a natural setting gained increasing authority in the early 1850s in defining both his aims as a writer and his way of life. Such experiences helped him to define his intellectual task as the delineation of the processes and seasonal cycles that governed the flow of natural energy.

Less overtly dramatic than the ascent of Ktaadn, but no less significant in impact, were the moonlight walks that Thoreau began to take with some frequency in the early 1850s, observing by the altering light of the moon the countryside around Concord which he knew so well. To see the world by moonlight and shadow was to see it anew, he discovered, and these experiments in observation began to take on an extraordinary importance in his search for an emotional and psychological balance in his middle thirties.

Escaping into a world that was both familiar and unknown, dreamlike and undeniably real, Thoreau sharpened his already remarkable skill as a nature observer and brought himself into contact with a form of intellectual and imaginative energy known and accessed by few others. This night walker yielded emotionally to a wholly new face of the planet, while also remaining intensely self-aware and precise in his observations.

Thoreau's moonlight walks were part of a larger strategy through which he continued to pursue "natural life" in the early 1850s, a strategy based on a devoted commitment to long daily rambles or "saunters" through the countryside, and a corresponding fidelity to his Journal, in which he meditated on these excursions and recorded the growing mass of natural history observations and data that they generated. The motto for this extremely productive phase of Thoreau's life after Walden is encapsulated in his great essay "Walking": "I think that I cannot preserve my health and spirits, unless I spend four hours a day at least—and it is commonly more than that—sauntering through the woods and over the hills and fields, absolutely free from all worldly engagements" (CEP 227).

The saunterer's way of life was conducive to meditative thinking and writing, and also, as Thoreau gradually realized, to the detailed observation of the cycles of change in the natural world. He had challenged himself in 1851 to begin to learn the names and classifications of the plants around Concord, and as he later remembered, he surprised himself at how quickly and thoroughly he was able to do so. This was valuable not only for introducing him to accepted scientific nomenclature but also for further sharpening the level of detail with which he noted natural phenomena. It also provided him with a more systematic overview of the structures of plants and the interconnections among plant species. The very specific local geography of his walks ("I have travelled a good deal in Concord . . ." [Wa 4]) also meant that of necessity he was studying what we now call ecology, the interactions of whole systems of life within a particular place.

Thoreau was able to enfold his literary ambitions into this way of life largely through his Journal, which became less a medium for drafting lectures or essays for publication than a work whose end was self-contained. But the Journal's variety, dynamism, and comprehensive scope also spawned several later projects that blurred the boundaries between literature and natural history, the texts of which have only recently come to light. *The Dispersion of Seeds* and *Wild Fruits*, substantial undertakings that were left unfinished at Thoreau's death, give us a better picture of how he was melding his poetic and naturalist sides through the growing compilation of natural "facts" and observations that his discipline of walking and journalizing made possible. These later projects also suggest that for Thoreau, the conventional idea of the literary life and the new idea of the natural life seemed to be rapidly diverging, the woods and fields becoming more important to him than the study desk as sites of inspiration. "Who is the most profitable companion?" he asked in 1857. "He who has been picking cranberries and chopping wood, or he who has been attending the opera all his days? I find when I have been building a fence or surveying a farm, or even collecting simples, that these were the true paths to perception and enjoyment. My being seems to have put forth new roots and to be more strongly planted. This is the true way to crack the nut of happiness" (J 10:146).

Thoreau's comment, with its references to organic growth and rootedness as measures of well-being, provides a striking example of how the lives of plants were beginning to serve him as representations of human life as well. It reminds us that his longing for a "natural life" was far more than an intellectual or artistic quest; its aims were productive fulfillment, a fruitful self-realization that Thoreau aptly names "the nut of happiness." Thus Thoreau's new commitment to botanical nomenclature and detailed field observation began to merge with his pursuit of a life that accorded more closely with what he came to see as the imperatives of the natural world. His study of natural life both instructed and reinforced his attempts to live a natural life. "It is in vain to dream of a wildness distant from ourselves. There is none such. It is the bog in our brain and bowels, the primitive vigor of Nature in us, that inspires that dream" (J 9:43). Thoreau affirms the close connection between human life and the wildness of nature, and, by implication, the importance of our own adherence to principles of tough-minded independence.

Thoreau's immersion into studies of natural history in the 1850s coincided with the national crisis over slavery and the dramatic acceleration of abolitionist sentiments in New England after the passage of the Fugitive Slave Law in 1850. Ardent and uncompromising in his antislavery convictions, Thoreau worked hard to maintain a cohesive tie between his commitment to the study of nature and his moral obligation as an opponent of slavery. This was not always easy, as he admitted in "Slavery in Massachusetts," his impassioned reaction to the tragedy of Anthony Burns's return into slavery. "Who can be serene in a country where both the rulers and the ruled are without principle? The remembrance of my country spoils my walk. My thoughts are murder to the State, and involuntarily go plotting against her" (RP 108). Thoreau's admission that he cannot put the political crisis out of his mind, that he is caught up in the events that surround him, is also an admission that the "natural life" he is seeking cannot be reclusive and asocial, and that nature cannot become a means of escape from moral responsibility and political duty. Thoreau's political writing remains thoughtful and moving, and in light of the wide currency of his "Civil Disobedience" in the modern discourse of dissent and political resistance, he has been one of the most influential political thinkers of our era.

Thoreau was not, however, engaged in politics as one interested in power for himself or for any particular group. As he admitted in "Civil Disobedience," it was often better to let the political world take care of itself than to be pulled into fruitless activity. "If the injustice is part of the necessary friction of the machine of government, let it go, let it go: perchance it will wear smooth,—certainly the machine will wear out" (CEP 211). It was when political conflict rose to the level of moral challenge that Thoreau understood its utter necessity. When governmental injustice "is of such a nature that it requires you to be the agent of injustice to another, then, I say, break the law. Let your life be a counter friction to stop the machine" (CEP 211). Woven through his later Journal and natural history writings is the awareness that the natural life must remain indistinguishable from the life of principle. Nature is no refuge from the moral responsibilities that political developments sometimes make inescapable.

Thoreau's later projects were focused on much vaster cycles of time than those generated by the American political system. His Journal shows an increasing fascination with the recurrent phenomenon of seasonal change— he seems to have come most passionately alive in the early spring and early fall—and he meditated extensively on the way these changes suggested both the constant alteration and the fundamental stability of nature. Studying the patterns and mechanisms of plant regeneration in some detail, and devoting particular attention to fruiting and seed production, he found his own way into an understanding of natural development that cohered with that of Darwin, whose *On the Origin of Species* he read with interest and approval soon after its publication. His later projects all seem to derive from the impossibly grand design of compiling a comprehensive "Kalendar" of all of Concord's natural phenomena. Even had he not died in his mid-forties, at a point when his command of both natural history and his own craft as an artist were expanding, this project would probably have remained a Grail-like quest. But this quest was nevertheless productive. Thoreau's deathbed harvest of his still unfinished papers yielded such fruits as "Walking," "Life without Principle," "Wild Apples," and "Autumnal Tints," essays that now seem destined to take an increasingly prominent place in the canons of American literature and of nature writing. The versions of his unfinished studies *Wild Fruits* and *The Dispersion of Seeds* edited by Bradley P. Dean are impressive in their revelation of Thoreau's eye for natural detail, but particularly notable for demonstrating his recognition of the vastness of nature's cycles, which dwarf human measurement and challenge the human capacity to imagine. These cycles teach a humility that is essential to knowing nature, and also to living in accord with it.

CHAPTER ONE

An Original Relation to the Universe

THE PHILOSOPHY OF THE NINETEENTH CENTURY

On a sunny winter Sunday in Concord, February 18, 1838, Thoreau meditated on the aptness of the day's name in a brief journal entry: "Rightly named Suna-day or day of the sun– One is satisfied in some angle by woodhouse and garden fence–to bask in his beams–to exist barely–the livelong day." It is on first glance a casual remark, a mildly contented comment on an excellent turn in the late winter weather and the appealing mood of lassitude that it promises. Soon after he added an entry on the first signs of the changing season: "I had not been out long to-day when it seemed that a new spring was already born–not quite weaned it is true, but verily entered upon existence" (JP 1:29).

The signs of revitalization that Thoreau finds in this hint of seasonal change are mirrored in his own mood. "Nature struck up 'the same old song in the grass', despite eighteen inches of snow, and I contrived to smuggle away a grin of satisfaction by a smothered—'pshaw—and is that all?'" (JP 1:29). Eighteen inches of snow would be for most of us quite enough, but Thoreau's swagger that he could take with complacency the worst that a New England winter had to offer is important beyond any usual concerns about seasonal conveniences and comforts. We can detect the barest of outlines for what would eventually develop into an arduous spiritual discipline in which seasonal change and other cycles and events of nature became signs and patterns for his own acts and attitudes, a spiritual language that required the most careful and attentive study. This particular Sunday, Thoreau saw the promise of a renewal of life, in which he would be both an enthralled spectator and a committed participant.

This moment of contentment, however, is only one part of the complicated texture of Thoreau's inner life, which was also marked by self-doubt, philosophical skepticism, and a growing need for a new vocational direction. These insecurities eventually led Thoreau to his famous experiment at Walden Pond, the act now most closely associated with his name. Facing in his two years at the pond questions that had been growing for a decade or more, he underwent an important period of growth that would advance and clarify, but by no means resolve, the drama of his inner life.

One notable sentence in his Sunday journal entry suggests an important element of his inner struggle, a desire to find in nature a tranquil and enveloping acceptance that would calm his sense of partiality or incompleteness. "One is satisfied in some angle by woodhouse and garden fence," he writes, "to bask in his beams–to exist barely." As innocent as this wish for serenity and self-acceptance may seem, it represented for Thoreau a largely unattainable emotional condition. It is the expression of a man whose intense desire for inner peace itself became, in extremes, the greatest barrier to his attainment of that peace.

Thoreau has much to teach us about the inner life and the conditions under which we can achieve there a just peace. But he teaches us most effectively if we are attentive to the difficulties that he faced, and the corresponding shifts in focus and direction that resulted from those difficulties. He offers an intricate pattern of aspiration and reconsideration, dependent in a fundamental sense on an ever-renewing capability to begin again. New England's dramatic seasonal changes taught this lesson repeatedly, and Thoreau thus became the philosopher of the spring and the fall, a naturalist detective always alert to the waxing and waning of the energies of the forests and fields around him.

Thoreau's private struggles, his restless dissatisfaction with the available models for fulfillment, were not, however, an isolated phenomenon. "The young men were born with knives in their brain," Emerson wrote of the religious and social upheaval in New England in the 1830s and 1840s that came to be known as Transcendentalism. He described "a tendency to introversion, self-dissection, anatomizing of motives" that captures Thoreau's inner turmoil and suggests that this critical inward turn was in part the result of the "many severe shocks" that had been dealt to "the popular religion of our fathers" (WE 10:329–30). In reading Thoreau's journals and letters, one finds an almost instinctive skepticism toward churches, sacraments, creeds, and conventional theologies, any of the formerly accepted patterns of religious expression and growth. As Thoreau came to intellectual maturity in the late 1830s, Emerson was leading an attack on all old institutions, seeking to formulate a new basis for religious belief and for the expression of that belief in action.

Two important encounters during Thoreau's formative years at Harvard College, 1833–37, helped to confirm this skepticism about the value of conventional beliefs and ways of life and to awaken the expectation of a spiritual and social renewal that was at the core of the Transcendentalist revolt. The most important of these was the emergence of Emerson as a prominent spokesman for a revitalized spiritual life. Having resigned his Boston pulpit in 1832, Emerson launched his career as a public lecturer just as Thoreau was beginning at Harvard. He gradually built an audience for lectures that covered a wide range of scientific, literary, historical, and religious issues. In 1836, the year before Thoreau graduated, Emerson published *Nature*, a book that brought together science, philosophical idealism, and poetic perception in an inspiriting call to personal and cultural renewal. In the fall of 1837, after he had graduated from Harvard and begun a short and unhappy stint of teaching, Thoreau met Emerson. At Emerson's suggestion, Thoreau began the Journal that would, more than any other activity, become his life's work: "'What are you doing now?' he asked, 'Do you keep a journal?'—So I make my first entry to-day" (JP 1:5).

"Why should not we also enjoy an original relation to the universe?" Emerson asked with a hint of both defiance and challenge at the beginning of *Nature* (CW 1:7). That new relation was built on a new attention to the natural world and to our modes of perceiving it, and a recognition that the natural world could serve as a crucial source of spiritual revitalization. *Nature* began with an edge of defiance, but moved toward an enraptured vision of new possibility, a dramatic call to a new way of life that must have impressed Thoreau. "So shall we come to look at the world with new eyes," Emerson declared. "Know then, that the world exists for you. For you is the phenomenon perfect. What we are, that only can we see. All that Adam had, all that Caesar could, you have and can do" (CW 1:44–45). Emerson understood that there were many young men and women who, like him, had felt that the social institutions most closely connected with the fostering of personal development, the church and the schools, were failing badly. His counterstrategy was to empower them to take charge of their own development.

Emerson's support was crucially important to Thoreau, and his influence was enormous, but Thoreau was not without an earlier introduction to the restless and questioning spirit of Transcendentalism, and had in fact already become a "Transcendentalist" before he met Emerson or read his work. In December 1835, during his junior year at Harvard, Thoreau began a six-week stint of teaching in Canton, Massachusetts, under the guidance of the local Unitarian minister, Orestes Brownson. Thoreau's work with Brownson was not only his introduction to teaching but also an initiation into the "new views" that came to be known as Transcendentalism. Brownson was a commanding personality and an energetic and forceful intellect, and when Thoreau came into his orbit, Brownson was engaged in some of his most original and influential work. Having freed himself from Calvinism, with its troubling doctrines of innate depravity and election to grace, by embracing Universalism, Brownson had eventually become a disciple of the principal spokesman for New England Unitarianism, William Ellery Channing. Impressed with Channing's unyielding resistance to dogma and his spiritual depth and intensity, Brownson saw Unitarianism as the wave of the future, and had committed himself to making it a theology for the working classes as well as for the elite.

Thoreau responded eagerly to Brownson's conviction that an important philosophical and social transformation was under way. They sat up all night discussing philosophy after they met, and undertook German study together so as to be more receptive to the philosophy that gave the edge to the progressive thinking of the day. These weeks, Thoreau later wrote, "were an era in my life" (Corr 19), and it is here that he first encountered the assumptions about the necessity of spiritual renewal that he would maintain and repeatedly test.[1]

Brownson believed that "religion is natural to man," but in a distinction that was repeated with variations by almost all the Transcendentalists, he argued that religion had to be distinguished from religious institutions.[2] Calling for a reconciliation of the seemingly antithetical principles of "spiritualism" and "materialism," Brownson argued that the materialistic principle had to be recovered in modern religion. "Instead of understanding Jesus to assert the holiness of both spirit and matter," Brownson wrote, the church "understood him to admit that matter was rightfully cursed, and to predicate holiness of spirit alone."[3] There were, Brownson believed, revolutionary implications to be drawn from a recognition of "the atonement" as a reconciliation of the spiritual and the material, and his emphasis on the recovery of the materialistic principle suggests the redemptive potential of a reclaimed material world.

Brownson was an energetic reader who cast a wide net, and when Thoreau met him in 1835, he was deeply engaged with the work of the French "eclectic" philosopher Victor Cousin, who believed that a new and comprehensive philosophical system could be melded from the best elements of the history of philosophy. Eclecticism, as Cousin used it, did not have the contemporary meaning of randomness and odd juxtaposition, but rather meant a progressive synthesis and unity. Cousin argued that the two major philosophical systems of the recent past, Lockean empiricism and Kantian idealism, had each embodied an inhibiting flaw. Kant had established that the mind's categories and modes of perception mediated knowledge, but had also fomented an extreme subjectivity that opened a troubling fissure between the mind and external reality. Locke had shown that philosophy must advance through the observation and testing of the information our senses provide, but had encouraged an excessive "sensualism" that drastically reduced the dimensions of human experience. Cousin argued that these systems had by now revealed both their strengths and their flaws, and that a new synthesis could thus be formulated: "After the subjective idealism of the school of Kant, and the empiricism and sensualism of that of Locke, have been developed and their last possible results exhausted, no new combination is in my opinion possible but the union of these two systems by centering them both in a vast and powerful eclecticism."[4]

Brownson published an exposition of Cousin's philosophy in the *Christian Examiner*, the leading Unitarian journal, in 1836, and that same year adapted eclecticism to the conditions of American religion in his *New Views of Christianity, Society, and the Church*, an initiating work of the Transcendentalist movement. Both these works revealed Brownson's fervent hope for a new era in human religious and social progress. He concurred strongly with Cousin's vision of the progressive nature of history, and his exposition of eclecticism is tinged with a millennialist fervor. He saw his historical moment as one of dramatic and revolutionary change, and while he recognized the importance of the rise of idealist philosophy in response to materialism, he saw it not as a completion or culmination of philosophical development but as a preparatory stage. The future lay in the union of the contrary principles of materialism and spiritualism, a synthesis that preserved the necessary elements of each system and balanced their respective excesses—the "eclecticism" that had been "all but perfected" by Cousin. Brownson declared it "the philosophy of the nineteenth century."[5]

Brownson's utopian conception of a coming era of harmony promised a transformed political world in which cooperation and association replaced competition. It would confirm the holiness of the human being, both soul and body, and transfigure all human activities and institutions. "Civil freedom will become universal," Brownson wrote, and "workingmen will be priests," invested with a reverence due the sacredness of labor.[6] But for Brownson the atonement would bring more than this egalitarian laborer's paradise. The natural world itself would also be transformed in the atonement, embodying the fusion of the material and spiritual that defined "atonement."[7] "The earth itself and the animals which inhabit it will be counted sacred. We shall study in them the manifestation of God's goodness, wisdom, and power, and be careful that we make of them none but a holy use."[8]

Thoreau had no particular love of the settled social order; he was, moreover, receptive to the idea that the natural world was sacred. He found similar ideas, though less prophetically proclaimed, in the work of Wordsworth and Goethe, and also in the new book *Nature* by his as yet unknown Concord neighbor, Emerson. In all of these works, the natural world was being reclaimed as a site of revelation and a source of harmonious energy.

Will this transformation of the natural world that Brownson describes be an actual material transformation of what now exists? Or will we be enabled to see completely what has always already been before us? Brownson's language is ambiguous, leaving the impression at times that the world will indeed be made new, and at others that it is human perception and moral character that will be changed. But the logic of his argument points to a perceptual transformation that will give individuals a clarified or revitalized way of seeing the world they have always partially and imperfectly known. Brownson argued that "the new doctrine of the atonement" reconciled the "warring systems" of spiritualism and materialism, teaching "that spirit is real and holy, that matter is real and holy, that God is holy and that man is holy." By ceasing to understand these as competing theories or conceptions of the world but rather as parts of a larger and inclusive whole, one could begin to comprehend reality in a different and much more exalted way. "Spirit and matter, then, are saved. One is not required to be sacrificed to the other; both may and should coexist as separate elements of the same grand and harmonious whole."[9]

Brownson's insistence on the shared identity of the material and the spiritual was of particular importance to Thoreau. The vigor of Brownson's refusal to diminish the significance of the material or to dismiss the presence of the spiritual allowed Thoreau to see the natural world as the potential embodiment of both principles. His subsequent intellectual life might be described as a preoccupation with precisely this imperative, to see the convergence of fact and truth. The contrasting portraits that later readers have drawn of Thoreau—as an Emersonian mystic or as a more empirically minded field naturalist—originate in this fundamental duality of material and ideal that Brownson was attempting to integrate. Given the caricature of the Transcendentalists in intellectual history as dreamy and otherworldly, it is important to remember Thoreau's early exposure to Brownson's conception of idealism as one of two constituent strands in the fabric of reality.

STRANGERS IN NATURE

Thoreau must have been struck forcibly by Emerson's declaration in *Nature* that "we are as much strangers in nature, as we are aliens from God." Emerson explained this estranged condition in terms that assume the visionary and utopian as the normative state of experience, and make ordinary perception evidence of the fall. "We do not understand the notes of birds. The fox and the deer run away from us; the bear and tiger rend us. We do not know the uses of more than a few plants, as corn and the apple, the potato and the vine" (CW 1:39). Emerson's depiction of the original state of innocence and perfect wisdom, now lost to men and women, is more immediate and more poetically suggestive than Brownson's, and carries an implicit agenda: know the natural world more deeply. What Brownson presented as a prophetic vision of history, Emerson proposed as a plan of action. Even if one did not share Brownson's confidence that history would inevitably progress toward the "atonement" (Thoreau was markedly disinclined to think in theological categories or use conventional theological language), one could nevertheless read in *Nature* an invitation, or a challenge, to reconsider one's patterns of experience or categories of perception.

We know that Thoreau had begun to read *Nature* as early as April 1837, during his senior year at Harvard, and Robert Sattelmeyer notes that "it impressed him deeply."[10] Emerson confirmed Brownson's conviction that a new era was opening, and dramatized this change as an internal revolution as well, tied to a new discipline of perception. In his most famous assertion Emerson proclaimed himself a "transparent eye-ball," merged absolutely into the nature around him while he simultaneously saw it all and felt circulating within himself "the currents of the Universal Being" (CW 1:10). But it was probably not this passage, however dramatic, that impressed Thoreau the most about *Nature*, but rather Emerson's later assertion that "nature is a discipline" (CW 1:23). By this he meant that nature should be seen as the primary teacher of men and women, the source of factual knowledge, and also the means by which each individual could come into the full possession of a more completely developed will and understanding.

Nature, characterized by Emerson as a "phenomenon" rather than inert or static matter, taught growth as its primary lesson. In November 1837, under the title "Discipline," Thoreau expressed a commitment to a patient and persistent program of perceptual growth. "I yet lack discernment to distinguish the whole lesson of to-day; but it is not lost–it will come to me at last. My desire is to know *what* I have lived, that I may know *how* to live henceforth." While Thoreau admits his lack of a larger framework to organize and integrate his accumulating knowledge, he places a provisional faith in the eventual reconciliation of discrete experience with larger truth. "Truth is ever returning into herself," he writes the next day. "I glimpse one feature to-day–another to-morrow–and the next day they are blended" (JP 1:11). He is committed less to a sudden revelation than to a work of patient and disciplined attention in which knowledge emerges in measured stages from a process of many steps.

Although he does not specify the "features" of truth that he is apprehending, it is safe to say that they arose from two sources: the voracious reading that would remain a central part of his daily discipline, and the observations of nature that would grow in both scope and precision over the next two decades. A month later he made an observation about the intertwined processes of nature study and philosophy that would characterize much of his later work: "How indispensable to a correct study of nature is a perception of her true meaning– The fact will one day flower out into a truth. The season will mature and fructify what the understanding had cultivated. Mere accumulators of facts–collectors of materials for the masterworkmen–are like those plants growing in dark forests, which 'put forth only leaves instead of blossoms'" (JP 1:19). Nature's "true meaning," though still only vaguely specified, is the principle by which the various facts of the natural world can be brought into harmony, the unified theory that will show the singularity and ultimate identity of the disparate parts of nature. Like Cousin and Brownson, and now like Emerson, Thoreau saw this work of unifying synthesis as the essential task of philosophy, and the fundamental purpose for the study of nature.

Emerson made one observation near the end of *Nature* that would also be of great importance to Thoreau. Noting the equivalent origins of "the world" and "the body of man," he argued that the world "is a remoter and inferior incarnation of God, a projection of God in the unconscious." But, he adds, the world "differs from the body in one important respect. It is not, like that, now subjected to the human will. Its serene order is inviolable by us. It is therefore, to us, the present expositor of the divine mind. It is a fixed point whereby we may measure our departure" (CW 1:38–39). The will-less natural order preserves and exhibits a perfected structural order that can be seen as the sign of a natural moral order as well. While in some senses Emerson's *Nature* reinforced the traditional conception of humanity as the pinnacle of nature, here Emerson subtly reverses that valuation, making the natural world both a perfected example and a teacher.

Thoreau's remarkable proclivity for natural experience and observation—"He knew the country like a fox or a bird," Emerson wrote (Trans 662)—was thus linked from the beginning with a faith in a unifying system of laws through which the particulars of nature could be more comprehensively understood. This meant that nature study was an inherently philosophical activity, an investigation of the order and meaning of reality. The laws that structured the natural world, Thoreau believed, also structured human consciousness and defined human action. The inner life was therefore inextricably tied to the life of nature.

DRIFTING

Brownson's theory of a redemptive history that would purify nature, and Emerson's call for a renewed perception that would allow us to see nature in its Edenic innocence, formed important points of reference for Thoreau. But his sensibility differed from both Brownson's and Emerson's in telling ways. An adept linguist who was deeply anchored in the Greek and Roman classics and fascinated by the ancient scriptures of various cultures, Thoreau was little inclined to think with Brownson in terms of the progress of Christian history. And while Emerson's enraptured calls to new vision no doubt moved him, his own epiphanies were likely to be grounded in the more mundane and tangible events of the natural world. He was in creative dialogue with both Brownson and Emerson, but he was decidedly a thinker who set his own direction.

Thoreau did, however, share with Brownson and Emerson a commitment to "self-culture," William Ellery Channing's translation of Christian theology into a conceptualization of the developing inner life. The early Unitarian advocates of self-culture reconceived the soul as a growing, dynamic organism that required assiduous cultivation. For Thoreau, who was disposed to see the organic as a measure of value, self-culture meant the discipline of bringing the inner life into harmony with the perfected order of nature.[11]

Thoreau's early journal entries reflect this attention to his inner development but also suggest that his pursuit of self-culture was interwoven with a complex struggle over vocational identity. Emerson's young men "with knives in their brain" were also in some sense displaced persons, unwilling to undertake the paths of life that their culture had laid for them. They waited for a high calling or an appropriate task that never seemed to materialize. Thoreau's vocational crisis was particularly acute, even though he was remarkably adept in a variety of practical skills. It also seems as if the fervor with which he pursued the cultivation of his inner life only exacerbated his difficulties in finding himself a suitable place and a suitable vocational task in the world.

Thoreau's varied and extensive reading and his personal encounters with working thinkers and authors like Brownson and Emerson were an important element of his process of self-culture, but for him, books were indeed for "idle times." However avid his reading, and however strong the pull of the literary life, he seemed to come fully alive only out of doors. The experience of nature was determinative for him, and this disposition grew more decided with time. But Thoreau's "experience" of nature was more accurately a series of discrete experiences, irreducibly separate and distinct in their character. His Journal became a rich resource for both observation and introspection. It is impressively miscellaneous and diverse, always open and responsive to the things he observed in the natural world, and ordered primarily by the sequence of those observations.

Thoreau's problem in compiling the Journal was how to make himself part of the scene that he saw and felt, how to enter fully into the natural world that so compelled him. One impulse was to study natural phenomena intently, to master their particulars. Knowing the particulars of nature would be a form of participation in it, as the human mind became the consciousness of nature, the means by which nature understood itself. Such a knowledge required an accumulation of detailed and verifiable facts, and it was for this reason that Thoreau took note of, and contributed to, the specialized science of his day. But as he understood from the outset, the kind of participatory knowledge that he sought also demanded a more integrative knowledge of the relationships among these facts. That was a more difficult achievement which the new science could not satisfactorily provide him.

Such detailed and comprehensive knowledge was not, however, the only path to achieving the sort of participatory experience of nature that Thoreau sought, and, he sometimes felt, not the best path either. We find him at times seeking a more passive surrender to the natural world, one based less on an intellectual mastery of it than on a sensuous merging with it. In such moments instinctive awareness and the reflex of the senses seemed a higher aspiration than systematic intelligence, and the effort of knowing was actually the principal barrier to be overcome. Taken to the extreme, such an act of complete merger required an extinction of consciousness and a life lived wholly in the body and the senses—a goal that the mind might paradoxically set for itself but that it could hardly achieve through planning or calculation.

The Journal is the best opening we have to Thoreau's pursuit of both factual knowledge and this other kind of bodily or instinctive knowledge. From its beginning the Journal was Thoreau's most important resource in his effort to construct a viable inner life. In some moments, such as the Sunday meditation quoted earlier, he was drawn to a stance of spiritual humility and passivity in which the self was in easy accord with the patterns of life and of nature. In such a mood indolence was a spiritual asset, and an enjoyment of the opulent present displaced any concern about the progress of the soul. The natural world was a gift, and living in the senses was the way one received it.

In other moments, however, Thoreau searched himself for signs of weakness or lethargy, and pressed on himself the urgency of an active pursuit of the moral life as he felt his grasp on it loosening. In moments like these, self-culture became a process of the severest discipline, comparable only to the rigors of military training and war itself. "There was somewhat military in his nature," Emerson later remarked, "not to be subdued, always manly and able, but rarely tender, as if he did not feel himself except in opposition" (Trans 656). Thoreau himself had admitted as much in 1840: "I have a deep sympathy with war it so apes the gait and bearing of the soul" (JP 1:146). The moral life was a disciplined and militant advance. "A man's life should be a stately march to a sweet but unheard music, and when to his fellows it shall seem irregular and inharmonious, he will only be stepping to a livelier measure" (JP 1:146).[12] In this march toward a better condition of existence, purpose and determination become the hallmarks of the self.

Thoreau understood, however, that many of the more important human actions and attitudes have roots in the subconscious or the instinctual, and exploring and defining the limits of self-discipline and self-control were of paramount importance to him in his early and middle twenties. His worried frustration over his inability to exert and sustain an absolute self-control is suggested by an 1841 journal entry: "I find my life growing slovenly when it does not exercise a constant supervision over itself" (JP 1:295). This self-involved, internally conflicted, and somewhat priggish Thoreau is a disquieting figure. The potential nobility of his moral aspiration can seem clouded by an adolescent self-absorption and a worried sense of inadequacy, and his eager fascination with the processes of nature is often accompanied by a troubling fear of disorder. "He was almost shockingly devoid of weaknesses," Robert Louis Stevenson wryly observed. "He was not easy, not ample, not urbane, not even kind; his enjoyment was hardly smiling, or the smile not broad enough to be convincing."[13]

In more constructive and self-confident moods, Thoreau seemed aware of his destructive tendency toward self-surveillance and moral censure. "What offends me most in my compositions is the moral element in them," he wrote in 1842. "The repentant say never a brave word–their resolves should be mumbled in silence. Strictly speaking morality is not healthy. Those undeserved joys, which come uncalled, and make us more pleased than grateful, are they that sing" (JP 1:361). In an 1839 journal entry titled "Self-culture," Thoreau recognizes that his vigilant self-scrutiny may initiate creative expression. "Who knows how incessant a surveillance a strong man may maintain over himself–how far subject passion and appetite to reason, and lead the life his imagination paints?" (JP 1:73). Painting here describes the formation of a life, a merging of the aesthetic with the ethical in the work of character building. "He is the true artist whose life is his material," he wrote in 1840. "Every stroke of the chisel must enter his own flesh and bone, and not grate dully on marble" (JP 1:139). Imagination and diligent craft, the focus and discipline of the artist, thus become the means of living as well as of art.

Thoreau insisted so emphatically on discipline in part because he felt a danger in his own passivity. We may admire his self-discipline, but it seems clear that the more intuitive dimension of his character made him a productive naturalist, an ethical thinker, and an original artist. While he spoke of self-culture as a military campaign to be executed or a blank canvas to be painted, a work of purpose and intention in which will and discipline were crucial tools, he also countered his imperative for a continual effort at self-culture with the realization that purpose itself has its limits. "My most essential progress must be to a sense of absolute rest," he wrote in 1840, in a meditation on the impossibility of knowing or controlling the secret springs of behavior. Using the analogy of instinctive animal behavior to capture the inscrutable quality of human motivation, he admitted that "some questions which are put to me, are as if I should ask a bird what she will do when her nest is built, and her brood reared." Recognizing the impossibility of either fully understanding or satisfactorily expressing himself, he tried to explain that the process of growth must remain enigmatic. "I cannot make a disclosure—you should see my secret.— Let me open my doors never so wide, still within and behind there, where it is unopened, does the sun rise and set—and day and night alternate.— No fruit will ripen on the common" (JP 1:191). Confessing the fundamental mystery of the inner life, Thoreau describes it in terms of the processes and functions of nature, from the bird's nesting behavior to the alternating pattern of night and day. The inner life can be understood only as part of the larger life of nature.

Thoreau represented the mysteries of nature and its processes in the language of stillness, acceptance, and non-resistance rather than militant willfulness. In a series of nine remarkable philosophical aphorisms in an 1840 journal entry (JP 1:143), he describes his program of self-culture in terms that suggest its active or willed pursuit is at times misguided. "He will get to the goal first who stands stillest" runs one of them, implying that any notion of the goal as somewhere beyond the present state of the self is illusory. The best strategy is not to attempt a linear progress but to understand and accept more fully the place one occupies now. In two other aphorisms Thoreau posits forms of stillness or quietism as methods of practical accomplishment. "By sufferance you may escape suffering," he writes, varying the proposition slightly with the admonition, "He who resists not at all will never surrender."[14]

Thoreau's quietism pushed him to examine more closely the apparent analogy between his inner life and the life of nature, and his Journal offers striking examples of the way that certain perceptions of nature could reinforce this paradoxically dynamic passivity. "I must receive my life as passively as the willow leaf that flutters over the brook," he wrote in 1842, using the leaf as an emblem of the sort of surrendered receptivity that he hoped to cultivate within himself. "I must not be for myself, but God's work and that is always good. I will wait the breezes patiently–and grow as nature shall de-termine– My fate cannot but be grand so" (JP 1:371). This desire for the leaf's passivity is mixed with a worried lack of direction which plagued Thoreau throughout his early adulthood. "I feel as if [I] could at any time re-sign my life and the responsibility of living into Gods hands–and become an innocent free from care as a plant or stone." Thoreau's desire to extinguish consciousness and care (to be "a plant or stone") suggests that he indeed feels care-weary, overburdened by the task of setting the correct course for his own program of self-development, and guilty over his lack of progress in achieving his goals. "My life my life–why will ye linger? Are the years short are the months of no account? How often has long delay quenched my aspi-rations– Can God afford that I should forget him– Is he so indifferent to my career– Can heaven be postponed with no more ado.–" (JP 1:371). These outbursts suggest the underlying restlessness and frustration to which the idea of a will-less, passive surrender was clearly a response.

In the passivity of the leaf or the unconsciousness of the stone, Thoreau found images of self-transcendence. "I must not be for myself," he had written, designating his drive toward self-development as a barrier to the course of nature. In place of the linear quality of purposeful development, he proposed another form of self-development after boating one day on Walden Pond: "Drifting in a sultry day on the sluggish waters of the pond, I almost cease to live–and begin to be." He titled the entry "Drifting," connoting the will-less surrender that he found crucial to his spiritual achievement. His distinction between "to live" and "to be" is both elusive and important; it suggests that in ceasing to "live," he surrendered will and purpose and thus began to "be," participating in a more encompassing ex-istence than that of the solitary and isolated ego. Such experiences tran-scend linear time and its mortality. "A boat-man stretched on the deck of his craft, and dallying with the noon, would be as apt an emblem of eter-nity for me, as the serpent with his tail in his mouth. I am never so prone to lose my identity. I am dissolved in the haze" (JP 1:69–70). Like Melville's Ishmael on the masthead of the *Pequod,* Thoreau seems here "lulled into such an opium-like listlessness of vacant unconscious reverie . . . that at last he loses his identity."[15] But for Thoreau there is no recoil from a sensed danger of what Ishmael saw as a deathlike merge with the universe. To let go, to find the crucial capacity of self-forgetfulness, to accept a place among the many other beings in the world, is the crucial spiritual step.

A rich contentment accompanies this mood of quiet passivity, when

Thoreau seems to have found a place beyond the necessity of striving. "Pray what things at present interest me?" he wrote in 1840. "A long soaking rain–the drops trickling down the stubble–while I lay drenched on a last year's bed of wild oats, by the side of some bare hill, ruminating. These things are of moment" (JP 1:120). There is both a meditative quiet and a sensuous presence in this self-description that captures the mood of fullness and realized self-acceptance central to this strand of Thoreau's sensibility. His moments of quietist passivity were moods not of abstraction or disengagement but of a fully realized presence in the natural world.

These moods of will-less but participatory engagement with the natural environment resulted in a habit of mind and expression that emerges in the early Journal and becomes characteristic of Thoreau's thought in *Walden* and other works—the use of nature and natural processes as an analogy for the various and changing self. Nature was the emblem of the perfected order of things, as Emerson had argued, and thus it became for Thoreau the best way to express his own aspiration toward wholeness. "A broad and roaming soul," he writes in 1841, "is as uncertain–what it may say or be–as a scraggy hill side or pasture." The valuable element in both is their capacity to surprise, to demonstrate something new and unexpected. "I may hear a fox bark–or a partridge drum–or some bird new to these localities may fly up. It lies out there as old, and yet as new." This ever-present possibility of change gives life to the landscape. "The aspect of the woods varys every day–what with their growth–and the changes of the seasons–and the influence of the elements–so that the eye of the forester never twice rests upon the same prospect," Thoreau observes. The same dynamic explains the nature of the inner life. "Much more does a character show newly and variedly, if directly seen. It is the highest compliment to suppose that in the intervals of conversation your companion has expanded and grown" (JP 1:305–6). Thoreau's effort to understand himself in terms of the natural world and model himself by that standard sometimes resulted in quite original moments of self-expression, as when he declared that he had "experienced a joy sometimes like that which yonder tree for so long, has budded and blossomed–and reflected the green rays" (JP 1:200). His comparison brings the tree to life in an unexpected way; the human emotion of joy is compared to the production of buds and blossoms.

"I feel that I draw nearest to understanding the great secret of my life in my closest intercourse with nature," he wrote in 1842, an important recognition that a deepened awareness of the impact of nature was crucial to his work of self-culture. This understanding takes on the gravity and import of religious worship. "There is a reality and health in (present) nature," he continues, "which is not to be found in any religion–and cannot be contemplated in antiquity– I suppose that what in other men is religion is in me love of nature" (JP 2:55). This is one of the most direct statements of self-understanding to be found in the Journal, and one of the most courageous. Though part of a culture that fiercely insisted on a reverence for religion, Thoreau declares that he is a man who finds his deepest religious self-expression in a much different form from that which is conventionally sanctioned. The Thoreau who declares his "love of nature" is not to be taken entirely as a harmless woodsy eccentric. Deeply interwoven in Thoreau's nature passion was an attitude of tough resistance, grounded in a determination to set an independent course of self-development. Seeing the growth of his character as one of many patterns of development in the natural world, he could derive both humble submissiveness and sturdy resolve. "Nothing is so attractive and unceasingly curious as character," he wrote in 1842. "There is no plant that needs such tender treatment, there is none that will endure so rough. It is at once the violet and the oak" (JP 2:36).

Those moments of awakening, when he seemed to achieve a clarity about himself and his place in the world, were usually almost indistinguishable from moments in which he had been out of doors, observing and absorbing the natural environment. In 1842, some three years before he began his sojourn at Walden Pond, he was both describing and theorizing the pond surface in his Journal. Recognizing the constant wear of moving water on partially submerged pine branches, he finds the "rotary" or circular patterns of movement that are the sources of natural beauty in all things, from pine branches to planets. "All things indeed are subjected to a rotary motion either gradual or partial or rapid and complete– From the planet and system to the simplest shell fish and pebbles on the beach. As if all beauty resulted from an object turning on its own axis or others turning about it. It establishes a new centre in the universe" (JP 1:376). He was learning to observe the details of the particular objects and processes before him while always exploring the common elements that gave them a place in the larger world.

Thoreau used his Journal most fruitfully in noting those moments in which particular natural phenomena yielded encompassing laws or patterns, and in which external nature mirrored the inner life. "In whatever moment we awake to life, as now I this same evening after walking along the bank, and hearing the same evening sounds (that were heard of yore) it seems to have slumbered just below the surface–as in the spring the new verdure which covers the fields has never retreated far from the winter" (JP 2:43). Thoreau's walk along the riverbank brings him to life again, awakens his slumbering awareness. This internal event is akin to the spring awakening of the hidden, slumbering life beneath the earth's surface. Nature and character are equivalents, driven by the same energies and shaped by the same laws. By seeing the development of his inner life in terms of the developing life of the natural world, he was able to balance his dedication to active character building with his passive acceptance of his identity as part of the larger identity of nature. "Though nature's laws are more immutable than any despots," he observed, "yet to our daily life they rarely seem rigid, but permit us to relax with license in summer weather" (JP 2:41).

THE TRAIL OF A FOX

Journal keeping, one of the New England Puritans' most important devotional tools, remained an important part of Thoreau's lifelong spiritual practice. He often understood and described journal writing in curiously passive terms, however, as if the words were simply the overflow of a brimming awareness, spilled onto the page. The Journal allowed Thoreau to think of writing as spontaneous, the natural product of the moment. In that sense, it reinforced his acceptance of unplanned and unintended spiritual progress.[16]

Behind his growing sense of the importance of the observation of nature, therefore, was an increasing dedication to the process of writing as a necessary correlative to this observation. Indeed, it seems as if Thoreau came to regard the writing as itself an integral part of observation, an attitude that blurs the lines of demarcation between cognition and expression and makes writing itself an act of reception or discovery. "Let the daily tide leave some deposit on these pages, as it leaves sand and shells on the shore," he writes in 1840, describing his work on the Journal. "This may be a calendar of the ebbs and flows of the soul; and on these sheets as a beach, the waves may cast up pearls and seaweed" (JP 1:151). The pages record the "ebb and flow" of observation and intellectual formulation, making the life of nature and the inner life as one. In comparing the journal page to a beach, he implied that thinking in its deepest sense was an exercise in receptive awareness, a process better understood in terms of apprehension than of creation. The intellect was to receive and to record rather than to create willfully.

While nature provided Thoreau with important analogues for his own thinking and writing, the representation of cognition in terms of the processes of the natural world also began to influence his conception of nature itself. He began to see the natural environment as a vast and complex web of signals that could be best understood as analogous to a language or a variety of languages. Each element of the natural environment, each interaction and process of nature, was some form of expression, and therefore potentially some form of communication. In January 1841 he tracked a fox across the frozen surface of Fair Haven Pond, which had been covered by a blanket of new snow. Walking in the fox's very tracks with "a tiptoe of expectation," he wrote that he felt "as if I were on the trail of the spirit itself which resides in these woods, and expected soon to catch it in its lair." These somewhat whimsical terms show an edge of self-mocking irony about his thrill over so inconsequential a thing as a fox's path through the snow, but beneath the superficial irony is a recognition that such tracking satisfies both physical desire and a spiritual aspiration. A sense of discovery, an elation over contact with something that is new and unknown, is evoked by the fox's track. "Here is the distinct trail of a fox stretching quarter of a mile across the pond. Now I am curious to know what has determined its graceful curvatures, its greater or less spaces and distinctness, and how surely they were coincident with the fluctuations of some mind" (JP 1:239–40).

It seems at first that Thoreau is asking what factors motivated the fox to take the path that it did. In what ways were the steps taken by the fox chosen responses to its environment? This would make the inquiry akin to what we would consider today a study of animal behavior. He is undertaking such a study in one sense, but what compels him is a feeling that his tracking of the fox implies something more significant, as the phrase "fluctuations of some mind" indicates. It is less the mind of the fox that Thoreau refers to in this phrase than a more inclusive consciousness that encompasses not only the fox but also Thoreau as he tracks it, and even perhaps the pond itself.

Thoreau is beginning to react to the natural environment as if the physical universe is a creative mind at work, expressing itself in the events and physical details of nature. This is, in a more concrete and dynamic conception, Brownson's redeemed earth expressing its creator. Thoreau knows that nature is speaking to him and that the perfected order of the creation that Emerson had posited in *Nature* is in fact continually unfolding. As he wonders about the logic of the fox's trail, he sees his pursuit as something quite profound, a tracking not just of a fox but of ultimate answers to fundamental questions about the nature and order of being. "If these things are not to be called up and accounted for in the Lamb's Book of Life, I shall set them down for careless accountants. Here was one expression of the divine mind this morning" (JP 1:240).

Thoreau's radical expansion of the boundaries of religious significance infused the world with a kind of newness and intensity of moment that was enormously invigorating. The inscription that we think of as nature was not only dazzlingly beautiful and complex but constantly renewing itself as well, its perpetual expression of new signs an indication of energy and health. This experiential realization of nature as a perpetually renewing scripture allowed Thoreau to understand his own desire for knowledge as somewhat more than the expression of the ravenous but narrow drive of his own ego. His Journal was, like the fox's track, the expression of something larger than himself, something that contained him and gave him definition. His own intellectual curiosity operated within this expanded conception of the world as an expressive, sign-making intelligence; his own acts of reading and speculative interpretation were themselves part of the larger operations of this world.

The fox's track thus mirrored Thoreau's speculation about it in his Journal. "The pond was his journal, and last nights snow made a *tabula rasa* for him. I know which way a mind wended this morning" (JP 1:240). The creation of his Journal was also one of a myriad of such acts occurring each moment. To understand nature's physical facts as expressions of consciousness was also to see his own expressions of consciousness in the Journal as the trail of a fox, facts of nature that embodied their own necessity and instinctive logic. The observation and interpretation of the natural world need not come, he believed, at the price of exclusion from it.

The Journal thus became Thoreau's means of participating in a larger community of expression. He compared the Journal to "a leaf which hangs over my head in the path– I bend the twig and then write my prayers on it then letting it go the bough springs up and shows the scrawl to heaven." In suggesting that God is the ultimate audience for his Journal, he admits its lack of a human audience, but equates his self-expression with that of the tree and with all nature. "As if [the Journal] were not kept shut in my desk," he explains, "but were as public a leaf as any in nature–it is papyrus by the river side–it is vellum in the pastures–it is parchment on the hills" (JP 1:259). The Journal takes its place within a natural world full of such expression. Its meaning, its value, must be measured in these expansive terms.

The line between language and nature, between thought and the physical attributes of the universe, are thus blurred for Thoreau in ways that are creatively stimulating. In seeing thought and nature in such a close merger, he was able to regard his own urge toward linguistic expression as part of a larger organization of natural energies. Thoreau was a man who deeply desired a wide readership and literary success, but was also suspicious of such success; his ambivalent efforts to establish himself as an author have been well documented.[17] These struggles and insecurities underline the importance of motivations other than that of public recognition in helping him continue to put words to the page day after day. To think that his work was an inherent and productive part of the flow of the energies of nature was surely an important aspect of those motivations. "I think I could write a poem to be called Concord," he declared in 1841. "For argument I should have the River–the Woods–the Ponds–the Hills–the Fields–the Swamps and Meadows–the Streets and Buildings–and the Villagers. Then Morning–Noon–and Evening–Spring Summer–Autumn and Winter–Night–Indian Summer–and the Mountains in the Horizon" (JP 1:330). This may in fact have been be a preliminary sketch for a poem of landscape description and local color that Thoreau was planning.[18] But even as he conceived of it, Thoreau knew that this poem had already been written and was being rewritten again with every passing moment.

CHAPTER TWO

The Scripture of All Nations

MISERABLE WITH INACTION

Through his own experience and his close relationships with several younger friends, Emerson recognized that "transcendentalism" signified a crisis of identity as well as a religious and literary movement. This identity crisis was in large measure a crisis of vocation, a desire for a task and a place in society that would be both socially useful and personally fulfilling. In his 1841 lecture "The Transcendentalist," he offered his most revealing description of this crisis as the dialogue between an idealistic and defiant but somewhat directionless "transcendentalist" and the commonsense voice of "the world." "We are miserable with inaction," declared the Transcendentalist. "We perish of rest and rust. But we do not like your work." The world's response, however predictable, is deflating. " 'Then,' says the world, 'show me your own.' " The Transcendentalist can only confess that "we have none," and refuse to perform any work "until I have the highest command" (CW 1:212). In the years following his graduation from Harvard in 1837, Thoreau was listening intently for the "highest command" but was largely unable to show his work to an unbending world. The literary and scholarly ambitions that he formed at Harvard continued to grow after his graduation, but they were vague in outline and, except for his Journal, had no ready outlet.

Thoreau's vocational aspirations took a more concrete form when he tested school teaching after his graduation. His decidedly mixed experiences in teaching were ultimately constructive in pushing him more firmly toward authorship and in underlining for him the necessity of living "free and uncommitted" (Wa 84), the first requirement of the poet's vocation. Most of the Transcendentalists who were not Unitarian ministers had some involvement in teaching, and progressive educational reform was a widely shared value among them. Bronson Alcott was a leader in educational innovation in his Temple School, and his work influenced both Margaret Fuller and Elizabeth Palmer Peabody, who also devoted significant efforts to teaching and educational theory. Although we remember Brook Farm principally as an agrarian commune, much of the group's energy was devoted to the school it operated. The doctrine of "self-culture," though it developed initially as a part of Unitarian theological discourse, had important implications for the formulation of educational theories and teaching methods, giving an intellectual rationale to a more dialogic model of the student-teacher relationship and reinforcing a more broadly democratic emphasis on the value of the experience of each individual.[1]

Thoreau's teaching apprenticeship in Canton with Brownson signaled an initial interest in teaching, and we can assume that Brownson's progressive views on religion and education and his supportive reception of Thoreau as a like-minded younger colleague helped to bolster that interest. Thoreau turned to Brownson for help in late 1837 when searching for "a situation as teacher of a small school, or assistant in a large one, or, what is more desirable, as private tutor in a gentleman's family." Thoreau told Brownson that he hoped to "make education a pleasant thing both to the teacher and the scholar," and affirmed a teaching philosophy characteristic of the Transcendentalists: "We should seek to be fellow students with the pupil, and we should learn of, as well as with him, if we would be most helpful to him." In this spirit, Thoreau added a seemingly humorous comment on his opposition to corporal punishment as a teaching method: "I have ever been disposed to regard the cowhide as a non-conductor. Methinks that, unlike the electric wire, not a single spark of truth is ever transmitted through its agency to the slumbering intellect it would address" (Corr 20).[2] This comment is of more importance than it might at first appear when we understand its immediate context: Thoreau's resignation from his first teaching position in Concord earlier that fall in a dispute over corporal punishment, long a puzzling incident in Thoreau's biography. Recent research by Dick

O'Connor has helped us understand more fully the nature and significance of this episode to Thoreau's maturing sense of his vocation.

Biographical accounts of the incident describe what seems one of Thoreau's oddest and most misanthropic public gestures. Shortly after he had begun teaching, he was visited by Deacon Nehemiah Ball, a school committee member, who took him to task for failing to keep the class sufficiently quiet and orderly. After Ball urged that it was his duty to use corporal punishment to maintain order and decorum, Thoreau complied by calling out several students apparently at random and feruling them. He then promptly resigned his position. Given this account, scholars have wondered exactly what Thoreau intended with the gesture, speculating that he wanted to demonstrate how pointless such punishment was, or that he acted out of anger and frustration.[3] His resignation left him out of work during the midst of the 1837 depression, and his letter to Brownson indicating his hope for a position as a "private tutor in a gentleman's family" no doubt reflects his wariness of the policies and procedures of the schools of the day.

O'Connor's reconstruction of what can be known about the incident, however, suggests a more understandable if less dramatic set of events, and gives a much better sense of Thoreau's early effort to find in teaching a vocation that would allow him to preserve his principles.[4] O'Connor believes that from the beginning of his teaching, Thoreau probably did occasionally use a mild form of physical punishment, striking a student's open hand with a ferule, a standard practice in the schools of the day. Deacon Ball was urging Thoreau to use a more severe form of punishment, striking with a leather strap or "cowhide." Thoreau had informed the school committee from the outset that he was opposed on principle to such severe punishment, and he responded to Ball's criticism by increasing the frequency and perhaps the severity of his use of the ferule, but not by punishing students at random. Finding after a brief experiment that he could not continue to teach in good faith using such techniques, and probably seeing that he would be in conflict with Ball and the school committee, he resigned his post, but finished the week rather than instantly leaving in protest. He began very soon to look for another teaching job. O'Connor classes the story of Thoreau's resignation in angry protest among "the various tales and legends concerning Henry Thoreau" (151), and depicts him less as a capricious and somewhat misanthropic resister of authority than as an idealistic teacher firmly committed to improving the educational process for his students.

Thoreau felt that the impulse to self-education should be developed within the student, rather than imposing on him a body of knowledge unrelated to his personal aspirations. In order to accomplish this, there must be a pleasant climate in which the student would feel himself a fellow-seeker with his teacher. Such a climate could not exist within the authoritarian structure of most schools where the success of a teacher was measured by how well his pupils obeyed him. (164)

That Thoreau did not abandon teaching immediately after this incident is some indication of the sense of possibility that he still invested in it, and perhaps also an indication of his dissatisfaction with the work he fell back on, helping his father in the family pencil-making business. He spent most of the rest of the 1837–38 school year in a frustrating search for a teaching job, almost heading west to Kentucky with his brother John in April, and undertaking a two-week tour of Maine villages in May in search of an open post. He finally established his own school in the Thoreau family home in the summer of 1838, and after a precarious beginning was able to move it to the Concord Academy. John soon joined him at the school, and their partnership was one of Thoreau's most rewarding vocational experiences. The school was innovative for its day, "a century ahead of its time" in Walter Harding's words, and also successful in the acceptance and support of the Concord community.[5] Thoreau might have settled into the life of a schoolmaster with his brother had not John's failing health forced him to quit teaching. Unwilling to continue the school alone, Thoreau closed it in April 1841.

During these first four years after finishing Harvard, Thoreau continued to develop his literary interests, though with little to show for them. His most important intellectual and literary stimulus was his growing friendship with Emerson, who treated him as both a friend and a promising young colleague. He was able to continue his wide reading, encouraged by Emerson's conversation and supported by his extensive library. Left adrift after his school closed in 1841, Thoreau accepted Emerson's invitation to live at his house as a kind of apprentice scholar, general handyman, and close family friend. Thoreau clearly understood this as an opportunity to begin his career as an author, and his response was to initiate two literary projects—a sheaf of poems centering on seasonal change and an anthology of early English and Scottish poems—which, while ultimately abandoned, offer crucial insights into his developing literary sensibility.[6] The course he was beginning to pursue, however, was violently disrupted by John's death from tetanus in January 1842, a tragedy that was followed shortly by the death of Emerson's five-year-old son Waldo, for whom Thoreau had developed a strong affection. These were devastating events.

Although Thoreau seemed at first to react calmly to John's death, he was actually repressing powerful emotions; he began to sink into a listlessness and depression, and eleven days later he too began to exhibit the symptoms of tetanus, or lockjaw, though he had not in fact contracted the disease. One can see in Thoreau's terrifying psychosomatic reenactment of John's symptoms a desperate reaching out in sympathy to a brother he could not help, and who had died in his arms. The accounts of his brother's illness also stress one other important element—John's remarkably selfless equanimity in the face of death. "On being told that he must die a speedy and painful death, he asked 'Is there no hope?' 'None,' replied the doctor. Then calmly he answered, 'The cup that my Father gives me, shall I not drink it?' and bade all his friends good-bye." Lidian Emerson reported that near the end, after John "had taken leave of all the family he said to Henry now sit down and talk to me of Nature and Poetry, I shall be a good listener for it is difficult for me to interrupt you."[7] John specified those things the brothers shared, poetry and nature, as a final gesture of love, but at that moment poetry must have seemed hollow and nature violently cruel. Thoreau's reenactment of John's illness was thus not only a sympathetic gesture of sharing his pain and his fate but also an emulation of the surrender of self that John had so heroically modeled. Thoreau's symptoms became so severe that his doctors and family were concerned that he would die, and even after he began to recover, he remained bedridden for a month, and was seriously weakened well into the spring. He had undergone a form of symbolic death, had lost the self that he once was, or had. The Thoreau who gradually emerged from the trauma was a man who had lost something precious and surrendered something of himself as a result.[8]

Thus in little less than a year, from the spring of 1841 to the winter of 1842, Thoreau saw the course of his life, and his emotional stability, profoundly shaken. Having lost his school, Thoreau was adrift vocationally; he was an aspirant to authorship with no solid accomplishments, utterly dependent on Emerson's support; and he had lost, in John, the closest human relationship that he would ever have.

NATURE'S BROTHER

Thoreau's desire to be a teacher was fundamentally a response to necessity; it had always been secondary to his aspiration to be a poet, and he concentrated much of his early intellectual energy into defining and clarifying what it meant to live the life of a poet. "There is no doubt but the highest morality in the books is rhymed or measured,—is in form as well as substance—poetry," he declared in 1840. "Such is the Scripture of all nations" (JP 1:141). Emerson had formulated a similar view of the poet as an idealized figure of prophetic vision, independence of mind, and spiritual wisdom, giving authoritative voice in *Nature* to the "Orphic Poet" who prophesied the coming of the new awakening. The Orphic Poet of *Nature*, however, spoke in prose. In both conception and practice, this "poet" was defined more by powers of perception and prophecy than by any concern with the process of composing verses. Even though Thoreau revered the "rhymed or measured" nature of poetic expression, and saw himself initially as a poet rather than an essayist or philosopher, he shared Emerson's view of the poet as the voice of the awakened consciousness rather than a practitioner of a particular literary craft. For Thoreau, being a poet signified the achievement of a state of mind, or the enactment of a set of values.[9]

In the summer before John's death, Thoreau had begun with some seriousness to write poetry, and had also thought much about the role and purpose of the poet. The closing of his school had given him the freedom to pursue literary projects more single-mindedly, and spurred his development of a sense of poetic identity and vocational purpose. The launching of the *Dial* in 1840 added fuel to Thoreau's literary aspirations and made the process of writing, editing, and publishing more immediate and tangible to him. He devoted several pages of his Journal in March 1841 to a detailed interpretation of one of the poems published in the *Dial*, Emerson's "The Sphinx" (JP 1:279–86), shortly before he moved in with the Emersons. A few months later he began what Elizabeth Witherell has identified as "a period of intensely productive poetic composition" culminating in a group of six poems that explore "the relationship between the season of autumn and the conditions of the poet's creative life." By the fall he had become, in Witherell's account, the "wildly inspired poet, writing furiously" (JP 1:330).[10]

One need not dissent from the consensus that Thoreau was at best a mediocre poet to understand that the conception of the Concord poem was important to his developing sense of literary purpose, and to recognize some moments of genuinely effective poetic expression that resulted from his intense work in the summer and fall of 1841. In these early poems Thoreau began to work out his rather complex understanding of nature's capacity to shape the insight of the poet, and the poet's corresponding duty

to create a world of perception and language that reflects the changing configurations of nature's energy.[11] Thoreau noted in his Journal that "nature
will not speak through but along with" the poet, whose role must be to
take "a fact out of nature into spirit." The poet thus re-creates in a shared
enterprise the energy of nature through poetic expression. The poet's
"thought is one world, her's [nature's] another. He is another nature—Nature's brother" (JP 1:69).

Thoreau's immersion in poetry coincided with his first reading in Hindu
philosophy, and as Witherell observes, *The Institutes of Hindu Law, or the Or-
dinances of Menu*, which he borrowed from Emerson, "seems almost to have
cast a spell over him."[12] He merged his interest in the study and observation
of nature with an awareness of the elusive arrivals of poetic and spiritual inspiration, the moments of intense elevation in which the individual is
brought into fuller and more complete recognition of a direct access to the
fundamental sources of both natural law and human discernment. Writing
in the poem "Inspiration" that his reverence for "the general show of
things" sometimes leads him to "forget that I am blind," he compared ordinary appreciation of nature with the moment of inspiration when "I who
had but sensual been, / Grow sensible, and as God is am wary." This transformation brings a new dimension of perception:

> *I hearing get who had but ears,*
> *And sight who had but eyes before,*
> *I moments live who lived but years,* ·
> *And truth discern who knew but learning's lore.*
>
> *I hear beyond the range of sound,*
> *I see beyond the verge of sight,*
> *New earths—new skies—new seas—around,*
> *And in my noon the sun doth pale his light. (CEP 557)*

Thoreau's avowal of "new earths—new skies—new seas—around" bears a
striking resemblance to Brownson's declaration that the merger of "materialism" and "spiritualism" would result in a new vision of the world in
which "all things are essentially holy," and to Emerson's declaration that
when a "faithful thinker" can "kindle science with the fire of the holiest af-
fections, then God will go forth anew into the creation" (CW 1:44).
Thoreau now began to work out his own distinct articulation of these
experiences.

"Inspiration" examines the paradoxical idea that inspiration disrupts and discredits the poet's more facile love for nature. Such visionary inspiration comes "in summer's broadest noon, / By a grey wall or some chance place," but it comes with such strange force that it "vexes the day with its presuming face" (CEP 558). Such revelation interrupts and unbalances ordinary experience. The tension between extraordinary perception and ordinary event is worked out in more detail in "The Fall of the Leaf," the poem that incorporates elements from "Inspiration" and other poems in the cluster, and appears to be the culminating achievement of this poetic project. The leaf, focal point of the natural world, signifies nature's perpetual state of flux, most dramatically exemplified in the change of the seasons, the fading of summer into fall.[13] The poem emphasizes, however, the way the seasons of nature shape and reflect the inner life. Seasonal change is thus a change in mood or intellectual tenor as well as a change in the weather; the conditions of the exterior world become difficult to distinguish from the state of the mind.

"The Fall of the Leaf" begins, like "Inspiration," with the problematic breach between nature and the mind, the difficult recognition that nature will not speak directly through the poet. The poet has "grown tired of this rank summer's wealth, / Its raw and superficial show," and seeks to "walk alone, / Apart from nature if need be" (CEP 561). The source of this restless dissatisfaction with "summer's wealth" is a suspicion of the superficiality of an attachment to the fullness of the natural world at its summer zenith. Such an attachment obscures a more truthful, and more complex, sense of the perpetually evolving energies of nature, energies that not only have generated abundance and beauty, but also are unraveling it even as nature is reaching its summer fullness. Nature cannot reveal or express this underlying energy, but the poet, walking "apart from nature if need be," can penetrate the layers of reality that time and season obscure. "Sometimes a late autumnal thought / Has crossed my mind in green July," Thoreau writes, attributing "Late ripend fruits and an autumnal sky" (CEP 561) to this unusual prescience of fall. The mind can recognize what is to come, seeing in fullness the shadow of completion. Autumn signifies ripeness and maturity, and when it is suggested to the mind by summer, it implies the inevitable development of knowledge, one thought generating another and leading the way to a fuller comprehension. It also signifies death, the inescapable limit of achievement and being.

Despite the stiffly formal language and awkwardly constricted rhythmic flow of Thoreau's poetry, he does capture the emblematic resonance of this confluence of seasonal change, enhanced perception, and mortality. He imaginatively anticipates the unexpected early fall of a leaf, an event he understands as a hint of his own mood, and of his own fate. The fall of a single leaf is thus an event of several dimensions. "So I have seen one yellow leaf / Amid the glossy leaves of June, Which pensive hung, though not with grief, / Like some fair flower, it had changed too soon" (CEP 561). Despite the poem's title, we do not at first see this leaf actually falling. It hangs, its golden color contrasting with the green around it and giving it a flower-like beauty. Its fall begins in the mind, its singularity and beauty a sign of its death. The poet who recognizes the contrast that lends the leaf its beauty is also able to connect that beauty with the leaf's fall. Although we eventually see a leaf "gently withdrawing from its stem" and lightly resigning itself "to sleep upon the old year's throng" (CEP 564), this is a later incident, representative of the myriad of "falls" that the initial leaf had contained.

The poem records the accumulating discernments of the fall, concealed within the gradually fading fullness of summer: the widening circle of shadows around the trees' trunks as the angle of the sun lengthens; the "scantier light, / Behind each needle of the pine"; the increasing but slightly muffled chirps of the cricket "beneath the sod, / Where he hath made his winter's bed" (CEP 562). These images eventually coalesce into a depiction of the bursting but nevertheless melancholy triumph of fall, when "the moon is ripe fruit in the sky" and "the sun doth break his stem well nigh / From summer's height he has declined so low" (CEP 563). With this full recognition of the arrival of autumn, Thoreau can declare that he too is "ripe," a claim that carries the weight of both achievement and decline. Here he incorporates the lines from "Inspiration" that signify a perceptual opening or revelation: "I hearing get who had but ears, / And sight who had but eyes before, / I moments live who lived but years, / And truth discern who knew but learning's lore" (CEP 564). His anticipation of the fall of the leaf has been an interpretation of the course of nature that he must not only express in words but also embody and enact.

Thoreau's foresight of the coming fall is not just understood rationally but felt emotionally. He is more than an observer of the processes of seasonal change; he is a participant in them, seeing in his own alteration a relationship between the mind and nature. It is as if the change of the seasons is in some way a chosen event, the will of the poet converging with the progression of natural occurrences. The first autumn breeze has "gently waved the birch tree tops" and "rustled the oak leaves," but before it died away, it also awoke a "melody . . . still faintly rising on my inward ear." Autumn has proved to be as much an internal as an external event, a state of mind as much as a season. The poet does not just observe and feel the evidence of the fall; he recapitulates its nature in his own processes of thought and emotion: "The crisped and yellow leaves around / Are hue and texture of my mood" (CEP 565).

Thoreau's season of poetic inspiration was productive, then, even though it did not bear the kind of fruit he hoped. He was able to construct an imaginative framework that addressed the fissure between nature and the poet, and formulated a valuable sign of that framework in the poet's recognition of the leaf and of the changing season. "The Fall of the Leaf" reveals a thinker of imaginative capacity who is struggling for a medium of expression. The figure of the poet had served Thoreau as an object of aspiration because the poet achieved inspired expression. Translating that poetic aspiration into rhymed verse would prove more problematic for him. By the end of the year he was beginning to curtail his efforts at poetry, in part because of Margaret Fuller's rejection of his submissions to the *Dial*, but also, one suspects, because he began to recognize that he had not found in the poem his authorial voice and vehicle.[14]

In the fall of 1841, almost exactly the high tide of his poetic inspiration, Thoreau also began a closely related project, compiling an anthology of English poetry that focused on the earliest English and Scottish verse. Noting Thoreau's hunger for publication at this moment and the encouragement that Emerson gave to this essentially archival and editorial project, Robert Sattelmeyer has seen it as an indication of "Thoreau's misguided appraisal of his literary vocation" and of "the deeply ambivalent effects of Emerson's patronage." Emerson apparently suggested the anthology to Thoreau, perhaps as a collaborative project, provided access to his books and his own collection of poetry selections, and lent Thoreau the expenses for a research excursion to the Harvard library in late November and December as he gathered material. Thoreau set about the work diligently, compiling four notebooks of extracts, and continued to work at it sporadically until 1844, when he focused his attentions on *A Week on the Concord and Merrimack Rivers*.[15]

While literary ambition and grateful loyalty to Emerson account in large part for Thoreau's initiation of the project, it is also clear that, given his very recent immersion in the composing of poetry, Thoreau had a genuine curiosity about the roots of English poetry and the conditions under which it was written. He was searching for fresh models, hoping to find them in archaic poems whose primitive and unadorned quality was a sign of closeness to inspiration and purity of purpose.[16] His thirst for such primal purity is suggested by an August 1841 journal entry in which he suggests that the tameness of the English poetry cannot capture the wildness that he associates with the American West and the Indian. "The best poets, after all, exhibit only a tame and civil side of nature– They have not seen the west side of any mountain." Thoreau was striving for that "west side," a view of the world unmediated by the norms of civilization. "Day and night–mountain and wood are visible from the wilderness as well as the village– They have their primeval aspects–sterner and savager–than any poet has sung. It is only the white man's poetry–we want the Indian's report. Wordsworth is too tame for the Chippeway" (JP 1:321). Thoreau hoped to find the spirit of wildness preserved in these ancient poems. His concurrent fascination with the literature of Hinduism shares some of the same hope. The Laws of Menu, he writes, "are the laws of you and me–a fragrance wafted down from those old times–and no more to be refuted than the wind." The remotely ancient signified the same purity that he associated with the western wilderness. "When my imagination travels eastward and backward to those remote years of the gods–I seem to draw near to the habitation of the morning–and the dawn at length has a place. I remember the book as an hour before sunrise" (JP 1:311).

On the whole he was disappointed by what he found in the records of early verse, and also, it appears, with the tedious process of scholarly compilation that his project required. "When looking over the dry and dusty volumes of the English poets," he commented, after beginning his work in the Harvard library, "I cannot believe that those fresh and fair creations I had imagined are contained in them." Disappointed that his search for new models and inspiration was in fact proving counterproductive, he declared that "poetry cannot breath in the scholar's atmosphere" (JP 1:337–38).

Thoreau's unrealized hopes for the project indicate his search for a medium of expression that could somehow embody the "lofty tone," the "simplicity of style" (JP 1:316), and the authoritative conciseness that he found in Hindu scripture. Much of what we now see in the truncated lines and the rough and sporadic rhythm of his poetry reflects this search for a "primitive" and pure literary form. Thoreau would distill some of his thoughts about the nature and place of poetry in an 1843 lecture on Homer, Ossian, and Chaucer that was published in the *Dial* and also incorporated into *A Week on the Concord and Merrimack Rivers*. There he declared that "the loftiest written wisdom is rhymed or measured," but also described poetry as "a natural fruit." "As naturally as the oak bears an acorn, and the vine a gourd, man bears a poem, either spoken or done" (EEM 154). While retaining a reverence for what is "rhymed and measured," Thoreau was also lending the dignity of poetry to the spoken word and the deed. His conception of the vocation of poetry was surviving his own limited success in the genre and taking on crucially new shapes.

A FOUNTAIN OF HEALTH

Thoreau's struggle to define his poetic vocation was tragically interrupted by John's death in January 1842, a blow that jeopardized the already fragile vocational and literary plans that he had begun to pursue, endangered the identity he had begun to construct, and deeply undermined his emotional stability. It forced him to begin anew, both emotionally and intellectually.

Thoreau's emergence from his grief was a slow process, and both his first books, *A Week on the Concord and Merrimack Rivers* and *Walden*, are in some senses chronicles of that recovery. But his 1842 essay "Natural History of Massachusetts" opened a way for him. As Barbara Packer has written, the essay "is the first of Thoreau's works to reveal his gift for evoking natural scenes in luminous, precise language."[17] Emerson, again, instigated the project, suggesting that Thoreau review an official survey of the plant and animal life of Massachusetts, and saw that it was published in the *Dial*. Emerson understood that the factual and empirical nature of the report would appeal to Thoreau and perhaps help spur his interests in natural history. The immersion in natural history that the essay required did open the way for Thoreau's accounts of his own excursions into nature, the genre that would become his most important medium of expression. We can only wonder whether Emerson also understood that the work would give Thoreau the opportunity, in Sherman Paul's words, "to state his faith in the 'health' of nature, and in the face of all his discontent—the mounting crises of vocation and friendship—to establish his relation to nature."[18]

Thoreau's new direction forward began with his declaration that one can "find health" only in nature, not in society, an attitude that seems especially striking in the aftermath of John's death. What follows is a celebration of health and vitality so clear-cut and assured that one must wonder at the force of will its statement required. "Unless our feet at least stood in the midst of nature, all our faces would be pale and livid. Society is always diseased, and the best is the most so. There is no scent in it so wholesome as that of the pines, nor any fragrance so penetrating and restorative as the life-everlasting in the high pastures" (CEP 22).

One may read the essay, as Paul does, as an indication that Thoreau "had turned to nature for his solace" after John's death,[19] but one should not overlook the vehemence of Thoreau's assertions of the health of nature, or the imagery of disease and restoration that colors them. They do suggest the beginnings of Thoreau's emotional recovery, but they also mask the pain, fear, and despair that he was still fighting off. His most confident assertions, read in their proper context, speak eloquently, if indirectly, of his struggle: "To the sick, indeed, nature is sick, but to the well, a fountain of health" (CEP 22). These are the words of one who has claimed his status as a survivor but who has yet to comprehend the reasons for it—and who remembers well his encounter with the sickness of nature. His tentative solution is to believe that the force that has enigmatically spared his body can also remake his spirit: "To him who contemplates a trait of natural beauty no harm nor disappointment can come. The doctrines of despair, of spiritual or political tyranny or servitude, were never taught by such as shared the serenity of nature" (CEP 22).

The culmination of this embrace of nature is the declaration "Surely joy is the condition of life" (CEP 22). The emphatic "surely," if we hear its undertone, carries an interrogative shadow. But Thoreau continues with a stirring catalogue of birth, spontaneous energy, and natural beauty that confirms his keen eye for the vigor and health of nature: "the young fry that leap in the ponds, the myriads of insects ushered into being on a summer evening, the incessant note of the hyla with which the woods ring in the spring, the nonchalance of the butterfly carrying accident and change painted in a thousand hues upon its wings, or the brook minnow stoutly stemming the current, the lustre of whose scales worn bright by the attrition is reflected upon the bank" (CEP 22–23). These images celebrate creatures whose life and energy are real but distinctly bounded. The insects are the creatures of "a summer evening"; the butterfly carries "accident and change" on its wings; the minnow is "worn bright" by the current's attrition. Thoreau's recognition of the quality of nature's beauty, while real and profoundly convincing here, carries with it a deepened sense of life's fragility.

Thoreau also sounds the note of withdrawal and simplicity that would grow in his work, linking it to the example of nature's innate humility. The beauty that one finds in "the recesses of nature," he writes, confirms "the inexpressible privacy of a life,—how silent and unambitious it is" (CEP 23). Ambition is in this sense the antithesis of "life," a superficiality that has no nurturing roots. Heroism is therefore a private and inward quality, a condition of integrity that cannot be earned by following the conventional demands for success. The life of the naturalist is one means of attaining this integrity. "What admirable training is science for the more active warfare of life," Thoreau declares. "Science is always brave, for to know, is to know good; doubt and danger quail before her eye" (CEP 23). Life indeed requires bravery, as Thoreau has recently come to see. In knowing that "nature will bear the closest inspection" (CEP 24), Thoreau hopes now to find a deliverance.

Given the praise of the bravery of science and the call for the close inspection of nature in "Natural History of Massachusetts," one might conclude that the "solace" Thoreau has found in nature is that of the empiricist, the observer and collector of fact, who rests satisfied with the premise that "to know, is to know good" (CEP 24). But Thoreau's conception of what it means to "know" renders a limited form of empiricism insufficient. To know means to be fully aware of the myriad aspects of seasonal change to which he devotes considerable attention in "Natural History of Massachusetts," arguing implicitly that one cannot enumerate and describe the flora and fauna of Massachusetts without due attention to the region's dramatic changes in season. The recognition of the omnipresence of change moves the observer beyond the present fact to the constant flow of natural energy and points to the unifying laws that account for nature's perpetual flux.

In one important description of a natural phenomenon that implicitly articulates a unifying natural law, a discussion to which Thoreau would return in a pivotal passage in *Walden*, he describes a December 1837 storm that covered "every tree, shrub, and spire of grass, that could raise its head above the snow . . . with a dense ice-foliage, answering, as it were, leaf for leaf to its summer dress" (CEP 38). The ice storm's odd mimicry of summer impresses Thoreau as more than a visual coincidence. He sees the ice formations as "ghost leaves" which result from the identical process that creates the actual leaf. "In obedience to the same law the vegetable juices swell gradually into the perfect leaf, on the one hand, and the crystalline particles troop to their standard in the same order, on the other." He has thus extended Goethe's principle of the leaf as nature's basic unit to the inorganic as well as the organic world, and seen an impressive visual exemplification of the idea that "the material [is] indifferent, but the law one and invariable" (CEP 38).

Thoreau was observing the natural world with an openness, but also with a purpose, not satisfied with locating the fact itself, but always conscious of it as the manifestation of a larger principle. He reaches back to his earlier journal entry to say, "Let us not underrate the value of a fact; it will one day flower in a truth" (CEP 41). His developing conception of the naturalist is still closely kin to the poet, a unifying intelligence capable of seeing the deeper origins and purposes that too often elude ordinary perception. He does not disguise his disdain for the superficiality of the natural history reports that occasion his essay, but he does recognize their potential value to the reader willing to probe those bare facts for the larger principles they embody. The probing is the real work. "It is much easier to discover," he wryly concludes, "than to see when the cover is off" (CEP 41).

WHERE GODS MIGHT WANDER

Goethe's exposition of the theory of the leaf as the fundamental botanical form in his *Italian Journey* provided Thoreau an imaginatively rich point of reference for his observations of natural law. Goethe also provided Thoreau another important imaginative framework by using the narrative of his journey as a structure through which external observation and inner discovery could be merged. Reading the book in late 1837, Thoreau was impressed with Goethe's "exact description of objects as they appear to him," noting that "his genius is exhibited in the points he seizes upon and illustrates." Such accurate observation "is chiefly to be prized in the book—even the reflections of the author do not interfere with his descriptions" (JP 1:16). Thoreau recognized that Goethe's selection and emphasis of detail from the myriad of impressions available to him was a fundamentally important creative act. Such descriptive observations and impressions, akin to the imaginative insights of the poet, constituted the texture of a kind of work to which Thoreau was increasingly drawn in the 1840s. Lawrence Buell, noting Thoreau's preference for the "romantic excursion" as a literary form, emphasizes its implicitly philosophical dimensions, explaining that the work of describing an excursion fully "tends to become, in effect, an account of the whole universe as it appears to the speaker."[20] The excursion allowed Thoreau to attend to the particulars of the natural world but to use that grounding for more ambitiously speculative ends as well, sustaining in his own work a poise between "fact" and "truth."

"A Walk to Wachusett" was the first such excursion narrative that Thoreau would write, the record of a hike to the top of Mount Wachusett in the summer of 1842 with Richard Fuller, Margaret Fuller's brother.[21] Thoreau had, with Margaret's urging, helped to tutor Richard for Harvard, and their new friendship had been helpful to Thoreau in his recovery from the loss of John. The tone of Thoreau's narration of the excursion is decidedly positive, and he seems to have experienced the trip, or at least to have reconstructed it, not just as a rejuvenating escape from social routine but as a revelatory exposure to an unusually powerful scene of natural beauty. Woven through the narrative is a building attitude of scorn for the falsifying demands of the modern social order, extending Thoreau's earlier conception of the poet-naturalist by fashioning him as a tough and exacting critic of his era.

Thoreau indicates the imaginative direction of the essay in his initial reference to their destination, "the dim outline of the mountains" a hovering presence whose "distance and indistinctness" give narrative shape to his quest for the intermingled authority of myth, antiquity, and scientific discovery.[22] "With Homer, on a spring morning, we sat down on the many-peaked Olympus, . . . with Virgil, and his compeers [we] roamed the Etrurian and Thessalian hills, . . . with Humboldt [we] measured the more modern Andes and Teneriffe" (CEP 42). Thoreau makes his expedition a heroic undertaking, equal in gravity to anything recounted in classical literature, or anything accomplished by modern science. His reference to the classics implies that modern experience, as represented in Humboldt's exploration, is the equivalent of the ancient experience recorded in Homer and Virgil, that the modern naturalist is the new maker of mythology and human meaning. The excursion tests this thesis. In it, Thoreau battles against the assumption that modernity is a diminished state.

The mood of mythical expectation and heroic quest in "A Walk to Wachusett" is reinforced by Thoreau's remarks on the exhilarating impact of the landscape, which seems to generate an intensified state of awareness. Leaving before daybreak, Thoreau and Fuller enter a natural world absent of all human activity. "As we traversed the cool woods of Acton, with stout staves in our hands, we were cheered by the song of the red-eye, the thrushes, the phoebe, and the cuckoo; and as we passed through the open country, we inhaled the fresh scent of every field, and all nature lay passive, to be viewed and travelled" (CEP 44). The journey enacts a new entry into the world, a first-seeing, in which the vitality of physical exertion and sensory experience coheres with a feeling of consonance with a landscape Edenic in its freshness and its benignity. The sense of renewal is heightened by the predawn quiet, in which human activity has almost completely subsided, and the world is restored to a pristine serenity. "Every rail, every farmhouse, seen dimly in the twilight, every tinkling sound told of peace and purity, and we moved happily along the dark roads, enjoying not such privacy as the day leaves when it withdraws, but such as it has not profaned" (CEP 44).

Thoreau's contrast between the ancient and modern worlds is reiterated in his opposition of nature and the village, with the ancient world and the natural world each serving as symbolic alternatives to the limitations of ordinary perception and experience. The sensuous appeal of the early morning scene has emphasized this contrast, for Thoreau feels not only as if he is exploring new territory in nature, but also that he is escaping the confinements and exhaustion of his accustomed social world. He enters a new landscape, and finds exhilaration in its freshness, but he is also conscious of entering it as a refuge from the ordinary patterns of human social and economic interaction which have been profaned by greed, competition, and the loss of real insight into the simplicity and harmony of nature. He links this landscape with the refuge of classical poetry. The walkers rest "in the shade of some oaks . . . reading Virgil, and enjoying the scenery" (CEP 46).

Though at first it seems a fulfillment, the entry of Virgil into the essay brings forward an underlying problem in Thoreau's imaginative depiction of his excursion. Is the world that Virgil represents still accessible? The heroic task of the excursion is the ascent of Wachusett the next morning. "It was only four miles to the base of the mountain, and the scenery was already more picturesque," he observes, communicating a level of rising expectation associated with ascending the mountain. Even though Mount Wachusett is a small summit, by its "slight elevation it is infinitely removed from the plain," and Thoreau reports that "when we reached it, we felt a sense of remoteness, as if we had traveled into distant regions, to Arabia Petrea, or the farthest East" (CEP 49). Here, finally, is the sense of difference for which Thoreau has been searching, the impression that he has indeed left his ordinary state of affairs behind.

The view is at first obscured by hazy conditions, but this phenomenon itself adds to the feeling of novelty, almost of dislocation. "It was like looking into the sky again, and the patches of forest here and there seemed to flit like clouds over a lower heaven" (CEP 50). The visual reversal here, in which heaven comes to look like earth, and earth like heaven, suggests a shift in seeing that has important metaphorical reverberations in the essay. Thoreau begins to look back on his home differently, finding the once familiar now interestingly disordered. The visual illusion caused by the mist leads him to see the earth as a strange and exotic place, "a blue Pacific island" (CEP 50). Thoreau confirms the theme that he had hinted at from the beginning: we must see the world as new.

That new world begins to open to Thoreau during the night he spends on the summit, "a place where gods might wander, so solemn and solitary, and removed from all contagion with the plain" (CEP 51). The revelatory experience continues the next morning when he sees "the sun rise up out of the sea, and shine on Massachusetts," allowing him to look down "over successive circles of towns, rising one above another, like the terraces of a vineyard" (CEP 52). He now recognizes nature as overwhelmingly powerful, framing and controlling all human activity. This comprehensive, Olympian view of human society is a release from "the follies of the plain" (CEP 54).

Thoreau has distanced himself temporarily from society in the ascent, and thus given himself a freeing sense of perspective on it. That perspective will be tested on his return, when he tells of passing the site of Mary Rowlandson's capture by Indians near Lancaster, the incident that is recounted in the most famous of the New England captivity narratives. The "unexpected refinement" of the scenery surprises him; its "level prairies of great extent, interspersed with elms and hop-fields, and groves of trees, give it almost a classic appearance." Such pastoral beauty contradicts the weight of the dark history of the place, making the past "seem as remote as the irruption of the Goths," far removed from tragic history. Thoreau is startled by his inability to connect the landscape with the violence of the past, and with his consequent ability to feel any connection with that "dark age of New England" (CEP 54).

Thoreau's interrogation of his own emotions as he passes through the captivity site is revealing. At the same time that he is asserting nature's authority over history, its capacity to cancel or override the past, he is in fact contemplating that very past, recalling its violence and tragedy. To say that the entire New England past is shaded in a kind of dim twilight is a confession of the burden of history, and even though he asserts the landscape's Edenic innocence, he is remembering the tragic history of this particular place. This meditation on the Indian wars, brief though it is, counters the mythical and antihistorical emphasis of "A Walk to Wachusett," with its allusions to Virgil and its quest for a timeless realm. When a particular natural place becomes the vehicle for historical memory, the simplified dichotomy of social contamination and natural purity on which Thoreau has built the essay is complicated and undercut. Thoreau's ascent has been an important achievement in understanding, but it cannot be a permanent condition of transcendence.

Thoreau thus returns from Mount Wachusett with renewed strength and purpose, reentering more bravely and constructively the social world that he temporarily left behind. "And now that we have returned to the desert life of the plain, let us endeavor to import a little of that mountain grandeur into it" (CEP 56). This declaration has something of the resolution to renewed engagement with the world that is the concluding note of Thoreau's later and more extensive excursions, *A Week*, "Ktaadn," and *Walden*. In all of these works, the removal from society paradoxically generates a renewed sense of presence and belonging in it.

CHAPTER THREE

No Higher Heaven

A WITHERED LEAF

The emotional trauma of John's loss intensified Thoreau's struggle to define his vocation and the course of his life, and for some three years, from 1842 to 1845, he remained extremely fragile emotionally, slowly regaining his balance and confidence. Fiercely independent in some respects, he nevertheless remained dependent on the Emersons financially and for the emotional stability that their home and family life provided. "I have been your pensioner for nearly two years, and still left free as under the sky," he wrote gratefully to Emerson in January 1843. "It has been as free a gift as the sun or the summer, though I have sometimes molested you with my mean acceptance of it" (Corr 78). While Emerson's support was crucial to Thoreau, his presence in Emerson's home was a constant reminder that he had not yet learned Emerson's fundamental lesson of self-reliance in a practical sense. He could justify his time there as a kind of literary apprenticeship, or as the "gift" of friendship, but as he understood more and more clearly, living with the Emersons could not be a permanent solution to the question of his life and calling.

John's death continued to weigh on him during these years, and as we saw in "Natural History of Massachusetts," Thoreau searched nature for understanding and acceptance, hoping to find an assurance of order and continuity in the face of sudden, destabilizing loss. His keen interest in the philosophical significance of natural events had become, after John's death, an "almost desperate faith in nature," as Linck C. Johnson has aptly termed it.[1] Thoreau's emotional recovery was real, if very gradual, during the early 1840s, but it was apparently punctuated by periods of lingering depression and self-accusation. Perhaps most telling is a moment of dark self-analysis in January 1843 (JP 1:447), a journal entry that is made more dramatic by the fact that the ninety-four pages following it are torn from the Journal. "I would fain describe myself though I am a rather uninterresting object to myself," he begins. "I force myself even now to write this." The imperative for self-examination was of course strong in the New England intellectual tradition, but as Thoreau surveys himself at age twenty-four self-examination becomes self-flagellation. "What am I at present? A diseased bundle of nerves standing between time and eternity like a withered leaf that still hangs shivering on its stem. A more miserable object one could not well imagine—but still very dull very insipid to think of." The leaf, a central emblem for life in Thoreau's figurative vocabulary, now becomes the vehicle for a moment of bleak self-representation that expresses the sense of mortal vulnerability that he had developed after John's death.[2] Hanging "between time and eternity," the withered leaf is a part of nature that has been spent or bypassed, less a sign of life than of death. Its fall is imminent.

The fall of this leaf, however, is invested with none of the ripeness, fulfillment, or melancholy beauty that characterized Thoreau's earlier poetic representations, and is instead the emblem of blighted achievement and thwarted hope. Although Thoreau had already begun the meditation with language that suggested his worried sense of mortality, as he continues, he makes death seem almost preferable to the hollow and meaningless existence that he foresees for himself: "I suppose I may live on not a few years—trailing this carcass after me—or perhaps trailing after it." It is as if his body has a will and a health of its own, quite apart from his essential identity. He admits that he has been healthy, "for periods perhaps healthier than most," but he adds a qualification, now lost to us, that seems more significant and determinative than his apparently sound physical health: "But there were short—" (JP 1:447). The passage ends here with ninety-four pages torn out.

Although we cannot know the directions that Thoreau's gloomy meditation took, it seems clear that his depression was connected with continuing emotional reverberations from the loss of John, and with his building frus-

tration over a lack of purpose and achievement in his life. Further complicating his situation was his complex relationship with Emerson. The friendship rested on a very solid foundation of mutual affinity, and it answered
important needs for both men. Emerson had lost his much-beloved
younger brother Charles in 1836, perhaps his closest male companion,
and Thoreau had in some ways helped to fill the gap that Charles had left.
And as we have seen, Emerson became a very important source of support
for Thoreau after John's death.

The two were also united in their dedication to scholarly and literary endeavors, with Emerson serving as a kind of example, mentor, and patron to
Thoreau, seeing in him a genuinely promising young writer and intellectual. This professional relationship, however informally it was conducted,
was a crucial element of their bond, but also a source of friction and frustration. Both of them were shy and somewhat awkward in interpersonal
relationships, so their shared literary work, especially their cooperative ad-
ministration of the *Dial*, provided a convenient vehicle for the expression of
mutual interests and supportive interaction. While Thoreau both wanted
and appreciated Emerson's advice and attention on literary matters, he also
needed more emotional support and openness than Emerson was capable of
providing. Their relationship was therefore somewhat delicate, with
Thoreau prone to feel at times that Emerson had failed him, or that he had
somehow failed Emerson. This insecurity further intensified those moments, such as the "withered leaf" meditation, when Thoreau struggled to
maintain a sense of his own worth.

Thoreau's bout of depression and self-deprecation in early 1843 may well
have been related to his anticipation of an imminent change, one that he either had discussed with Emerson or felt that he must soon discuss. Some
four months later, in May 1843, he would leave for New York to accept a
position as tutor to the son of Emerson's brother William.[3] Both Thoreau
and Emerson felt that this move could be a launching place for Thoreau's
literary career, giving him proximity to the growing New York magazine,
newspaper, and book publishing industry.

Emerson had of course helped to orchestrate Thoreau's tutoring position
with his brother, an arrangement that promised both the advancement of
Thoreau's literary career and relief from Thoreau's two-year residence.
Hawthorne's comment after a visit with Emerson in April 1843, a month
before Thoreau left for New York, suggests that Emerson may indeed have
hoped the experiment would succeed: "Next Mr. Thoreau was discussed,
and his approaching departure; in respect to which we agreed pretty well;

but Mr. Emerson appears to have suffered some inconveniency from his experience of Mr. Thoreau as an inmate. It may well be that such a sturdy and uncompromising person is fitter to meet occasionally in the open air, than to have as a permanent guest at table and fireside."[4] It would be wrong to exaggerate the tension between Emerson and Thoreau at this time, given their close affinity and mutually supportive relationship.[5] But it is also clear that both of them recognized that some change in Thoreau's living arrangements was necessary. The position with William Emerson in New York helped them circumvent a potentially awkward separation.

It was also becoming apparent that Emerson was beginning to exhaust his ability to advance Thoreau's literary career. When Emerson had taken over the editorship of the *Dial* from Margaret Fuller in 1842, he had been able to sustain the editorial and administrative duties largely because of Thoreau's untiring help. The *Dial* had provided Thoreau with important exposure to the operations of a literary magazine, given him access to the works of other like-minded writers, and, most important, offered him an outlet for his work and a small but influential audience. But by the spring of 1843 Emerson had realized that the days of the *Dial* were numbered, "for Miss Peabody shows me that it no longer pays its expenses" (ELet 3:154–55).[6] Both Emerson and Thoreau recognized that New York was a growing commercial center of the publishing industry, and Thoreau had a potentially important ally there in Horace Greeley, editor of the *New York Tribune*.[7]

In his discussion of Thoreau's move to New York, Steven Fink has stressed the lasting impact of Thoreau's ultimate failure there, largely the product of the hostile literary market of the day. "Thoreau's hope and that of his mentors, that he might earn his living by his pen in New York," Fink explains, "was in fact a naïve one; almost no writer could expect to do so, and especially not an unknown writer." The experience did not kill Thoreau's literary ambitions, but it made him decidedly suspicious of the literary marketplace as it then existed, forcing him to reconsider the extent to which he was willing to tailor his works in response to the demands of editors and the popular readership.[8]

Disillusioned with the New York literary scene, and somewhat uncomfortable in the William Emerson household, Thoreau moved in with his parents at the end of 1843. While such a return home at age twenty-five may have seemed something of a personal defeat, Thoreau was very glad to be back, and determined to make himself useful to his family. He began to work more intensively in the family pencil business to further perfect their product, laying the foundation for his family's improving finances. Their increasing prosperity was signaled by the new house that he and his father built for the family in the fall of 1844, a reflection of both his sense of loyalty and responsibility and of his growing array of practical skills.[9]

Throughout these somewhat unsettled years, Thoreau had nursed a project that addressed both his loss of John and his ambitions as a writer—a memorial narrative of their 1839 boating excursion on the Concord and Merrimack rivers. It was a project that grew slowly from 1842 to 1844 in his Journal, taking shape as a narrative of the voyage interspersed with loosely related philosophical meditations, and thus providing the kind of flowing structure that was conducive to Thoreau's still developing authorial purposes.[10] As the project grew, Thoreau understood more clearly its potential importance to his self-understanding. He also recognized his need for the kind of sustained and concentrated effort that only a period of uninterrupted study could provide.

During one of his meditative walks at Walden Pond in October 1844, Emerson happened upon two men engaged in a discussion of selling some of the land bordering the pond; he purchased eleven acres, returning the next day to buy three or four acres of adjoining woods. Seeing it as a potential rural retreat for himself, he was also eager for his friends to make use of it. Although Thoreau had by now returned home and was contributing to the well-being of his family, he was still somewhat unsettled about his future direction. He had taken a long hike with Ellery Channing through the Berkshires and Catskills in the summer of 1844, and perhaps shared his restlessness with Channing then. The next March, Channing, then in New York, wrote him with this now famous diagnosis: "I see nothing for you in this earth but that field which I once christened 'Briars'; go out upon that, build yourself a hut, & there begin the grand process of devouring yourself alive. I see no alternative, no other hope for you" (Corr 161). Channing's tone has a sardonic edge, but his recognition of Thoreau's fundamental restiveness was astute. The next March, Thoreau accepted Emerson's invitation to use the Walden land, putting his recently augmented skill in house building to work on the cabin that would provide the space he needed not only for self-devouring but also to bring his developing manuscript to completion, and to begin the most important phase of his literary career (ELet 3:262–63).[11]

A Week has suffered some pointed criticism for its rambling structure, but a certain looseness was the necessary cost of Thoreau's concurrent desires to memorialize, philosophize, engage in social critique, and construct an accurate and detailed narrative. The manuscript thus became a repository for his most recent ideas and concerns, and the reader must bear in mind that it principally reflects Thoreau's thinking just before he went to the pond and during his first year there. He superimposes, that is to say, the Thoreau of 1844 and 1845 onto an earlier self who had made the journey in 1839.

Over these four or five years he had undergone rapid intellectual growth, reading widely, conversing frequently with Emerson and others, and taking an important role in the *Dial*, an intellectually capacious and philosophically unorthodox journal. One of the uses Thoreau made of *A Week* was to give himself a more prominent voice in the dialogue of Transcendentalism, a movement that had largely determined his intellectual frame of reference. The book's probing of the relationship between Christianity and mythology, its critique of the narrowness of conventional society, its passionate concern with the dynamics of conversation and friendship, and its keen awareness of the natural world all reflect important strands of Transcendentalist discourse.

A Week was thus a summation and also a step forward. Thoreau stakes out his positions and marshals his arguments on several important Transcendentalist themes, interspersing these disquisitions into the more experientially oriented narrative of his boating trip. Under the powerful magnetism of narrative, readers over the years have preferred the Thoreau they found on the river or at his shoreline camp to the book's extended philosophical reflections. But the more abstract and discursive elements of his book were essential to its composition, part of the necessary fuel that sustained Thoreau's commitment to his first long project by allowing him to weigh in on the major concerns of what was still his primary intellectual community.

The questions of religious authority and religious inspiration, the formative concerns of Transcendentalism, dominate the first half of his account of the river journey. While he was not generally inclined to think in the categories of theology or to use theological terminology, he was deeply engaged by the kind of poetic and anti-doctrinal religious and ethical speculation that Emerson had instigated. But his orientation was by no means ecclesiastical. The Christian Church, its history, forms, and doctrinal disputes, were not his concerns, and he included the church and its supporters in his general indictment of the ills and shortcomings of American society. Nor was he willing to grant Christianity any unique or particular authority. This challenge to New England's religious institutions certainly caught the attention of the early reviewers of *A Week*, and marked the book for controversy.[12]

On the river Sunday morning Thoreau describes the "auroral rosy and white" light that "dated from earlier than the fall of man, and still preserved a heathenish integrity" (Week 43). His natural Sabbath on the river is of course set against all that Sunday represented in New England. In place of the formalities and conventions of worship and the "quiet and very civil" lives of the farmers and villagers whose fields he passes, he avows his "singular yearning toward all wildness" (Week 54). Yet he feels he must come to terms with his era's "one memorable addition to the old mythology . . . the Christian fable" (Week 66). Thoreau wants to separate "absolute religion," as Theodore Parker termed it, from the present-day church, to separate Christ from the Christians.[13] "I know that some will have hard thoughts of me, when they hear their Christ named beside my Buddha," he admits. "Yet I am sure that I am willing they should love their Christ more than my Buddha, for the love is the main thing, and I like him too" (Week 67).

In referring to "my Buddha," Thoreau is offering less a declaration of a faith in a particular religion than an openness to guidance from a variety of sources. The New Testament is "an invaluable book," but he also recognizes that no culture or religion can claim an exclusive or authoritative truth. "The book has never been written which is to be accepted without any allowance" (Week 71, 73). What he hopes for instead is a receptivity to all sources of ancient wisdom. "The reading which I love best is the scriptures of the several nations, though it happens that I am better acquainted with those of the Hindoos, the Chinese, and the Persians, than of the Hebrews, which I have come to last" (Week 71–72).[14] Each reader must gather his or her own scriptures, Thoreau believes, making an engaged and critical use of every available resource.

Thoreau's meditation on religious authority is closely connected with an issue of deep personal concern to him, the conflict between the contemplative and the active life. He drafted most of *A Week* during the first year of his stay at Walden Pond, a time during which he was living in a comparatively isolated situation, and weighing that isolation as a potentially permanent course of life. Yet he undertook this experiment at a time when the call for political engagement, collective action, and "association" was making a huge impact on the Transcendental circle.[15] This call to a deeper engagement with social and political issues was the still available alternative to his life of contemplative withdrawal, nature study, disciplined reading, and sustained literary projects. Thoreau's inner conflict over these alternatives is reflected in his discussion of what he terms the "pure morality" of Christianity and the "pure intellectuality" of Hindu scripture (Week 137).

While Thoreau takes an antagonistic view of American political culture in general, characterizing it as the enemy of the contemplative life, he also recognizes that certain barriers to both social progress and personal growth must be addressed in political terms. "In my short experience of human life, the *outward* obstacles, if there were any such, have not been living men, but the institutions of the dead" (Week 130). If dead institutions and not living men represent the principal barriers to change, then one can more confidently expect the transformation of society and more concretely work toward it. In a phrase that he would soon repeat in "Civil Disobedience," he declares that "I do not wish, it happens, to be associated with Massachusetts, either in holding slaves or in conquering Mexico" (Week 130). Such moral dissociation from evil is the first step in recognizing that it is not a necessary evil, that political institutions and policies that have been created in the process of history can also be changed in that same process.

Thoreau continued to struggle, however, with what at times seemed the incompatible demands of politics and philosophy, and he read this struggle into his description of the prevailing characteristics of "Eastern" and "Western" religion. He believed that New England's established forms of Christianity were too purely pragmatic and worldly, and thus lacked contemplative balance and spiritual depth. He was fascinated by the alternative image of the purely withdrawn and contemplative East, yet understood it finally as a compelling but limited answer to the question of how we should live.

Thoreau's representation of Eastern religion, one that followed the general contours of the limited and somewhat distorted European reception of Asiatic religious texts, emphasized its meditative and deterministic aspects, qualities he found both appealing and disquieting.[16] "The wisest conservatism is that of the Hindoos," he observes. "'Immemorial custom is transcendent law,' says Menu. That is, it was the custom of the gods before men used it" (Week 135). He contrasts Hinduism with the narrowly parochial conservatism of New England, which relies on a custom that is instead "memorial," or tied to arbitrary and inflexible human traditions (Week 135). By anchoring itself in usages that seem to transcend "the inevitability and unchangeableness of laws" (Week 136), Hinduism achieved a form of permanence missing in the comparatively new culture of New England Christianity. His attraction to Hinduism's "wisest conservatism" thus reflects in some aspects his own hunger for a permanent moral foundation that seemed absent in his own religious culture.

Yet even as Thoreau praises the Hindu concentration on permanent law, he prepares the grounds on which he will show himself finally dissatisfied with its vision. The emphasis on permanence excludes the element of vitality and transition that is a fundamental expression of spiritual energy, and a crucial religious value for Thoreau. "Buoyancy, freedom, flexibility, variety, possibility, which also are qualities of the Unnamed, they deal not with" (Week 136). A reverence for the "permanent" also implies an element of the static, a concept with problematic connotations for the development of Thoreau's spiritual stance.

The meditative and contemplative religious orientation that Thoreau associates with the East becomes, as his analysis continues, the basis for a different claim on the meaning of Christianity, one in which Jesus is presented as an agent of change and reform rather than the founder of the present order of things. Hinduism is "so infinitely wise, yet infinitely stagnant," while Christianity "is humane, practical, and, in a large sense, radical" (Week 136). This contrast leads Thoreau to envision a Christianity that returns to its origins as a movement of activism and social justice, much like the "new" church that Orestes Brownson has called for in his *New Views*. "The Brahman had never thought to be a brother of mankind as well as a child of God. Christ is the prince of Reformers and Radicals" (Week 136–37).

It is ironic that a book whose immediate reception centered on its critique of Christianity actually represented Christianity as an enlivened and redemptive alternative to the potential stasis of Eastern spirituality. But the new Christianity that Thoreau described was also unsettling, and potentially threatening, to the conventional practices of the New England churches of the day. This activist Jesus, much more a politically oriented figure than Emerson's Jesus-poet of the Divinity School *Address*, is a teacher of transformation and social change. "Many expressions in the New Testament come naturally to the lips of all protestants, and it furnishes the most pregnant and practical texts. There is no harmless dreaming, no wise speculation in it, but every where a substratum of good sense. It never *reflects*, but it *repents*" (Week 137). The determinism of Hinduism, however, limits the Brahman's potential response: "His active faculties are paralyzed by the idea of cast, of impassable limits, of destiny and the tyranny of time" (Week 140).

These meditations on the forms of religious inspiration and authority, and the competing demands of politics and the contemplative life, come to a dramatic but somewhat enigmatic culmination in the narrative of a hike Thoreau had made to the top of Saddleback Mountain which he includes in the "Tuesday" chapter. Here he extends his speculations on Asian religions and Christianity into an embodied narrative of the search for enlightenment, a journey that parallels his earlier hike to Wachusett and anticipates his later ascent of Mount Ktaadn. His seven- to eight-mile path to the summit of Saddleback is "a road for the pilgrim to enter upon who would climb to the gates of heaven" (Week 181). Like a true pilgrim, Thoreau has taken a solitary path, trusting himself and the natural world, and has thereby developed his capacity to know that world more completely. He spends a cold night at the summit, keeping warm by encasing himself, corpse-like, in boards that he gathers nearby, and in a symbolic resurrection arises early and climbs the tower of the mountain's observatory to witness the dawn: "As the light increased I discovered around me an ocean of mist, which by chance reached up exactly to the base of the tower, and shut out every vestige of the earth, while I was left floating on this fragment of the wreck of a world, on my carved plank in cloudland; a situation which required no aid from the imagination to render it impressive" (Week 188). Thoreau's isolation in an ethereal atmosphere, free from all connections with the world, momentarily rewards his arduous and self-directed ascent, providing an entry into "the new terra-firma perchance of my future life" (Week 188).

The dichotomy between matter and spirit, imaged here as the gulf between earth and heaven, colors Thoreau's interpretive response to the scene. He associates the ethereal world of the clouds with purity, finding "no spot nor stain" in these "immense snowy pastures," and comparing his vista to "a country as we might see in dreams, with all the delights of paradise" (Week 188). The earth becomes "a flitting thing of lights and shadows," having "passed away like the phantom of a shadow" (Week 188–89). But Thoreau remains conscious that these conditions are rare, that his experience is temporary. As the clouds finally engulf him, he returns to earth with memories of having seen, during his ascent, "new and yet higher mountains, the Catskills, by which I might hope to climb to heaven again" (Week 190). He descends from Saddleback with the recognition that to ascend to "heaven" he must continue to explore the earth.

The climbing of Saddleback seems a parable of enlightenment in which the pilgrim's struggle is rewarded with illumination. Thus in his influential reading of *A Week*, Sherman Paul found the Saddleback narrative Thoreau's "finest anecdote of inspiration." The description of his sense of "ecstasy" in nature on the mountain's peak, Paul believes, was essential to his construction of *A Week* as "an extended Sabbath devoted to the headwaters of inspiration."[17] But Thoreau's importation of this event into the quite different narrative of the river voyage raises difficult questions. The Saddleback ascent is actually the product of a quite different excursion that took place in 1844 *after* the 1839 trip with John. Both Frederick Garber and H. Daniel Peck have emphasized the interpretive significance of Thoreau's interpolation of this distinct event into his larger narrative. As Peck writes, the Saddleback climb "is called up from memory rather than the present voyage" in such a way that it "interrupts and temporarily arrests *A Week*'s developing motion of discovery."[18]

The potential significance of Thoreau's placement of the episode is further magnified when we examine Linck C. Johnson's text of the first draft of *A Week*, in which Thoreau had sketched only a description of the unusual view from the mountaintop, with no account of his climb to the summit or·his overnight vigil, and none of the revelatory intensity we find in the final draft.[19] Those who prefer a more "de-Transcendentalized" Thoreau may actually like this portion of the earlier draft better than the final edition. It certainly shows the extent to which the final account of the Saddleback excursion was self-conscious mythologizing interposing itself into the ordinary progression of the voyage. The ascent of Saddleback is followed, indeed undercut in some senses, by a very different set of concerns in the "Wednesday" chapter, which centers less on the spiritual quest in nature than on the grittier questions of death, grief, survival, guilt, and the problematics of friendship. The centrality of the ascent is thus progressively undermined by the continuing narrative, its mystical disembodiment in tension with an increasingly this-worldly Thoreau, who seems more at ease on the river or on the bank than in the clouds.[20]

When his account of the voyage resumes, Thoreau seems even more immersed in the descriptive details of the Merrimack. His "descent" from Saddleback Mountain, a reentry into the flowing current of life, diverges dramatically from the unearthly withdrawal at the mountain's summit. The episode seems instead to mark a point of renewal in which Thoreau is reintroduced to a world whose newness and complexity are constantly revealed as he advances upstream.[21] It is as if his glimpse of cloudland, however unusual and awe-inspiring, had attuned him to a more serious and detailed observation of the actual earth. The river and its surrounding landscape are now the embodiment of the vision he had attained at the summit, and Thoreau is intent on examining it at firsthand.

What initially seemed a disjuncture in his narrative becomes, as the "Tuesday" chapter proceeds, an occasion through which the significance of the natural world is further magnified. In fact, the "Tuesday" chapter contains some of Thoreau's most interesting scenic prose, with descriptions of the effects of the mists and vapors that make the river's atmosphere unique, of the many spring-fed rivulets that flow off the river's banks to replenish it, of their sighting of the Goffstown Mountain, of Uncannunuc, of their passing Cromwell's Falls and their arrival at Plum Island. We find in these moments a determined new absorption in the worldly. While Thoreau had felt momentarily disconnected from the earth by the fog surrounding the summit, that seeming disconnection had in fact been the means by which his appreciation of the earth had been renewed. Even though he saw nature for a moment as "the phantom of a shadow" (Week 188–89), he was reborn not to an ethereal heaven but to an actual "terra-firma."

Typifying this new engagement with the world as he finds it is Thoreau's gently humorous account of making a meal of a roasted pigeon which had "lingered too long upon its perch" (Week 223). His description of the "handsome" bird seems equally apologetic and ironic, a complexity of tone that we associate with his most interesting writing in *Walden* or the Journal. "It is true, it did not seem to be putting this bird to its right use, to pluck off its feathers, and extract its entrails, and broil its carcass on the coals; but we heroically persevered, nevertheless, waiting for further information" (Week 223). Thoreau neither spares us the unappealing details of the meal's preparation, nor indulges in guilty self-accusation or retrospective moral censure. The brothers' heroic perseverance, as Thoreau terms it, signifies a tacit acceptance of the conditions of the world, a recognition that life persists, even flourishes, under conditions that are also in some senses brutal and tragic. "The same regard for Nature which excited our sympathy for her creatures, nerved our hands to carry through what we had begun" (Week 223).

With this observation Thoreau strikes an entirely different tone from the one he used at the summit of Saddleback Mountain. If the world seemed both impure and far removed from that vantage, it seems undeniably present at the campsite by the riverbank, and Thoreau admits that to be part of it, and to act within it, is the order of life, even though we must always await "further information" to understand it fully. "We would fulfil fate, and so at length, perhaps, detect the secret innocence of these incessant tragedies which Heaven allows" (Week 223). This search for the "secret innocence" among the tragedies of living and dying becomes a prominent concern as Thoreau turns his attention to John and himself.

YET THIS SUFFICES

Thoreau wrote *A Week* to relive imaginatively an experience that was intimately connected with his relationship with John. Its dual and sometimes conflicting celebration of both immediate experience and memory reflects Thoreau's complex sense of the fragility and the miraculous continuance of life. He is alive while John is dead, the victim of a trivial accident. Yet he and John shared the same experiences in their river trip, experiences which now demand that Thoreau recover and reconstruct them, and that he accept his own continuing life under the terms of a new wakefulness in the world.[22]

Thoreau not only remembers his brother but remembers *for* his brother, assuming a voice in his narrative that seems to speak for them both. Linck C. Johnson notes the peculiar fact that "John is neither described nor characterized" in *A Week*, and it is indeed unusual to encounter a book conceived as a memorial that contains almost no description of the person memorialized.[23] With John hardly to be found in the narrative, Thoreau presents the experiences of the voyage as those of a remarkably unified "we," essentially absorbing John's vision into himself, or, in another sense, giving John new life through his own eyes.

Thoreau's effort to make the voyage yield a more profound moral perception and a deeper commitment to new experience is clear in his description of making camp on Wednesday evening of the journey, one of the most compelling moments of self-reflection in the narrative. A mixture of confident celebration and melancholic reverie, it reflects the conflicting emotions associated with the entire journey. Its strategic placement in the narrative also gives it a structural importance, bridging the earlier disquisition on friendship in the "Wednesday" chapter and the somewhat autumnal mood of the later chapters.

Thoreau's memory of the evening keeps alive the fact that the trip was something of a lark in which he and John enjoyed an exhilarating sense of freedom from the routines of school-keeping and family life. Amid the book's detailed descriptions and earnest philosophy, this moment reminds us of the playfulness and camaraderie that made the trip so meaningful. The brothers secure the boat "at the mouth of a small brook," and the evening unfolds into a buoyantly optimistic affirmation of the possibilities of life, enhanced by the beauty of the natural light in this secure harbor. "As we sat on the bank eating our supper, the clear light of the western sky fell on the eastern trees and was reflected in the water, and we enjoyed so serene an evening as left nothing to describe" (Week 291).

Thoreau does not, however, dwell at length on this moment of beauty, but hastens to add that it should be regarded only as one of a series of always unfolding experiences. "For the most part we think that there are a few degrees of sublimity, and that the highest is but a little higher than that which we now behold; but we are always deceived. Sublimer visions appear, and the former pale and fade away" (Week 291). In a book created to preserve memory, this is a somewhat surprising claim. The principle is closely related to Emerson's proposition in "Circles" (1841) that the soul is always capable of drawing a new circle or of further expanding its knowledge or power beyond any level of achievement. A cardinal tenet of the Transcendentalist movement, it expresses faith in the continually renewing creative powers of the self. Because of John's death, Thoreau inevitably remembers this particularly sublime moment at the riverside as something irretrievably lost. His assertion that this experience is only a prelude to greater ones is an avowal of hope, an essential part of his recovery from grief. That "sublimer visions appear" is the assurance that this past experience, as serenely beautiful as it was, is capable of being superseded. My life, if lived to its limit, Thoreau implies, is my best testament to the memory of John.

Thoreau transforms this moment into a call for living with an intensity and self-directed purpose that make the world "canvass to our imaginations" (Week 292). When the soul awakens, the imagination becomes an engine of power through which the world can be made over. "All things are as I am," he writes, emphasizing the coordinated synergy between the awakened soul and the newly perceived world. "Our circumstances answer to our expectations and the demand of our natures" (Week 292).

This declaration of the capacity of renewed perception to alter the world is one of the most radical claims of Transcendentalism, echoing directly Emerson's prophetic avowal in *Nature* that "a correspondent revolution in things will attend the influx of the spirit" (CW 1:45). Thoreau craves the assurance that such moments of awakening are indeed possible. His recollection, or reconstruction, of his experience at Wednesday's campsite is thus an important element in the developing theory of the new life he is living at Walden Pond.

The description of the power of such an awakening, however, begs the question of its cause. Can such moments be willed or caused to happen? That question gnawed at Thoreau throughout his life. His conception of the awakened soul emphasizes will and active engagement, a seizing and re-making of the world in one's image. But he is forced to acknowledge that his own survival is a kind of mystery, and that "the singular pertinacity and endurance of our lives" (Week 293) is both inexplicable and uncontrollable. "The miracle is, that what is *is*," he writes, "when it is so difficult, if not impossible, for anything else to be" (Week 293).

The intensity of Thoreau's language here suggests his emotional entangle-ment in the questions of survival and meaningful self-determination. His own life seems miraculous to him because of his inescapable recognition that John's life is no more. While he is grateful for his continuing life, he is also troubled by how little, finally, he had to do with his own survival, and how little John had to do with his own death. He praises the "endurance" of life, but his praise also evokes a sense of life's fragility. To endure can seem to be less a triumph than a fatalistic resignation to the nature of things, making the "miracle" of life seem more like an inexplicable burden: "We walk on in our particular paths so far, before we fall on death and fate, merely because we must walk in some path" (Week 293). And yet this resignation, with its im-plied acknowledgment of limit, carries an ironically liberating corollary: "So much only can I accomplish ere health and strength are gone, and yet this suffices" (Week 293).

Life not only endures, it suffices. This realization is, for Thoreau, a break-through. His examples of this principle of "sufficiency" imply that our de-sire to control events or even to read them as significant is misguided. "If debts are incurred, why, debts are in the course of events cancelled, as it were by the same law by which they were incurred. I heard that an engage-ment was entered into between a certain youth and a maiden, and then I heard that it was broken off, but I did not know the reason in either case" (Week 293). While Thoreau speaks in somewhat abstract and depersonal-ized language, his examples are biographically revealing. The anxiety over debt in part reflects his ongoing concern about his dependency on Emerson and his desire for financial self-sufficiency, which he was pursuing at Walden while he wrote *A Week*. His reference to the canceled engagement has particular biographical significance, given John Thoreau's brief engage-ment with Ellen Sewall in 1840, and Thoreau's own infatuation with her and subsequent unsuccessful marriage proposal.[24] Thoreau thus preaches his new faith in life to himself, addressing his own anxieties and disappointments. Life will run its course, and carry us with it. This potentially dark recognition seems curiously liberating to him.

Thoreau's liberating fatalism provides a surprising counterpoint to the celebration of the power of the newly aware consciousness which begins his meditation. Survival itself, the very fact of continuing, Thoreau comes to argue, has its own quite different capacity to empower; that insight is crucial when one is forced to admit that the coming of awakening is not connected with will or choice. The empowerment conferred by survival and continuance thus becomes the theme of one of the book's most intriguing declarations:

> Our particular lives seem of such fortune and confident strength and durability as piers of solid rock thrown forward into the tide of circumstance. When every other path would fail, with singular and unerring confidence we advance on our particular course. What risks we run! famine and fire and pestilence, and the thousand forms of cruel fate,—and yet every man lives till he ——dies. How did he manage that? (Week 293–94)

Thoreau's dark humor about the limits of survival reinforces the narrative's veiled lament over the death of John, and underlines his own conception of himself as one who has somehow managed to live on. "My life will wait for nobody, but is being matured still without delay," he declares, "while I go about the streets and chaffer with this man and that to secure a living. It is as indifferent and easy meanwhile as a poor man's dog, and making acquaintance of its kind" (Week 294). Life continues; our responsibility is to recognize and embrace that continuance.

Thoreau's realization that "my life will wait for nobody" is also a significant step of healing, if we take the "nobody" here to refer primarily to John, and recognize the complex mix of guilt, pain, surprise, and joy at his own survival that he underwent in the face of John's death. What he seems to recognize as he remembers camping on the river shore is that the same buoyant freedom he enjoyed that evening with John is still his. Despite his grief, his own life has gathered force and has begun to set a direction beyond his sense of a conscious capacity to plan and progress. My life, he asserts, "will cut its own channel like a mountain stream, and by the longest ridge is not kept from the sea at last. I have found all things thus far, persons and inanimate matter, elements and seasons, strangely adapted to my resources" (Week 294).[25]

This revelatory and empowering discussion is not completed, however, until Thoreau recounts the dream that left him "unspeakably soothed and rejoiced" after he awoke the next morning. Burdened by the feeling that an unnamed friend blamed him for some wrong of which he was innocent, Thoreau achieves an absolution, dreaming that "ideal justice was at length done me for his suspicions" (Week 296–97). His dream of reconciliation reaches back to an earlier meditation on friendship in the "Wednesday" chapter, in part an homage to John, but also a reflection on his complicated relationship with Emerson.

Remaking and revitalizing the concept and practice of friendship was a fundamental concern of the Transcendentalists, and discussions of the workings of human relationships were very much in the air in the late 1830s and early 1840s. Linck C. Johnson traced the origins of Thoreau's discussion of friendship in the "Wednesday" chapter to journal entries in the late 1830s, a period shortly before Emerson began to draft his essay "Friendship," which was included in his *Essays* (1841). Thoreau's concern with the subject intensified, Johnson notes, after John's death, becoming a central part of the first draft of *A Week*.[26] He hoped to memorialize John as the ideal friend and companion, and portray their boating trip as a key moment in their brotherly bond.

Emerson had replaced John at the center of Thoreau's emotional life after John's death, offering a profound friendship, but one knotted with difficulties. Each man valued the other deeply and worked toward an idealized conception of friendship, but certain troubling barriers persisted between them. In *A Week*, Thoreau is responding to these hopes and difficulties and also responding to Emerson's attempt to theorize his own relationships in the essays "Love" and "Friendship." It is inconceivable that Thoreau would not have read "Friendship," in particular, without a sense of the dynamics of his own relationship with Emerson. It is equally clear that what he says in *A Week* was in part determined by Emerson's representation of the possibilities and limits of friendship. "Friends, such as we desire, are dreams and fables" (CW 2:125), Emerson had concluded, and this chilling observation weighs heavily in Thoreau's consideration of friendship.[27]

To see Thoreau and Emerson as deeply engaged in a discourse on friendship runs counter to the customary idea that Thoreau enacted Emerson's "Self-Reliance" in his solitary life at Walden Pond. Self-reliance and unfettered independence of action and thought were indeed important elements in both Emerson's and Thoreau's conception of a successful life. But the interest in friendship, both as a lived reality and as a philosophical category, was also a principal concern. Emerson and Thoreau both praised and disparaged friendship simultaneously, but they placed extraordinary hopes on a form of perfected friendship that was an extremely rare and difficult achievement. Their idealization of the unlimited possibilities of human relationships, ironically, made the daily practice of friendship all the more difficult.

Fundamental to their shared conceptions of friendship was the observation that it was not willed or chosen, that the individual was not free in the choice of friends but was pulled toward them by an involuntary and ordained power of attraction. "My friends have come to me unsought," Emerson wrote. "The great God gave them to me" (CW 2:115). Commenting on the same sense that friendship is a decree or power working beyond the scope of the will, Thoreau disparaged the conventional guidebook advice about the choice of friends. "The books for young people say a great deal about the *selection* of Friends; it is because they really have nothing to say about *Friends*. They mean associates and confidants merely" (Week 269). That power which makes friendship predestined is named "affinity" by Thoreau, a natural energy whose course is irresistible.[28] "Friendship takes place between those who have an affinity for one another, and is a perfectly natural and inevitable result. No professions or advances will avail" (Week 269).

The hope for such deep emotional bonds among the Transcendentalists arose not only from personal needs but also from their disappointment with the sterility of conventional middle-class life. Creation of a world in which meaningful relationships could flourish was part of their agenda of social change.[29] Thoreau understood that this power of affinity was not necessarily sanctioned by his culture. Real friendship was wild or uncivilized, "an essentially heathenish intercourse, free and irresponsible in its nature" (Week 276). Herein lay its enormous power. "There is on the earth no institution which Friendship has established; it is not taught by any religion; no scripture contains its maxims" (Week 263). Surrender to our affinity for another is an act of profound self-discovery and self-expression, not a learned, artificial practice.

Friendship reflects a power working through the self but not limited to it, an energy that finds its expression in the blending of separate identities. The power of affinity therefore seems to affirm the transcendent. Both Emerson and Thoreau believed that the apotheosis of a relationship is not its expression or gratification of individuality but its capacity to express, through the bonding of separate selves, something universal. Loving a universal law or transcendent principle through a friend may seem abstract and passionless, but listen to Thoreau's ardor when he portrays the ideal utterance of "the true and not despairing Friend": "I never asked thy leave to let me love thee,—I have a right. I love thee not as something private and personal, which is *your own*, but as something universal and worthy of love, *which I have found*. O how I think of you! You are purely good,—you are infinitely good. I can trust you forever. I did not think that humanity was so rich. Give me an opportunity to live" (Week 269). To love another as "something universal" is to love some power in which we too can participate and derive new identity. While Thoreau's language seems at first to idealize the loved one as theoretical or unreal ("You are purely good,—you are infinitely good"), his deeper purpose is to suggest that the love of another brings us a greater sense of our own unrealized capabilities for goodness, which we see exemplified in the one we love. It is for this reason that he adds the important observation "I did not think that humanity was so rich," emphasizing how love grants us a larger perception and makes us more confident of our ability to enlarge ourselves morally and spiritually. He follows this observation with a declaration, or a plea, that grounds his idealism in moral purpose: "Give me an opportunity to live."

No sentence in *A Week* is more resonant with meaning than this deep wish for the "opportunity to live," when we remember its context in Thoreau's grief for John and his complex struggle to accept his fate as a survivor and thus to live, in a sense, as John's surrogate. In the face of the doubts that John's death raised, Thoreau presents friendship as the means of opening life to a greater richness and moral intensity. He situates friendship as the antithesis of death, a condition that, through a force or power as mysteriously determined as that of death, lends meaning and possibility to life.

The obvious danger of friendship conceived as the unwilled love of "something universal" in another is that it threatens to transform the most intensely personal of inner drives into something coldly impersonal. While it may seem that we are drawn to a friend's unique character, this desire for the particular qualities of the individual finally dissolves into a pursuit of something abstract or disembodied. This converts the inescapable passion that drives friendship into a means of moral aspiration. The closely intertwined qualities of the pursuit of friendship and the desire for moral betterment are echoed repeatedly by Thoreau and Emerson, and their depictions of the nature of successful relationships are thus permeated with images of strife and conflict.

Emerson argued that friendship depends on some measure of difference and resistance, and that it requires "that rare mean betwixt likeness and un-likeness, that piques each with the presence of power and of consent in the other party." Unless that difference exists, and is enacted in full honesty, there is an irreparable loss. "Let me be alone to the end of the world," Emerson declared, "rather than that my friend should overstep by a word or a look his real sympathy. I am equally baulked by antagonism and by com-pliance." A harmony of opinion or of action is not necessary and sometimes not even desirable. Friendship is less the hunger for sameness than for dif-ference, the separate identity of a friend serving to goad us into a fuller self-possession. "Let him not cease an instant to be himself. The only joy I have in his being mine, is that the *not mine* is *mine*" (CW 2:122). With the recog-nition of difference comes a joy, the self brought to a more profound fulfill-ment through the stimulus of the other.

This form of friendship entails a perpetual tension between friends and generates a relationship built on plain speaking and sharp-edged encounters. "I hate, where I looked for a manly furtherance, or at least a manly resis-tance, to find a mush of concession," Emerson says. "Better be a nettle in the side of your friend than his echo" (CW 2:122–23). This nettlesome quality is the sign of valid difference and necessary honesty, guaranteeing that a relationship has not settled into complacency or evasion. But its ulti-mate demand is that one live as if friendship itself is expendable. "The con-dition which high friendship demands, is, ability to do without it" (CW 2:123).

Thoreau concurred with this demanding view of friendship, but we can imagine how it must have complicated his desire for Emerson's support and approval, and added further layers of reticence and coolness to his shy per-sonality. Nevertheless, he celebrated friendship as an important element in his pursuit of a more complete self-realization. "For a companion, I require one who will make an equal demand on me with my own genius" (Week 279), he wrote, much in the same spirit in which Emerson had defined the ideal relationship as "a nettle in the side of your friend." For Thoreau, the greatest expression of loving generosity between two persons was a high ex-pectation, a belief that one's friend was capable of moral excellence. "After years of vain familiarity, some distant gesture or unconscious behavior, which we remember, speaks to us with more emphasis than the wisest or kindest words." The power of such acts is that they reveal that our friend "treated us not as what we were, but as what we aspired to be" (Week 259), an expectation that actually confirms the better self toward which we aspire. Demanding and potentially conflict-laden as it might prove to be, Thoreau believed that such a relationship would deepen our hold on experience.

The problem was, however, that friendship had been conventionalized, made routine, and had thus become hollow and dissatisfying. Writing of friendship in an age given to lavishing friendship with sentimental approbation, Thoreau had to write against the grain to emphasize his sense of its rarity. Thus he adopts Emerson's seemingly hard attitude that relationships must have edges to be real and valuable.

> We are continually acting a part in a more interesting drama than any written. We are dreaming that our Friends are our *Friends*, and that we are our Friends' *Friends*. Our actual Friends are but distant relations of those to whom we are pledged. We never exchange more than three words with a Friend in our lives, on that level to which our thoughts and feelings almost habitually rise. One goes forth prepared to say "Sweet Friends!" and the salutation is "Damn your eyes!" (Week 265)

The "Friend" is of course the conventional name for our daily companions; but Thoreau also uses its italicized version to signify our true companion, and the deeper relationship that we desire when we use that term. The gap between the ordinary state of interpersonal relationships in the culture and what we both expect and demand from such relationships is maddeningly wide.

Thoreau's meditation on friendship is thus simultaneously a sternly critical piece of social commentary and a cry from the heart. His judgmental impulses alternate with his deep desire for meaningful relationships. The tension is clear in his observation of the perpetual and disappointing search that constitutes the daily lives of almost everyone. "No word is oftener on the lips of men than Friendship, and indeed no thought is more familiar to their aspirations. All men are dreaming of it, and its drama, which is always a tragedy, is enacted daily. It is the secret of the universe" (Week 264–65). The superficiality of most relationships is fundamentally unsatisfying, and does not quiet the urge for a more complete communication and mutual understanding.

Thoreau's representation of a fulfilling friendship is striking, however, because it does not include the kind of verbal interchange that would seem to be the foundation of mutual understanding. In fact, he specifically excludes a dependence on language as the means of securing the bond of friendship. "Let me never have to tell thee what I have not to tell. Let our intercourse be wholly above ourselves, and draw us up to it. The language of Friendship is not words but meanings. It is an intelligence above language" (Week 273). He imagines instead a tacit understanding between friends that makes conversation unnecessary and even disruptive. Recognizing that language is beset with imprecision and a source of potential misunderstanding, he envisions instead a state of unspoken trust between friends, "an intelligence above language," in which the separation of individuals implied by language is overcome. While friendship "is a miracle which requires constant proofs," its perpetual reaffirmation is not the work of language but of "a silent but eloquent behavior" that Thoreau terms a "divine courtesy" (Week 272). Each member of the relationship, that is, must demonstrate to the other a kind of ideal behavior, modeling a moral excellence that becomes a constantly renewing declaration of love.

The etiquette of such friendships seems to be a strange mixture of casualness and formalized distance, in which the discussion of the relationship itself, or any allusion to the needs of the parties for each other, is a sign of something amiss. "He [the friend] never asks for a sign of love, but can distinguish it by the features which it naturally wears. We never need to stand upon ceremony with him with regard to his visits. Wait not till I invite thee, but observe that I am glad to see thee when thou comest. It would be paying too dear for thy visit to ask for it" (Week 272). Such invitations or requests, ordinary as they may seem, constitute a sign of weakness, a hint that the perfect independence necessary for friendship will be compromised. Only in a situation in which nothing needs to be or can be said can one feel that understanding is complete and that the friendship is secure.

Emerson too was troubled by a friendship that was too overtly expressive or demanding, and his rejection of such developments is even blunter:

Why should we desecrate noble and beautiful souls by intruding on them? Why insist on rash personal relations with your friend? Why go to his house, or know his mother and brother and sisters? Why be visited by him at your own? Are these things material to our covenant? Leave this touching and clawing. Let him be to me a spirit. A message, a thought, a sincerity, a glance from him, I want, but not news, nor pottage. (CW 2:123)

Emerson's insinuation that contact is the source of all troubles among friends summarizes the paradox of this austere philosophy. The more one loves a friend, the less one should want to see her. The more one understands a friend, the less one should want to speak with him. "We must be our own," he insists, "before we can be another's" (CW 2:124). Emerson translates the drive for relationship into a drive for independence, making passion for another the fuel for self-development. Ultimately, he argues, such independence is the necessary requisite of the friendship we crave. "There can never be deep peace between two spirits, never mutual respect until, in their dialogue, each stands for the whole world" (CW 2:124).

These depictions of friendship are of course public statements, part of a larger philosophical and ethical project in which Emerson, Thoreau, and their Transcendentalist associates were engaged. They understood these writings as part of a larger effort at social reform and educational advancement, attempts to bring modern culture to a more satisfying and ethically sustainable way of life. But reading these commentaries on friendship by two friends side by side reminds us of how intertwined such texts were in the actual relationships that Emerson, Thoreau, and their circle of friends were attempting to practice. These essays contain quite specific interpersonal signals, translating the daily experience of their own interactions into broader theoretical axioms. Certainly, Thoreau's reading of Emerson's "Friendship" was more than a philosophical encounter, for he understood that insofar as Emerson was writing from his own life and experience, he was writing in part, and perhaps in large part, about Thoreau. He was also setting the goals and conditions of their continuing friendship. By the same token, Thoreau's essay on friendship in *A Week* has to be taken as his response to Emerson's challenge—for challenge it certainly was, if Thoreau aspired to friendship with him. Thoreau's response is not just to accept Emerson's challenge through his own depiction of an austerely restrained enactment of friendship, but to go even beyond Emerson in his insistence on the "divine courtesy" of the silent but knowing friends.

Emerson's plea for separation between friends relieved the essentially shy and reclusive Thoreau of the annoyance of social niceties and the discomfort of frequent or prolonged conversation. In that sense it accorded with his own temperament, even as it promised a new form of relationship that avoided the mannered superficiality of conventional friendships. In *A Week*, Thoreau is therefore signaling his agreement with Emerson's desire to discard the trivialities and decorum that encrust themselves on most relationships. He is signaling to Emerson his worthiness as a friend, and his desire for friendship on these new and demanding terms. Beneath the brave talk of independence, talk that Thoreau certainly believed in one sense, there is also the hope for a bond that, by Thoreau's own assent, cannot be directly expressed.

It would of course be illuminating to know more exactly how Thoreau and Emerson conversed and interacted; their journals do offer occasional glimpses into their conversations which, though sparse in detail, provide some clues. Emerson's record of a conversation in October 1841, some six months after he had published his "Friendship" essay,[30] is particularly arresting:

> I have seen scores of people who can silence me, but I seek one who shall take me off my feet, and make me forget or overcome those sudden frigidities & imbecilities to which I am prone to fall. I told H.T. that his freedom is in the form, but he does not disclose new matter. I am very familiar with all his thoughts,—they are my own quite originally drest. But if the question be, what new ideas has he thrown into circulation, he has not yet told what that is which he was created to say. (JMN 8:96)

Emerson's frankness about his expectations must certainly have placed a burden on his friendship with Thoreau. His demand for originality was sure to produce at least some anxiety in his friend, a feeling that his worthiness hinged in part on a kind of intellectual performance, and on a willingness not to seek accord with Emerson but rather to contradict or go beyond Emerson's own premises.

As their relationship grew, and strains became more and more prominent, Thoreau developed his own distinctive approach to the set of intellectual issues that Emerson had addressed in his early works. But Thoreau's first response, one that seems to have been operative for the most part through the writing of *Walden*, was to extend Emerson's viewpoint radically, turning Emerson's own words against him. Emerson preached the spiritual value of nature, and Thoreau became a dedicated naturalist; Emerson preached nonconformity and self-reliance, and Thoreau refused any ordinary professional path and went to live in the woods. Emerson preached an austere, rigorously demanding, and essentially self-denying form of friendship, and Thoreau echoed his sentiments in thunder, even while he craved Emerson's acceptance, support, and intellectual guidance.

Perhaps the most poignant aspect of Thoreau's discussion of friendship in *A Week* is his frank admission that the key to friendship, a silence that signals a mutual understanding that goes beyond language, can also be its undoing. "I sometimes hear my Friends complain finely that I do not appreciate their fineness," he writes. "I shall not tell them whether I do or not. As if they expected a vote of thanks for every fine thing which they uttered or did" (Week 277–78). For Thoreau, this need to communicate approval directly compromises the motives for goodness and taints the undertaking of human relationships with the threat of flattery. "There are some things which a man never speaks of, which are much finer kept silent about. To the highest communications we only lend a silent ear" (Week 278). This is a silence grounded in respect and approval, a silence that emphasizes the surety of the shared perception and values between the friends. The more profound the friendship, Thoreau reasons, the deeper the silence. "Our finest relations are not simply kept silent about, but buried under a positive depth of silence, never to be revealed" (Week 278). He attributes to such relations a kind of awed reverence, a holiness that should not be profaned by speech.

The problem, of course, is that such unspoken faith is extremely open to misinterpretation. Its aim is to express a trust, yet its effect is to ward off conversation and therefore leave open the possibility of mistrust. Although he affirms the holiness of silence, Thoreau recognizes its tragic potential within a relationship. "In human intercourse the tragedy begins, not when there is misunderstanding about words, but when silence is misunderstood. Then there can never be an explanation" (Week 278). When the tacit agreement between friends, sealed by a reverent silence, somehow becomes derailed, a relationship is undermined at its foundation. "What avails it that another loves you, if he does not understand you," he asks. "Such love is a curse" (Week 278). Although Thoreau demands, like Emerson, that a friend be the "other" who goads him into a deeper understanding of himself and the world, he is equally insistent that the relationship be based on a complete unity of mutual perception—perhaps the hardest accomplishment in the work of friendship.

WE ARE STILL BEING BORN

The remembered ascent of Saddleback Mountain on Tuesday and the meditation on friendship occasioned by the camaraderie of the riverbank campsite on Wednesday are dissonant sections that emphasize *A Week*'s reflection of Thoreau's inner tensions. But insofar as the narrative gains thematic coherence, it does so through its accumulating realizations of nature's sharp and uncompromising realities, facts of experience that, joyful or tragic, challenge the individual to more comprehensive acts of perception, free of distorting assumptions and expectations, and lead to a more absolute engagement in the texture of life. The momentum of this emphasis on engagement accelerates in the final chapters, as Thoreau recounts his return to Concord and considers its implications. The last days of the voyage mark the end of the idyllic retreat with John and the return to a life that would end, he knows in retrospect, in tragedy. That tragedy is not, of course, something that Thoreau could or would make explicit in the text, but its reality is always just beneath the surface of the narrative.

Beginning the return on Thursday, now gliding downstream with the current, Thoreau starts to recount the captivity narrative of Hannah Dustan, an early settler who was captured by Indians and saw her baby killed by them. The same river and the same landscape in which he now finds himself had been the scene of violent struggle and desperate flight a century and a half earlier. "This seems a long while ago," Thoreau comments, "and yet it happened since Milton wrote his Paradise Lost" (Week 324). The unfallen forest retains an essential innocence despite the blood that has been spilled in it by fallen humans.[31] The historical context of this violence is significant—a battle over the control and ownership of land in which one people were seeking to displace another. It was the Indians who ultimately lost a paradise in this conflict, and despite his ancestry and tradition, Thoreau feels a kinship with their experience.

One of the most revealing moments in Thoreau's account of the Dustan narrative is his imaginative reconstruction of the landscape as the fleeing Dustan might have seen it, while "the spring is opening" and "a few faint-singing forest birds, perchance, fly across the river to the northernmost shore." These details are lost to the fleeing captives, who "do not smile or chat all day" (Week 322–23). These comments establish Thoreau's distance from Dustan and link him to her enemies, who lived with a sense of belonging in a world that the European found alien. "On either side, the primeval forest stretches away uninterrupted to Canada or to the 'South Sea;' to the white man a drear and howling wilderness, but to the Indian a home, adapted to his nature, and cheerful as the smile of the Great Spirit" (Week 323).

Different as his experience seems from Dustan's, Thoreau is nevertheless a product of the same culture that has set itself so decidedly apart from the natural world. This tragedy of separation is embodied in the apple tree against which Dustan's baby was crushed, a complex symbol of the lost Eden. Thoreau recognizes the melancholy fact that in returning, he too is returning to a fallen world. Only through his voyage back into the world from which Dustan had fled in terror, his momentary "escape" from civilization we might say, is Thoreau able to recognize his complicity with the "civilization" that the European settlers advanced.[32]

Thoreau's river trip has provided him with a Transcendentalist version of the Miltonic "fortunate fall," however. If there has been a fall, there must have been an Eden. Although he returns to Concord burdened with a sense of fundamental spiritual loss, he also returns with the ironic surety that this loss provides. The Indian, the "fabulous wild man" (Week 323) from whom Dustan fled, signifies both loss and hope, a figure whose demise before modern European civilization is a tragedy, but whose presumed harmony with nature signifies the possibility of the recovery of paradise. While his memory of the trip includes the pain of his subsequent loss of John, it also contains the reassurance that he has journeyed into Eden, even though he may not have recognized it until later.

The changing colors on the riverbank elaborate the motif of the "fall" as the Thoreau brothers return to civilization.[33] Thoreau's pensive mood suggests the difficulty of bidding Eden farewell, and of relinquishing his memories of the bond with John that the journey represented. The imperative that energizes the end of *A Week* is Thoreau's determination to make the journey a sign of hope, and to believe that the autumnal mood that he feels as he concludes the journey (and its narrative) can be fruitful. He must convert his sense of loss into a motive for positive change and reaffirm his commitment to purposeful living.

Thoreau embodies his hopes for a transformed life in the figure of the "naturalist," whose engagement in studying the processes of natural history is also a project that is life-affirming and life-transforming. "The eye which can appreciate the naked and absolute beauty of a scientific truth is far more rare than that which is attracted by a moral one," Thoreau observes. "Few detect the morality in the former, or the science in the latter" (Week 361). The naturalist is a figure of reconciliation who can bring together superficially opposed modes of intellectual endeavor and satisfy Thoreau's conflicting inner demands. The question is how to live such a life. "The fact which interests us most is the life of the naturalist," he writes, not the facts or subjects that the naturalist studies (Week 362).

The natural study to which he aspires is more than factual accumulation; its aim is "law" rather than "fact," and it is akin to the poet's synthesizing consciousness, or the instinctual capacities of the individual untainted by modern civilization. "The power to perceive a law is equally rare in all ages of the world, and depends but little on the number of facts observed. The senses of the savage will furnish him with facts enough to set him up as a philosopher" (Week 364). Thoreau connects true knowledge with experience and divorces it from the corruptions of civilization, arguing that the accumulation of knowledge lacks value for those who come to it simply as fact. "Knowledge is to be acquired only by a corresponding experience. How can we *know* what we are *told* merely?" (Week 365).

This is a call to a kind of nature study that emphasizes close personal observation of phenomena in the field and a general disposition to search for the underlying patterns and natural systems, a work that would grow increasingly important to Thoreau in the years following his completion of *A Week*. The ties between his loose theorizing about the methodology of science and his attempts to mark and define a vocational route for himself suggest that the ending of *A Week* was an important exercise of preparatory orientation for the set of interlinked environmental, agrarian, literary, and ethical projects that characterized his experience at Walden. These originate in Thoreau's resolve to recover, or reinvent, what it means to live a "*natural life*" (Week 379).[34]

The "Friday" chapter thus becomes a festival of celebration of the "*natural life*," fueled in part by the motif of the "fall" that had proceeded it. Thoreau's sense of a departure from Eden generates a determination to rediscover the natural world that will still remain for him when he returns to Concord. "Men nowhere, east or west, live yet a *natural life*, round which the vine clings, and which the elm willingly shadows" (Week 379). This dedication to "natural life" is Thoreau's new credo, the vision that best describes his aspirations at Walden and afterwards. In emphatic distinction from the image of spiritual transcendence at the summit of Saddleback, Thoreau here presents a much fuller picture of the kind of being in the world that would fulfill humanity's highest religious and moral aspirations. Natural life is oriented to worldly experience and marked by a renewed sensuous awareness. "Man would desecrate [nature] by his touch, and so the beauty of the world remains veiled to him. He needs not only to be spiritualized, but *naturalized*" (Week 379). To be "naturalized" entails a purification and revivification of our "touch," our fundamental contact with the world. "We need pray for no higher heaven," he declares, "than the pure senses can furnish, a *purely* sensuous life" (Week 382). Thoreau finds this recovery and development of the life of the senses the primary work of self-culture. "We are comparatively deaf and dumb and blind, and without smell or taste or feeling. Every generation makes the discovery, that its divine vigor has been dissipated, and each sense and faculty misapplied and debauched" (Week 382). Thoreau catalogs the senses, linking hearing, speech, sight, smell, taste, and touch with the "divine vigor." The restoration of the senses means the restoration of divinity as well. "The ears were made, not for such trivial uses as men are wont to suppose, but to hear celestial sounds. The eyes were not made for such grovelling uses as they are now put to and worn out by, but to behold beauty now invisible. May we not *see* God?" (Week 382).

The quest to see, hear, and touch God is Thoreau's language for a reawakened life in the world. "It is easier to discover another such a new world as Columbus did, than to go within one fold of this which we appear to know so well" (Week 383). Despite the difficulties, it is this effort at "discovering" the world we presume to know already that is the essence of the "natural life" he envisions. Noting the bracing and clarifying impact that such seemingly small things as the sounds of echoing music or the fragrance of ripening fruit can have on us, Thoreau declares that "we live on the edge of another and purer realm, from which these odors and sounds are wafted over to us" (Week 381). Our situation on the border of Eden is revealed to us primarily through our senses rather than through any process of rational calculation, and it is thus the further purification and perfection of the senses that becomes imperative. "The borders of our plot are set with flowers, whose seeds were blown from more Elysian fields adjacent. They are the pot-herbs of the Gods. Some fairer fruits and sweeter fragrances wafted over to us, betray another realm's vicinity" (Week 381). Such glimpses of the actual nature of a realm that we inhabit but do not really know in detail are the hints of a new and more perfected life that Thoreau is now advocating with such intensity. "This world has many rings, like Saturn, and we live now on the outmost of them all" (Week 384). The goal is to move inward toward the center and source of the gravity that we sense but do not fully comprehend. "We are still being born" (Week 385).

Thoreau's insistence on our proximity to "another realm" dramatically alters the mood of the closing of *A Week*. The course of the narrative itself, with its burden of grief and melancholy, its confrontation with the limits of perception, time, and will, and its moments of stoical resignation to fate, amplifies the significance of these closing affirmations, making them compelling declarations of new purpose. This vision of a "natural life," with its emphasis on the new responsibility to live intensely, is the prophetic call that concludes *A Week*. It carries into *Walden*, progressively shaping that text as a prolonged investigation of the natural life.

CHAPTER FOUR

Devour Yourself Alive

A DRAMA OF MANY SCENES

There is irony in Thoreau's closing call for a "natural life" in *A Week*, since he had presumably led and then abandoned such a life in his secluded cabin at Walden Pond before completing and publishing *A Week*. Thoreau worked intensively on his reflective reconstruction of his voyage with John during his two-year stay at Walden (1845–47), continued after he left his cabin at the pond to stay with Lidian Emerson while Ralph Emerson traveled in England, and finally completed and published the book in May 1849, after Emerson had come home and Thoreau had returned to live with his family in Concord. *A Week* is a book of memory, but it also reflects Thoreau's experience and thinking in the middle and late 1840s, one of the most intellectually vital and emotionally complex periods of his life. He found his literary voice in these years, writing and publishing not only *A Week* but also "Civil Disobedience" and "Ktaadn," and drafting the first versions of *Walden*. In these years he also began to establish a certain freedom *from* authorship, and to develop alternative arrangements of living and working that allowed him to manage constructively the demands of writing and integrate them into the larger pattern of his life. This freedom was bought with some pain, in both the disappointment and the financial burden that resulted from the commercial failure of *A Week*, and in the strains of his relationship with Emerson, whose role as close friend was sometimes in conflict with his role as a professional adviser.

But Emerson never gave Thoreau a better gift than the use of his land at Walden Pond. There Thoreau translated Emerson's call to "build your own world" into the search for a "natural life." In almost every respect Thoreau's two years at Walden were an enormously positive period of growth in which he began to achieve a measure of personal independence and to make himself into an accomplished literary artist. "I wish to meet the facts of life–the vital facts, which where the phenomena or actuality the Gods meant to show us,—face to face, And so I came down here." His journal entry of July 6, 1845, two days after he had taken up residence at the pond, suggests the combination of determined purpose and open experimentation that marked his decision to live at Walden. His mixed mood of confidence, anxiety, and curiosity suggests that he understood his departure to the woods as a significant turning point, an opportunity for both discovery and self-formation. He was unsure of the result of his experiment, but certain that the engagement with life that it brought was worth the risk. "Life! who knows what it is–what it does? If I am not quite right here I am less wrong than before" (JP 2:156).

We can now recognize the Walden experiment as an important phase of Thoreau's development, but not the ultimate answer to his emotional needs and vocational struggles, nor the culmination of his intellectual life. To understand it fully we must ask not only why he went to the pond but also why he left it. "I left the woods for as good a reason as I went there," he tells us near the end of *Walden*, but his explanation is somewhat indirect and suggests a measure of indecisiveness or uncertainty: "Perhaps it seemed to me that I had several more lives to live, and could not spare any more time for that one." This restlessness is one of the bedrock principles of Thoreau's personal ethic: the unchanging need for self-renewal. "It is remarkable how easily and insensibly we fall into a particular route, and make a beaten track for ourselves. I had not lived there a week before my feet wore a path from my door to the pond-side; and though it is five or six years since I trod it, it is still quite distinct" (Wa 323). Not just going to Walden but leaving it, too, were necessary and positive gestures, the signs of an essential stance of openness to new experience.[1]

The journal entry on which this passage is based is revealing for the way it amplifies Thoreau's initial ambivalence and puzzlement about his reasons for leaving the pond. Written in January 1852, as he was beginning the second phase of the revision and expansion of *Walden*, it suggests a reaching back to attempt to comprehend a decision that is no longer comprehensible, and perhaps never was. "But Why I changed–? Why I left the woods? I do not think that I can tell. I have often wished myself back– I do not know any better how I ever came to go there–." There is a quality of bewilderment, and even an edge of disappointed bitterness, that is surprising in the entry, and the impact of his statement is sharpened by his confession that "I have often wished myself back" at the pond. He continues with a series of conjectural hypotheses about the end of his Walden stay that seem less explanations than rationalizations, and it is on these that he eventually builds the passage that he published in *Walden*:

> Perhaps I wanted a change– There was a little stagnation it may be–about 2 o'clock in the afternoon the world's axle—creaked as if it needed greasing–as if the oxen labored–& could hardly get their load over the ridge of the day– Perhaps if I lived there much longer I might live there forever – One would think twice before he accepted heaven on such terms– A ticket to Heaven must include tickets to Limbo–Purgatory–& Hell." (JP 4:275)

Thoreau's tangled and elusive train of thought signifies his unclear intentions and unresolved regrets. If the laboring oxen represent Thoreau himself, he seems to suggest that a failure of strength or of capability, or some insurmountable obstacle, led to his abandonment of the experiment.

While the tentative quality of this introspective meditation makes Thoreau's reason for leaving Walden unclear, more concrete and immediate reasons seem to lie in his literary goals and emotional needs. After all, the Walden sojourn was in large measure a writer's retreat, a step in Thoreau's larger strategy for his literary career, and a signal that his experience in New York by no means destroyed his literary ambitions.[2] After two years at the pond, Thoreau felt that he had two books within reach and had completed (in "Civil Disobedience") or begun (in "Ktaadn") two of his most important essays. In this very practical sense the experiment was successful, providing Thoreau with the most productive period of his literary life.

The aggressively self-reliant narrator of *Walden*, an important expression of Thoreau's personality and aspirations in the middle and late 1840s, has obscured the even stronger need for belonging and relationship that continued to haunt Thoreau in these years. This is perhaps most convincingly demonstrated when we recognize that it was an invitation to move into the Emerson household during Emerson's lecture tour in England that occasioned his leaving the pond. A frequenter and sometime resident of the Emerson home since 1841, Thoreau continued to fill the complicated role of intimate friend, intellectual ally and apprentice, and loyal family retainer. Thoreau's need for independence was growing, and he was beginning to chafe at Emerson's expectations, but his underlying sense of loyalty and gratitude, and his personal affection for both the Emersons, remained strong. The promise of Thoreau's availability as a companion and helper to Lidian had no doubt helped the Emersons negotiate the difficulties of Emerson's plans for extended travel overseas. On August 30, 1847, some two months before he left for England, Emerson wrote to his brother William that "Lidian has invited Henry Thoreau to spend the winter here, & will probably take Mrs Brown to board (ELet 3:415). That both Emersons seemed to need Thoreau at this moment was undoubtedly important to him. And the prospect of a winter in Emerson's comfortable house, with access to Emerson's sizable library, no doubt added to the attraction of Lidian's invitation, the simple and secluded life at the pond notwithstanding.

It was also probably important to Thoreau that the invitation had come from Lidian. His relationship with her had been warm, and he had written her somewhat emotional letters from Staten Island that communicate a very deep attachment (Corr 103, 119–20).[3] That his attachment deepened during Emerson's extended absence in England is suggested by a journal entry of 1849 in which he describes his devotion to an unnamed "Sister": "You are of me & I of you I can not tell where I leave off and you begin" (JP 3:17). The passage is abstract and highly spiritualized, but it is also surprisingly passionate, and reveals the inner turmoil and profound need for close emotional bonds that Thoreau continued to feel. It suggests that Lidian stirred his emotions deeply:

When I love you I feel as if I were annexing another world to mine. We splice the heavens. Can there be a rich man who does not own a friend?

My sister, it is glorious to me that you live. Thou art a hushed music to me—a thousand melodies commingled and filling the air. Thou art transfigured to me, and I see a perfect being– O Do not disappoint me. (JP 3:18)

Thoreau describes and addresses a "sister" here, and later describes this figure maternally ("my young mother–I thy eldest son") and even as a part of himself, "the feminine of me" (JP 3:18).[4] But the passage suggests a deep yearning in which idealizing language is straining hard to contain emotional longing and displace sexual desire. Henry Seidel Canby's blunt assertion that "Thoreau was what the common man would call in love with Emerson's wife" has of course been controversial since he made it in his 1939 biography, but Thoreau's letters to Lidian and journal entries that seem to be about her suggest that his loneliness and emotional needs played a large role in his decision to leave his Walden cabin.[5] Thoreau moved in with the Emersons in September 1847, some two months before Emerson left for England, and so the Walden experiment ended.

His leaving the pond should not obscure, however, the shaping impact of his experience there, something that grew in importance as he reconstructed it in *Walden*. His opening emphasis on thrift and simple living, based on his first lectures about his Walden life, had a practical source in his particular economic situation, as did the work in the bean field which Thoreau undertook during his stay at the pond. Life at Walden promised to answer a number of philosophical questions for him, but it also promised to answer, or at least render temporarily irrelevant, the question of his vocation. There he would be not only free from considerations of work in the conventional sense, but also free for the extended projects that he felt necessary to fulfill his literary ambitions. Readers and commentators who have noted that Thoreau was not completely cut off from the potential economic support of his family and of Emerson in Concord have a point. It is a mistake to read *Walden* as a narrative of a survivalist experiment in the wilderness, as modern readers are sometimes prone to do. But that is not to dismiss the vitally important nexus of economic and vocational forces that made the experiment a logical and practical step for him.

Thoreau's remark that he had "private business" to conduct at the pond highlights another crucial motivation in his undertaking the experiment, one raised in Ellery Channing's somewhat teasing suggestion that Thoreau's only hope was to "begin the grand process of devouring yourself alive" (Corr 161). Although financial and vocational motivations were central to Thoreau's decision to launch the experiment, he also understood that a life in the woods offered extraordinary opportunities to establish a daily life centered on contemplative self-discovery and spiritual discipline. While life at Walden may have been conducive to his literary work—the evidence is overwhelming on this—and may also have provided him with a measure of self-confident maturity, he portrayed the most important accomplishment of the experiment as the development of his inner life: "I grew in those seasons like corn in the night, and they were far better than any work of the hands would have been" (Wa 111).

Thoreau's feeling that he was coming into closer contact with fundamental ethical laws and bedrock ontological realities permeates both the text of

Walden and the journal entries that were the basis of his early drafts of the text, especially the Journals designated as "Walden 1," "Walden 2," and the "Berg Journal," collected in the second volume of the Princeton edition of the *Journal*. The world seems to open to him in these texts, and that newness is paralleled by the inner discovery that arose from the meditative seclusion and self-discipline that his new way of life demanded. In mustering the necessary strength and ingenuity to live his radically simplified life, he was simultaneously putting himself in direct and constant touch with the laws that also revealed the workings of nature:

> I had this advantage, at least, in my mode of life, over those who were obliged to look abroad for amusement, to society and the theatre, that my life itself was become my amusement and never ceased to be novel. It was a drama of many scenes and without an end. If we were always indeed getting our living, and regulating our lives according to the last and best mode we had learned, we should never be troubled with ennui. (Wa 112)

A life that is "a drama of many scenes" is a life that is constantly evolving and reinventing itself. Thoreau understood more and more clearly that self-knowledge entailed a recognition of the fluid boundaries of the "self." He searched for ways to express the self's broad affinities and porous boundaries, finding important emotional sustenance in a "self" that was defined through its dynamic interactions with the natural world.

His description of the companionship he found in a rainstorm at the pond dramatizes his efforts to make peace with the isolation of his new life, depicting the self as a more flexible and amorphous entity than we ordinarily imagine. Remembering what he claims to be his one moment of loneliness at Walden, he dismisses the incident as "a slight insanity in my mood" during which he could, at every moment, anticipate his "recovery." It was then that he came to understand more completely the companionship of nature's many selves, to understand that "the most innocent and encouraging society may be found in any natural object, even for the poor misanthrope and most melancholy man" (Wa 131). As the rain continued, keeping Thoreau in his cabin, he became "suddenly sensible of such sweet and beneficent society in Nature, in the very pattering of the drops, and in every sound and sight around my house." The sensations of the storm converge with his mood of "slight insanity," and as the aural and visual stimuli increase dramatically, he is reminded of his exposure and vulnerability to forces beyond human control. But he also senses "an infinite and unaccountable friendliness all at once like an atmosphere sustaining me" (Wa 132). He has crossed an important threshold. He no longer witnesses the rainstorm; he is part of it, its physical manifestations both familiar and sustaining to him. The rain does not happen *to* him; he is, rather, a part of its larger occurrence. He embraces the whole of nature as the raindrops do, and also, as part of nature, feels the rain's embrace. He not only overcomes the brooding feeling of loneliness and melancholy but also becomes more fully "aware of the presence of something kindred to me" (Wa 132).

Thoreau's "self" was being "devoured," merging with all that was around him and all that he was aware of. Both his surroundings at the pond and the disciplined awareness that they helped to make possible worked to undermine the dichotomy of participant and observer that structures ordinary perceptual awareness. The moments of greatest philosophical and poetic intensity in *Walden* are these experiences of perceptual reorientation that reveal the inadequacy of conventional self-understanding.

A FOOL'S LIFE

Thoreau's difficulties in settling into a vocation, while rooted in his unique personality and circumstances, also yielded a powerful attack on America's obsession with work and consumption. Woven into the description of the life he lived at Walden is an aggressive critique of the life that most people around him led, exposing the thralldom of endless labor that depleted them of both perspective and energy, and the pointless and wasteful search for satisfaction and social status through the ownership and consumption of goods. "Men labor under a mistake," he warns. "By a seeming fate, commonly called necessity, they are employed, as it says in an old book, laying up treasures which moth and rust will corrupt and thieves break through and steal. It is a fool's life, as they will find when they get to the end of it, if not before" (Wa 5). Thoreau contrasts his "natural life" at the pond with this "fool's life," using its values as a reverse guide to his own reconstruction of possibility. Almost everything he shows his readers about the reformation of his way of life in the chapter on "Economy" also reflects his rejection, explicit or implicit, of commonly accepted axioms about the requirements of living and the prevalent but unexamined practices of ordinary life. "The whole ground of human life seems to some to have been gone over by their predecessors, both the heights and the valleys, and all things to have been cared for" (Wa 9). Such habitual and unquestioning comportment, revealing an apathetic acceptance of the inevitability of present social conditions, fuels an ire that adds a social dimension to Thoreau's work of autobiography. The move to the pond may be one individual's experiment in solitary living, but the significance of Thoreau's solitude is amplified by its continual reflection of the life of the town, the farm, and the family that it implicitly repudiates.

Thoreau's move to the pond was also a response to the rising interest in utopian experimentation in the early 1840s. The same sense of the futility and apathy of ordinary life that Thoreau articulates so sharply in "Economy" was widely shared among the Transcendentalists, whose initial intervention in the religious discourse of the day quickly evolved into an interest in programs of social reform and communal economic experiments. By the time Thoreau had taken up residence at the pond in 1845, the Brook Farm commune had already been in existence four years, and had refashioned itself, at least in theory, into a Fourierist phalanx. Bronson Alcott and his beleaguered family had returned to Concord after the failure of their Fruitlands communal experiment, an episode that tested the limits of Alcott's idealism, his wife, Abigail's, strength, and some of the assumptions of utopian reform thinking. Thoreau was keenly aware of these experiments, of course, and was steeped in the discourse surrounding them, in which he and Emerson had participated with both a sincere interest and an instinctive skepticism.[6]

Emerson's skepticism toward utopian communalism and the Fourierist movement in particular has been most heavily emphasized in the existing accounts of the Transcendentalist movement, and despite his genuinely divided mind on many issues connected with the movements, his reservations about them have come to seem prophetic. The pull of his conflicting inclinations about the possibility of utopian success is evident after a visit to the Alcotts just as they had begun the Fruitlands collective in July 1843. Emerson is struck by their serenity and seeming command of their course of life as they embark on the new experiment: "The sun & evening sky do not look calmer than Alcott & his family at Fruitlands. They seemed to have arrived at the fact, to have got rid of the show, & so to be serene." Emerson's reference to "the fact" and "the show" suggests a certain uneasiness about the grandiosity of Alcott's plans for the commune with the English reformer Charles Lane. Emerson worried that Alcott and Lane tended to see Fruitlands less as a new way of life than as a demonstration of certain social principles. Undertaking the project on such terms tended to falsify it, as if it were a stage production meant to impress an audience rather than a direct engagement with life. What relieved him during this visit was the lack of such staging or posing, the sense that Alcott was not playing a role but doing his work with a self-contained dignity and purpose. "Their manners & behavior in the house & in the field were those of superiour men, of men at rest. What had they to conceal? What had they to exhibit?" Nevertheless, Emerson could not dismiss the suspicion that uncontrollable forces shaped the terms of life more decidedly than most utopian reformers were willing to admit. "I will not prejudge them successful," he observed. "They look well in July. We will see them in December" (JMN 8:433). By then, Fruitlands had unraveled in utter failure.

Emerson's intimation of the ultimate collapse of Fruitlands is perhaps less important to us now than his praise of the Alcotts' simplicity and directness at the beginning of the experiment. Such praise carries the underlying conviction that theory did not motivate the attempt at reformation so much as it falsified it, turning experimentation into theater and reducing alienation to a pose. One can sense here Emerson's initial relief that the Fruitlanders do not seem to be playing to an audience, their parts scripted in the imaginations and conversations of Lane and Alcott and in the theorizing of the Fourierists. But his meditation raises the question of whether a social experiment can degenerate into performance, and whether such performance usurps the inner drive toward a more satisfactory social life and internal experience that is the fuel of utopianism.

Thoreau's stay at Walden Pond can only problematically be thought of as utopian, since it was by design an antisocial rather than a social experiment, a turning away from society. Nevertheless, he took with him to the pond the attitude of experimentation and hope that is vital to utopian thinking, and also a keen sense of the problematics of performance and audience that we detect in Emerson's comments on Fruitlands. We encounter some indication of his anxiety about role-playing in his life at the pond in the first pages of *Walden*, when he explains that "I should not obtrude my affairs so much on the notice of my readers if very particular inquiries had not been made by my townsmen concerning my mode of life" (Wa 3). As a respondent to his neighbors, even as a defender of his way of life, Thoreau can justify the lengthy and detailed account he gives of his Walden experiment, and while he thereby admits that his *narrative* has an audience, he preserves the idea that his living itself did not. Moreover, such skeptical questions from his townsmen establish the tone of embattled irony that works so effectively in the opening chapter; the very statement of the questions seems to defuse them as serious challenges, reflecting only the insecurity or self-righteousness behind them. "Some have asked what I got to eat; if I did not feel lonesome; if I was not afraid; and the like. Others have been curious to learn what portion of my income I devoted to charitable purposes; and some, who have large families, how many poor children I maintained" (Wa 3). Thoreau's retention of "the *I*, or first person," and his characterization of his book as "a simple and sincere account of his own life" (Wa 3), may indeed be crafted elements of the persona that he creates in *Walden*, as a long tradition of literary analysis has shown us. But Thoreau had implicitly considered this problem, and his persona is shaped by the worry that his life at the pond might be seen merely as the performance of a role rather than the logically inevitable action that he had taken to solve specific problems in the living of his life.

Thoreau also felt another form of pressure from both churches and social reformers as he undertook his solitary experiment. In referring to questions about his contributions to the poor or his support of children, Thoreau was broaching the larger question of the social relevance of his experiment, something crucial to his opening description and defense of his simplified economy and natural life. Although his initial response is to emphasize the monotonous imprisonment of conventional life, and to illustrate his own way of breaking those bonds, he addresses the question of the social relevance of his life more directly near the end of the "Economy" chapter, again using the challenge of those observing him as an opportunity for fuller self-explanation. "But all this is very selfish, I have heard some of my townsmen say" (Wa 72). This objection comes straight to the point, a point that has bothered many of Thoreau's readers over the years who have found in *Walden* a highly problematic individualism that, manifest in American culture at large, has been the source of a litany of social problems. Thoreau's *Walden* is in some ways the quintessential expression of American individualism. "The history of the New England tradition," Perry Miller wrote, "is a series of splinterings, of divisions, and subdivisions and the subdivision of subdivisions, until you are left breathless as you try to keep pace with the accelerating pace of Yankee individualism." Ultimately this process results in the lone individual, the church of one, whose self-sufficiency can be seen as dangerous to the hope of community. "Where," Miller asks, "beyond Emerson and Theodore Parker could the tradition of New England individualism go? Where indeed, but either to Walden Pond or into Big Business?" It is the implicit similarity of these last alternatives that concerns Miller, and has concerned many others.[7]

But the more pointed the objection to his experiment on the grounds of its individual narrowness, the more sharp and sarcastic is Thoreau's dismissal. "I confess that I have hitherto indulged very little in philanthropic enterprises. I have made some sacrifices to a sense of duty, and among others have sacrificed this pleasure also" (Wa 72). This is one of the most notable instances of Thoreau's rhetoric of inversion, the transformation of the duty of charity and good works into one of the indulgences and luxuries that he has demonstrated to be obstacles to fulfillment earlier in the chapter. "Most of the luxuries, and many of the so-called comforts of life, are not only not indispensable, but positive hinderances to the elevation of mankind" (Wa 14), he had argued, and he now turns the force of this argument on the demand for philanthropy, including it among those luxuries. This description of philanthropy as a suspect indulgence is of course related to the issue of performance and role-playing at Walden, for each case raises the question of sincerity and artificiality, and makes the clear distinction of one's motives for action crucial.

Thoreau uses the challenge of philanthropy to emphasize that his life at Walden is a genuine and necessary step of self-expression, the enactment of a calling whose moral grounding is as secure as that of any duty to work for the betterment of society or the help of others. "You must have a genius for charity as well as for anything else," he argues. "As for Doing-good, that is one of the professions which are full" (Wa 73). The "genius" he refers to is the sense of inner compulsion or calling that leads one to undertake a way of life or a project of activity that is both self-fulfilling and a contribution to the larger good of the world. Although he does not himself engage in philanthropic work—"I have tried it fairly, and, strange as it may seem, am satisfied that it does not agree with my constitution"—Thoreau understands his experiment as itself important. By fulfilling the duty of his calling, he is remaining faithful to a vision that is uniquely his own, the consequences of which may have a larger impact than he knows. It is finally an act of faith that a larger good will arise when individuals work in accordance with their own reason and conscience. "Probably I should not consciously and deliberately forsake my particular calling to do the good which society demands of me, to save the universe from annihilation; and I believe that a like but infinitely greater steadfastness elsewhere is all that preserves it" (Wa 73). This determination is of course linked to his diagnosis that the ills of conventional life are the result of the inability of men and women to maintain the integrity of their moral decision making in the face of the demands for conformity, status, and material gain. Rather than doing good, the motto of the philanthropists, Thoreau has other advice: "Set about being good" (Wa 73). To *do* good without the conviction of its necessity is inherently external and superficial; to *be* good forces us to accept a singular, self-directed responsibility.[8]

The false obligation of philanthropy is the last of the obstacles to the reformation of life that Thoreau considers in his initial chapter. The others are social and economic barriers, rooted in false or shallow aims, or the inability to forgo unnecessary physical comforts. "Economy" is an effort to clear the decks of these obstacles, using Thoreau's counterexample at Walden as decisive evidence. By beginning life anew at the pond—he moved into his cabin, as he tells us, on "the 4th of July" (Wa 45)—Thoreau was able to reconsider his economic needs in the strictest of terms, and fulfill only those that were absolute. This radical simplification of his wants is grounded in a strict discrimination between luxuries and necessities, with the resulting observation that modern civilization has redefined many luxuries as necessities. Thoreau insists on returning to a more fundamental set of definitions. "By the word *necessary of life*, I mean whatever, of all that man obtains by his own exertions, has been from the first, or from long use has become, so important to human life that few, if any, whether from savageness, or poverty, or philosophy, ever attempt to do without it" (Wa 12). Using this exacting standard, Thoreau is able to dismiss most of the ordinary patterns of consumption and ownership as superfluous to a fulfilling life, and demonstrate how such superfluities account for most of the worry and exertion, and most of the excessive labor, that bedevil the American middle class.

In this redefinition of the patterns of consumption and work, Thoreau is interrogating the concept of "freedom" that is central to the American national ideology, and insisting that it must be examined in the light of the daily experience of the majority of Americans. "Most men, even in this comparatively free country, through mere ignorance and mistake, are so preoccupied with the factitious cares and superfluously coarse labors of life that its finer fruits cannot be plucked by them." Thoreau's metaphor gains additional force when he extends it with a depiction of the debilitation and exhaustion that are the physical signs of overwork: "Their fingers, from excessive toil, are too clumsy and tremble too much for that" (Wa 6).

Obtaining the necessities must not, however, become an end in itself; it is only a necessary preliminary to the real work of living. "When he has obtained those things which are necessary to life," Thoreau argues, "there is another alternative than to obtain the superfluities; and that is, to adventure on life now, his vacation from humbler toil having commenced" (Wa 15). Not to begin this "adventure," to remain enmeshed in a never-completed struggle to achieve and then augment the material necessities, was thus to lose the point of living. "The mass of men lead lives of quiet desperation" (Wa 8). They have become convinced that their financial entrapment is inescapable, and thus have lost any larger sense of the purpose of life. The Walden experiment was only in a preliminary and superficial sense about getting a living more easily; the "natural life," as Thoreau conceived it, encompassed the pursuit of much larger means of self-expression and fulfillment.[9] "I know of no more encouraging fact than the unquestionable ability of man to elevate his life by a conscious endeavor" (Wa 90). This endeavor could not overlook the material and economic requirements of living, but it could not rest there either.

MERELY A SQUATTER

Acknowledging the primacy of economy, Thoreau began by explaining his frugal existence, peppering his descriptions with references to the agrarian life he hoped to lead, and the situation of other farmers that he saw around him. Writing at the outset of the industrial age, and aware of technological changes such as the railroad that were altering both the landscape and human society significantly, Thoreau saw his experiment at Walden as a return to fundamentals. In the summer of 1845, after he had begun his stay at the pond, he alluded to Wordsworth's rural life as a modern example of the kind of "serene and contented" life led by "the ancients." He aspired to this "simple epic country life–in these days of confusion and turmoil" (JP 2:200–201). That he based his "simple epic" life on farming, or at least on growing a crop, as a primary means of economic support further signified an act of recovery or a return to a lost essential. "Husbandry is a universally sacred art," he wrote in 1846, "pursued with too much heedlessness and haste by us" (JP 2:234). Thoreau believed himself to be returning to a direct relationship with nature and redefining human economic activity in terms of the fundamental productive energy of the natural world. Explaining his need "to earn ten or twelve dollars by some honest and agreeable method," he "planted about two acres and a half of light and sandy soil near [his hut] chiefly with beans, but also a small part with potatoes, corn, peas, and turnips" (Wa 54). Thoreau explains his farming as an act of necessity and practicality, the easiest way to solve an inescapable problem, but he sets himself apart from other farmers by making it clear that his methods cut against the grain of the conventional wisdom. Of his land, "one farmer said that it was 'good for nothing but to raise cheeping squirrels on.' I put no manure on this land, not being the owner, but merely a squatter, and not expecting to cultivate so much again, and I did not quite hoe it all at once" (Wa 54). This is farming of a kind, but Thoreau is also thumbing his nose at the farm community around him, taking a certain pride in his defiance of the established patterns of work.

There is, however, a set of counterexamples to which he makes frequent reference, the lives and cultures of "primitive" or "savage" peoples, and the similar examples of the earliest New England settlers and the contemporary dwellers on the American frontier. These all offer an alternative to the values of the settled New England farmer, whose work has become an entrapment. Thoreau was always careful to keep the object of his labor in mind, to earn "ten or twelve dollars by some honest and agreeable method," and to accommodate his work to that specific and limited goal. He scaled back his efforts in the fields his second year at Walden when he recognized that he did not need two and a half acres of beans. Throughout his explanation of his work, he strives to distinguish his life as a farmer from the lives of most of those around him, even as he recognizes the dignity and high purposefulness in the act of cultivating one's food. He rejected the advice of the farmers around him as well as "many celebrated works on husbandry" to confirm through his own experience that farming could be radically simplified, "if one would live simply and eat only the crop which he raised," and "raise no more than he ate" (Wa 55). This agrarian application of Thoreau's grand principle of simplification allowed him to preserve a sense of farming as a fundamental activity that explicitly linked human life to the productive capacity of nature.

It is in this sense that Thoreau's bean field, limited in aims and artless in method though it was, can be regarded as an agrarian experiment, as several critics have noted. Sherman Paul referred to *Walden* as in part "a modern epic of farming," noting the "Bean-Field" chapter as "an example of Thoreau's idea of organic social reform, of the reform that returned to the economy of nature rather than to economy," one that also entailed "self-reform." Leo Marx analyzed it as a "report of an experiment in transcendental pastoralism," weighing the extent to which Thoreau both affirmed and circumscribed the pastoral impulse.[10]

The experimental and potentially impermanent nature of his stay, however, militated against his conceiving it wholly in Jeffersonian terms of rootedness and permanence in a place that one owns. His description of what he regarded as his near mistake in negotiating for the purchase of the Hollowell Farm suggests his fear of the entanglements that a permanent commitment to a particular farm might bring. "I even had the refusal of several farms,—the refusal was all I wanted,—but I never got my fingers burned by actual possession" (Wa 82). In a journal entry of March 1841, when Thoreau was seriously considering buying a farm as a way of solving his problem of vocation, he reveals even more emphatically the wariness he felt about committing himself to a farm, or to any limiting profession, all of which threatened to imprison him in a stifling routine. "I must not lose any of my freedom by being a farmer and land holder," he writes. "Most who enter on any profession are doomed men–the world might as well sing a dirge over them forthwith. The farmer's muscles are rigid–he can do one thing long not many well. His pace seems determined henceforth–he never quickens it. A very rigid Nemesis is his fate" (JP 1:291). His Walden acreage, borrowed from Emerson, and richer in scenery than in humus, suited his needs more closely because it would be less likely to become an impediment to the spiritual restructuring of his life that he was also undertaking.

Even under these limited conditions, Thoreau's farming was an important part of his experiment, and eventually a prominent part of his narrative. Early versions of what came to be *Walden*, delivered first as lectures, included an account of "White Beans and Walden Pond."[11] The final text of *Walden* is saturated with references to the work of farming and the attitudes of farmers, which, despite his attempts to separate himself from them, suggest an unresolved tension in his thinking. Thoreau sees farming as an ennobling and empowering form of work which cuts against the grain of the social malaise that characterizes modern American society. His act of retiring to the country and *farming* it, and the prominence that he gives to his agrarian work in the text, are signs of his fundamental faith in country life as a valid social alternative. Despite his attacks on the farmers' misuse of their resources, Thoreau recognizes the potential of the farm as a means of economic self-sufficiency. This is of particular importance to him because he offers in *Walden* one of our earliest warnings against an incipient consumer culture, depicting agrarian life as a potential insulation from it: "Every New Englander might easily raise all his own breadstuffs in this land of rye and Indian corn, and not depend on distant and fluctuating markets for them" (Wa 63).

Thoreau also recognized, however, that in practice farming was often an enslaving drudgery. His critique of the ordinary patterns of middle-class life seems to focus most directly on the farmers.[12] He characterizes them as victims of their own greed and shortsightedness, individuals who have ironically defeated themselves through their misguided striving for betterment. "I see young men, my townsmen, whose misfortune it is to have inherited farms, houses, barns, cattle, and farming tools; for these are more easily acquired than got rid of" (Wa 5). The farm is a kind of prison that bends one to its own demands. "Who made them serfs of the soil?" he asks pointedly, playing against the Jeffersonian belief in the independence of the farmer. "Why should they eat their sixty acres, when man is condemned to eat only his peck of dirt? Why should they begin digging their graves as soon as they are born?" (Wa 5). The analogy between farm work and grave digging, between labor and death, is a powerful challenge to the assumptions that had enshrined the work of farming with a moral authority in American culture.

Thoreau chooses the analogy with a full sense of its provocative nature, and a clear understanding that he is undermining the social sanction that farming enjoyed in American culture. "The better part of the man is soon ploughed into the soil for compost" (Wa 5). The farmer is thus broken down and consumed by the farm he supposedly owns. The relationship between farm and farmer epitomizes Thoreau's general observation that material ownership or possession is often inverted in modern society. The laboring man thus "has no time to be any thing but a machine" (Wa 6), a loss of purpose and higher endeavor that drains life of any meaning.

These doubts about farming cannot be wholly overcome even by the simplified and purified version of it that Thoreau practices. One senses that his work in the field is always secondary to him, and that it remains somehow threatening, as if its demands must be kept closely in check lest they devour him. He is less proud of his success in growing his crop of beans the first summer at Walden than in his resulting resolution that "I will not plant beans and corn with so much industry another summer" (Wa 163–64). The farm is, in the last analysis, a place outside Eden, and its necessary work the reminder of a lost harmony between nature and humanity. "The very simplicity and nakedness of man's life in the primitive ages imply this advantage at least, that they left him still but a sojourner in nature." These "primitive ages" held for Thoreau the promise of a natural life, whose grace, ease, directness, and freedom had been lost to civilization. "The man who independently plucked the fruits when he was hungry is become a farmer; and he who stood under a tree for shelter, a housekeeper." This was not progress but decline, and its costs were primarily spiritual. "We now no longer camp as for a night, but have settled down on earth and forgotten heaven" (Wa 37). Uncertainty, vulnerability, direct exposure to and reliance upon natural forces, and a life of constant change and variety were not, as modern society had defined them, harmful or destructive conditions but rather spiritually enriching ones. Their gradual erosion, now accelerating rapidly in the industrial age, were calamities that Thoreau had set out to rectify within the confines of his own life. Farming was thus always the warning sign of the fall to him, a sure indicator that human life had not finally resolved itself into natural life. He would be a farmer at Walden, but he would do so with a double consciousness, aware of the farm's potential for self-reliant nobility but also of its tendency toward a subtle form of enslavement.

UNCHRONICLED NATIONS

Thoreau protects himself against the threat of the farm's becoming a prison of drudgery by assuming the attitude of a loafer. *Walden* contains a series of amusing incidents in which he mocks the conventional standards of responsible hard work.[13] "What demon possessed me that I behaved so well?" (Wa 10), he asks ironically. His well-known descriptions of his Walden occupations, such as "reporter to a journal, of no very wide circulation," and "self-appointed inspector of snow storms and rain storms" (Wa 18), are a calculated satire on the farmer's work ethic. "I have had an eye to the unfrequented nooks and corners of the farm" (Wa 18), he remarks slyly. His preference for geographical margins is the correlative of his intention to stay away from the pull of conventional expectations, especially as they concern work.

Attempting to protect himself from any rigid daily schedule, Thoreau emphasizes a quality of openness and spontaneity, especially in his depiction of his responses to the natural world. "There were times when I could not afford to sacrifice the bloom of the present moment to any work, whether of the head or hands." Some mornings he did not hoe beans but instead "sat in [his] sunny doorway from sunrise till noon, rapt in revery" (Wa 111), finding this gift of time and acceptance an important enhancement to his life.

Then again, he did hoe beans many mornings during that first year, and his crop of nine bushels and twelve quarts (Wa 163) is evidence of at least a moderate degree of diligence. It is with some pride that he mentions that "when they were growing, I used to hoe from five o'clock in the morning till noon" (Wa 161). Loafing constituted an important counterstatement to the debilitating work ethic of the farmer, but it was not Thoreau's only response. His nonchalance about work accounts for only one side of his strategy for countering the work ethic, for in another sense he remained deeply committed to it.[14] In *Walden* he aimed not to deny the absolute claims of work but to reformulate the spirit and awareness in which work is conducted. He hoped to demonstrate that moral self-fashioning required an unremitting spiritual labor, and that the physical labor necessary to sustain our daily lives must also be considered an integral part of this larger pattern of spiritual work. "To affect the quality of the day, that is the highest of arts" (Wa 90), he declared, and that change necessarily implied both a new mode of self-conception and a change of perception that would entail a reformulation of the quality of daily labor.

That reformulation was enabled by Thoreau's nurturing of what we might call the ecological orientation of his consciousness. "Ecology" was not a term available to Thoreau, but it has come to represent for our era a direction of thinking in which Thoreau was an originating participant.[15] I use it here to express the dramatically enlarged frame of reference that *Walden* adduces in its depictions of the human observation of, and interaction with, the natural world. This changed mode of interaction with the world is of particular importance in dictating the valuation of labor and other economic activities. "It was no longer beans that I hoed, nor I that hoed beans" (Wa 159), he writes in describing his morning work at one point. This mutual elision of identities signifies Thoreau's broadening perception, which breaks through the usual hierarchical relationship between the observing and use-making self and the observed and used object.

The cultivation of this capacity of knowing, the foundation of an ecological sensitivity, informs the agrarian aim of *Walden*, representing the larger spiritual and ethical attainment that is Thoreau's dearest hope. It is epitomized in the famous discussion in "Spring" of the "sand foliage" on the banks of the deep cut for the railroad tracks, in which the human body, the organic world, and the earth itself are shown to be a single evolving entity.[16] But it is important to remember how deeply that vision of wholeness is grounded in the particulars of Thoreau's observation and the detail of his description. The delicacy and precision of his seeing and knowing exemplify the state of awareness, or condition of being "awake," that he had hoped to recover at Walden. "Moral reform is the effort to throw off sleep," he had explained. "Why is it that men give so poor an account of their day if they have not been slumbering?" (Wa 90).

Being "awake" is Thoreau's most pointed metaphor for the enlargement of perspective that is fundamental to his ecological stance, and its antithesis, the condition of slumber, implies a world of events and objects from which the mind is cut off in isolation. Thoreau's acts of observation always imply an act of joining, a discovery of some fundamental quality of relatedness. His observation of the sand foliage, for instance, moves him to think in terms of the body. "What is man but a mass of thawing clay? The ball of the human finger is but a drop congealed" (Wa 307). Even his fanciful descriptions of the trumping of bullfrogs around the pond, "*tr-r-r-oonk, tr-r-r-oonk, tr-r-r-oonk!*" is given a humorously human context, as the bullfrogs are presented as "ancient wine-bibbers and wassailers" (Wa 126), passing the cup in increasingly sodden drunkenness. The passage tells us more about Thoreau than it does about bullfrogs, for his imaginative description exemplifies the acutely alert and energetically charged consciousness that Thoreau strives to maintain at Walden.

Thoreau's rhetoric of wakefulness is intended to make us aware of the rich network of affinities that constitutes the interlacing of human experience and the natural world. In one vivid metaphorical articulation of this connection, Thoreau referred to his head as "an organ for burrowing, as some creatures use their snout and fore-paws," and declared his intention to "mine and burrow my way through these hills" (Wa 98). The search for precious ore, typifying a human preoccupation, is here spoken of in the same phrase with the animal-like act of burrowing in the earth. Both of these operations signify the delving of the mind into nature, a metaphor of destructive conquest and use, but also of surrender and burial, suggesting the desire to be one with the earth. We may initially consider an image of burial as one of diminishment, but Thoreau's implication is quite the opposite. "I think the richest vein is somewhere hereabouts" (Wa 98), he declares, ending the paragraph on a note of active expectation.

Thoreau's concern with the promise of agrarian life and his parallel concern with an expansive ecological way of knowing come together in his representation of his work in the bean field (Wa 158–60), a significant assertion of the possibility of a union between labor and knowledge. His labor begins with a reference to another form of digging in the earth, drawing "a still fresher soil about the rows with my hoe," an act that is linked with life rather than burial because it brings nutriment not only to his beans but to himself as well. For a nation founded on the taxing, incessant labor of clearing, plowing, planting, cultivating, and harvesting, we have had surprisingly few literary representations of manual labor, a subject that most aspiring writers have regarded as decidedly unpromising territory. Thoreau's refusal to gloss over the effort it takes to get nine bushels of beans from an unfertilized field, frequented by a voracious woodchuck, is therefore important, both in its honest factuality and in its depiction of such work as an appropriate literary and ethical subject.

Perhaps most significant to the poetic representation of this work is the discovery that he makes with his hoe. "I disturbed the ashes of unchronicled nations who in primeval years lived under these heavens, and their small implements of war and hunting were brought to the light of this modern day" (Wa 158). Thoreau was well known in his Concord circle for his knowledge of Native American artifacts and culture, and his discovery of such artifacts here is a reminder of the displacement of the Indian from the land. Thoreau transforms his discovery, initially a sign of the gulf between the cultures, into the bridge between himself and the cultures that have been linked to the land before him. As he recognizes, the presence of these remnants places his work in a greatly enlarged temporal framework, transforming an ordinary, and some might even say irksome, task into a mode of communion within a larger human family. In this way the day's customary and routine activities are represented as life-sustaining. They are necessary, as economic acts, for the maintenance of life at the level of commodity, and they also show Thoreau, the worker, his place in the fabric of human history. His connection with these "unchronicled nations" sacramentally deepens his humanity by returning him to the fundamental work that has sustained the human race.

The "ashes" that he disturbs with his hoe are those of "unchronicled nations," making his work a form of reading and reporting the "chronicle" of their past. The earth serves as a text from which he uncovers meaning, his very labor an enactment of their story. As Thoreau uncovers this buried narrative of human life, he also reformulates his important earlier trope of the farmer's cultivation of the earth as a form of burial. "Why should they begin digging their graves as soon as they are born?" he had asked, meaning then that the farmer's work, and by extension much of the work of modern life, was a form of slow death. These buried ashes, the remnants of fire, but also, by implication, the ashes of the men and women who built those fires, force him to see the death of farmers in a new and not entirely tragic light. The "compost" that these ashes represent suggests the process by which successive generations have rejoined themselves to the earth, not only through their deaths but through their lives and works as well. The earlier allusions to the degrading and tragic implications of the farmer's plowing himself into the ground as compost have here become something more ennobling. Thoreau uncovers with his hoe a purpose and a dignity that stretch across generations and cultures. These generations and cultures find a common point of reference in the earth itself.

As the allusion to the Indian ashes suggests, hoeing beans is a particularly suggestive activity for Thoreau, the reverie that often accompanies repetitive physical labor proving in this case to be a rich imaginative resource. Linking Thoreau's thoughtful attitude toward his work in the field with meditative practices anchored in the American Indian religious traditions, Robert F. Sayre has noted that "the bean-field and the beans were teachers," and Stanley Cavell, among others, has shown persuasively that hoeing serves Thoreau as a metaphor for writing and for reading: "For the writer's hoe, the earth is a page."[17] Thoreau's uncovering the remnants of Indian cultures with his hoe is an instance of such learning, reading, and writing, a chronicling of the past in which he himself is absorbed into the narrative he uncovers. But it is important to keep in mind that Thoreau's hoe is also a tool for cultivation. His discovery of these remnants ties him to the human narrative in the first instance as a cultivator, the performer of an ancient but never completed labor.

Thoreau therefore makes much of the distinction between labor and leisure as he hoes, finding his work less drudgery than diversion, and cultivating not just his beans but his awareness of his surroundings. "When my hoe tinkled against the stones, that music echoed to the woods and sky, and was an accompaniment to my labor which yielded an instant and immeasurable crop" (Wa 159). Work is hereby transformed into a celebratory music making, and he comes to see the "crop," or end product of his work, as the process of work itself. The "music of the hoe" leads him to pity his "acquaintances who had gone to the city to attend the oratorios" (Wa 159); he has discovered a truer music arising organically from the rhythm of his daily activity.

Midway through his description of his work, Thoreau speaks of the "night-hawk" that "circled overhead," a skyward shift of his heretofore earth-focused vision. The hawk falls "with a swoop and a sound as if the heavens were rent, torn at last to very rags and tatters," and the bird's sweeping flight expands the spatial frame within which Thoreau performs his labor. He sees the hawk's soaring and diving as gestures of expansion that balance the digging and delving of his hoe. The heavens remain "a seamless cope" despite the power of the hawk as it rips through the air, for such power, however superficially disruptive it may seem, remains in fundamental harmony with the larger framework of earth and sky. For Thoreau, the hawk is "graceful and slender like ripples caught up from the pond, as leaves are raised by the wind to float in the heavens." This is more than ornamental poetic description, for it indicates the profound likeness of the forms and processes of nature. "Such kindredship is in Nature" (Wa 159), Thoreau says, reflecting both the hawk's likeness to other natural things and his own sense of kinship with the things around him.

The nighthawk is one of what soon becomes a throng of creatures that populate the frame of Thoreau's picture. He observes "a pair of hen-hawks" whose "soaring and descending, approaching and leaving one another," seem to be "the imbodiment of my own thoughts." Those thoughts are not sequentially rational, it is important to note, and their erratic ebb and flow, their lack of predictable pattern, suggests the freedom of reverie that his labor yields. Such surging and turning thoughts are those of a poet or a writer of the imagination, who is capable of reveling in pure energy, even at the price of an organized or rationalized form. When the imagination is freed, suggestions and traces of the exotic can come even from the most unlikely sources, as when, "from under a rotten stump," he turns up "a sluggish portentous and outlandish spotted salamander, a trace of Egypt and the Nile, yet our contemporary" (Wa 159).

The expansive direction of the passage is the reflection of the growing energy of Thoreau's imagination as he pursues his labor, and it suggests the growing web of connections with life in all its forms that becomes apparent to him through his work.[18] This is a crucial moment in *Walden*, a binding together of Thoreau's agrarian with his ecological experiment, a union whose catalyst is the most fundamental and prosaic aspect of agrarian life—the repetitive and physically demanding labor of the hands and back that farming requires. Thoreau will redeem the life of the farm not only on the level of theory, in which he calls the motives of the typical farmer into question, but on the level of sweat as well, by illustrating the redemptive possibility of work itself.

It is of course important to remember that Thoreau's work transpires within a framework of reformed economic objectives, free from exploitation. He will later discuss his meeting with the Irish immigrant John Field, who "worked 'bogging' for a neighboring farmer, turning up a meadow with a spade or bog hoe at the rate of ten dollars an acre and the use of the land with manure for one year" (Wa 204). There is little that is redeeming or imaginatively expansive in Field's situation, as Thoreau frankly recognized. The celebration of labor that we find in "The Bean-Field" is tied closely to the social experimentalism that Thoreau's life at Walden represented. Labor in and of itself may well be unable to overcome oppressive social conditions or exploitative economic relationships. But Thoreau is also intent on showing that the work of the hoe is not necessarily drudgery either, and that any form of social change must entail a conception of the necessity and dignity of work, and even of its beauty and intrinsic satisfaction.

The labor that Thoreau performs with his hoe is superficially similar to that of most Concord farmers, but Thoreau has represented that labor to his readers, and to himself, as a qualitatively different enterprise. His work is not an act of resignation or desperation, nor is he a "serf" to the soil that he works. He has a demanding crop of beans to nurture and cultivate, and he remembers to tell us how much he sold them for, but he also has a freedom of mind about his work that originates in the economic freedom that his Walden experiment represents. His beans, linked as they are to his plan for his life at the pond, are part of his independent means; his spirit of independence, conversely, allows him to find in his agrarian labor a more expansive vision of his belonging in the natural world. That belonging is rooted in work, the structured expression of his own creaturely necessity to survive and flourish.

In his work in the bean field Thoreau therefore found the conceptual and experiential link between his hope to live in the world freely and his drive to know the world ecologically. The work rooted him, an expression of his necessary search for sustenance, even as his beans were themselves rooted in a similar search. The gradual process of self-recognition that the work in the bean field records is augmented by the way his own agrarian work mirrors that of the lost, unchronicled nations he discovers with his hoe, his work providing the missing chronicle through a re-creation of the same experience.

Despite its mockery of most forms of human toil, *Walden* is nevertheless a book that attempts to redeem the concept of work, using the open and thoughtful response to bodily necessity, the foundation of our economic identities, as a means of spiritual redemption. The harmony that Thoreau hears when he hoes the stone in the bean field is the confirming signal that work has transfigured itself into art of the highest kind, that which can "carve and paint the very atmosphere and medium through which we look" (Wa 90).

CHAPTER FIVE

Living Poetry

THE BLOOM OF THE PRESENT MOMENT

The blistering critique of conventional life and artificial values that opens *Walden* is extended by implication in "The Beanfield" and other chapters in which we see Thoreau enacting a new way of living in the natural world. This new way of life is grounded in a meticulous and discerning awareness of the particularities of nature, which includes the human body and the operations of consciousness and perception as part of an interrelated, constantly interactive whole.

Life at Walden provided much but by no means all of the impetus and fabric for this representation of a new experience. The text of *Walden* evolved through an extended process of composition, enlargement, and revision—seven versions in all. It therefore reflects both Thoreau's immediate experience at the pond and his later recollection, interpretation, and shaping of that experience in the seven-year period, 1847–54, between his leaving Walden and his publication of the book. Those years were pivotal in his development, providing the perspective that allowed him both to expand and complete *Walden* and to begin a new phase of his work that has only recently begun to come into full appreciation.

Building on the earlier work on the *Walden* manuscripts by J. Lyndon

Shanley, Robert Sattelmeyer explains that the book evolved through two major phases of composition, an initial set of four versions written while Thoreau was at the pond and in the years immediately following his leaving, and a later series of three revisions (1852–54). The later revisions provided the seasonal shape and "organic form" that brought *Walden* recognition as a literary masterpiece in the mid-twentieth century.[1] The most important changes in these years were Thoreau's return from Walden in 1847, his family's move in August 1850 to the larger "yellow house" on Concord's Main Street, and his resolution to make a serious and detailed study of plant characteristics and classification in the early 1850s. Thoreau occupied an attic room in the new house which was more private, and also spacious enough to accommodate his books and various botanical and artifact collections.[2] Although he was no longer at Walden Pond, he now had in some ways more freedom and opportunity to explore the countryside and study the natural world through his pattern of afternoon walks. He began to use his Journal as an extension of these walks, compiling both observations and interpretive insights there, and gradually transforming it into a rich compendium of information about the climate, seasonal cycles, and ecosystems of the Concord area.

Thoreau's new pattern of life after Walden, especially his deepening engagement with field observation and natural history, generated an intellectual tension that is evident both in the Journal and in *Walden*. A fact collector, fascinated with the working details of the natural world, Thoreau also wanted to understand the larger patterns that gave meaning and connection to these facts. He remained a believer in nature's unity even as he noted its disparate details. His study of Hindu scriptures in the late 1840s reinforced the holistic perspective he had absorbed from Brownson, Emerson, and others, as did his continuing commitment to a Transcendentalist idea of a higher law that informed human conduct. That principle was becoming increasingly prominent in his thinking as the slavery crisis intensified in the late 1840s and early 1850s.

Walden thus evolved through its several revisions as a work in which Thoreau attempts to depict his life as a thing of the moment and of the eternal simultaneously. His burden is to maintain the recognition that every object and every perception bears an enormous weight of significance. *Walden* thus urges a new way of comprehending nature and also a new way of living in nature. Each of these emphases informs and reinforces the other.

In rejecting the life of "quiet desperation" that so many of his contemporaries were living, Thoreau resolved to "live deliberately," assuming a new responsibility for the decisions that constituted the quality of daily life. "Every man is tasked to make his life, even in its details, worthy of the contemplation of his most elevated and critical hour" (Wa 90). The patterns of the day became the artist's medium at Walden, demanding the same balance, economy of means, detailed craft, and sense of purpose that the canvas or the blank page demanded. It also required a constantly renewed effort to see the world afresh. To live a natural life, one must shed the inherited categories of perception and refuse to take appearances as truths. "I perceive that we inhabitants in New England live this mean life that we do because our vision does not penetrate the surface of things. We think that that *is* which *appears* to be" (Wa 96).

Thoreau's wish to live deliberately, artistically shaping the experience of each successive day, entailed a demanding commitment to literature, both as a reader and as a writer. His Walden sojourn was in part a writer's sabbatical, and while he makes almost no mention of his literary projects in the text of *Walden*, he does devote an early chapter to the centrality of disciplined "Reading" as the first of his enterprises at the pond. Reading is thus the first call of the natural life. In "The American Scholar" Emerson described a fundamental tension between books and nature, arguing that reading posed a certain danger to the formation and cultivation of the intellect, and was capable of transforming "Man Thinking" into "the bookworm": "The sacredness which attaches to the act of creation,—the act of thought,— is instantly transferred to the record. The poet chanting, was felt to be a divine man. Henceforth the chant is divine also. The writer was a just and wise spirit. Henceforward it is settled, the book is perfect; as love of the hero corrupts into worship of his statue. Instantly, the book becomes noxious. The guide is a tyrant" (CW 1:56). Although he shared Emerson's suspicions of the artificiality and potential corruption of reading that was a substitute for original thought, Thoreau works to defuse the inherent tension between reading and natural experience by portraying reading as a natural and essential act, a means by which the individual can become part of an expansive and liberating dialogue that spans ages and cultures.[3]

"My residence was more favorable, not only to thought, but to serious reading, than a university" (Wa 99), he remarks, beginning a series of observations through which he transforms reading from an artificial activity associated with social norms and institutions into an organic one, connate with the self and its continuing development. Living deliberately, returning to a freedom beyond any set of imposed social expectations, will inevitably incline us toward reading and study. "With a little more deliberation in the choice of their pursuits, all men would perhaps become essentially students and observers, for certainly their nature and destiny are interesting to all alike" (Wa 99). The problem, of course, is achieving that degree of deliberation in our choice of pursuits. The sort of reading he demands of himself requires an openness and freedom, and also a disciplined commitment. He insists that reading is neither an emotional escape nor a means of mental or physical relaxation; it is a difficult achievement, one that engages and challenges all the resources of the self.

Admitting these demands, and confessing even his own failures to meet them, is one of the most important achievements of Thoreau's chapter on his reading. "I kept Homer's Iliad on my table through the summer," he reports, "though I looked at his page only now and then" (Wa 99). Thoreau's open Homer is the symbol of so many well-intended but never-completed reading projects—the ever-growing list that we always carry mentally, waiting for that magical summer of absolute freedom. But Thoreau had to postpone this obligation. "Incessant labor with my hands, at first, for I had my house to finish and my beans to hoe at the same time, made more study impossible" (Wa 99–100). This is a frank but not a rueful admission, because of the sense of ultimate priorities that his house-building embodied. "Yet I sustained myself," he tells us, "by the prospect of such reading in the future" (Wa 100). He made his open book a kind of promise, the reminder of a commitment that predated his work on the house and in the field and made it meaningful. Homer had been postponed, but not postponed indefinitely. Thoreau knows himself to be creating the conditions within which he can sustain the sort of reading necessary to his reformed living. That "prospect" was implicit in Homer's narrative of the heroic search for one's rightful place.

Thoreau's reading was primarily a morning exercise, the kind of intensive activity that required a depth of attention available only to what he called an awakening mind. His praise of the morning comes with the related observation that few individuals are fully awake as they experience the world. "Every morning was a cheerful invitation to make my life of equal simplicity, and I may say innocence, with Nature herself" (Wa 88). This repeated invitation, triggered by the rhythms of nature, signified the possibility of a fresh access to the buried powers of thought and observation that were the necessary constituents for the reformulation of life. "That man who does not believe that each day contains an earlier, more sacred, and auroral hour than he has yet profaned, has despaired of life, and is pursuing a descending and darkening way" (Wa 89). The realm of dreams, like the realm of fable or poetry, signified a larger life of varied, metamorphic identity. One awoke with this newly enlarged sense of possibility, which amplified the significance of the natural world and added acuity and discernment to reading.

Thoreau's proposition that "morning brings back the heroic ages" (Wa 88) is thus echoed in his conception of his morning work with the classics. "The student may read Homer or Aeschylus in the Greek without danger of dissipation or luxuriousness, for it implies that he in some measure emulate their heroes, and consecrate morning hours to their pages" (Wa 100). The mind, fresh in the morning from its immersion in dreams, is capable of meeting the conceptual and imaginative demands of literature and more effective in responding to the voice of the text with its own inner voice.

Although it is engendered by the natural rhythms of the night and morning, and is part of the process by which the self is remade in the mold of nature, such reading is nevertheless an act of will and discipline, demanding an unusual dedication and tenacity. Such labor "will task the reader more than any exercise which the customs of the day esteem," Thoreau warns. "It requires a training such as the athletes underwent, the steady intention almost of the whole life to this object" (Wa 101). Again he links the act of reading to that definitive word "deliberate," placing reading on the same plane of importance as the highest decisions of life: "Books must be read as deliberately and reservedly as they were written" (Wa 101). The complex and sometimes painful work of choosing words, building intellectual structures out of them, and revising and refining a growing text is a mirror of the process of reading, in which each word is weighed as it contributes to the emerging patterns of the text. In Stanley Cavell's apt explication, "reading is not merely the other side of writing, its eventual fate; it is another metaphor of writing itself."[4]

Reading of this kind is a determined and skeptical scrutiny of a work, breaking it into its constituent parts and rewriting it as if one were its author. We thus become the author in the highest acts of reading. But the strain and severity of this conception belies the element of passion in reading, the keen desire that finds fulfillment in it. In the deepest acts of reading, something compels us; we are pulled into the text and through the pages almost will-lessly. Although both formulations of the act of reading help us to understand the intensity and all-consuming nature of "deliberate" reading, their difference also suggests the tension that Thoreau continued to wrestle with, one akin to the dichotomy between grace and works in the explanation of religious experience. The text is a gift, an offering of "the treasured wealth of the world" from authors who constitute "a natural and irresistible aristocracy in every society" (Wa 102, 103). But it is also an earned attainment, available only to those who have paid the cost of devotion and discipline required for its acceptance.

Thoreau expands his analysis of the nature of reading in "Sounds," integrating the internal voices of books with the myriad voices of the natural world.[5] Reading must be seen, he argues, as one aspect of a much larger process of listening, translating, and decoding that includes our entire experience of the natural world. Confinement to books, even "the most select and classic," may cause us to forget "the language which all things and events speak without metaphor" (Wa 111). Thoreau's move from the written world to the natural world is important, not because it signals any abandonment of language as a crucial medium of the understanding, but because it synthesizes reading and writing with other acts of perception and self-expression.

He laid the groundwork for that synthesis in "Reading" by maintaining that the written word "is something at once more intimate with us and more universal than any other work of art. It is the work of art nearest to life itself" (Wa 102). Reading as he had depicted it was a complete absorption of the words of another, an internalization of the very processes of thought and feeling that are the necessary prerequisites of authorship. In taking the thoughts of another within us and reconstituting the grounds on which the words took the form they did, we reanimate the record of human experience. The written word may "not only be read but actually breathed from all human lips;—not be represented on canvas or in marble only, but be carved out of the breath of life itself. The symbol of an ancient man's thought becomes a modern man's speech" (Wa 102).

If the written word can bring the past into a living present, the sounds of the natural world are the constant reminder of the "now" in which we are immersed. An essential step in Thoreau's recovery of a "natural life" is to reawaken and expand his awareness of the present moment, in the sense not only of "knowing" more of the world around him but also of entering into it fully. Thoreau hoped to give himself over to his senses, finding a fulfillment in his own attentive presence at the pond and the surrounding hills. "Much is published, but little printed" (Wa 111), he observed, comparing the vast text of nature with the more limited books written by men. If books made certain thoughts and expressions permanent, the expressions of nature were confined to their moment, and were in a sense all the more valuable because of their transience. Such events, however, were not necessarily laden with a meaning that somehow transcended their present manifestation. Thoreau warned against "forgetting the language which all things and events speak without metaphor," a language wholly contained within itself and within the moment in which it comes into being. An event as seemingly incidental as the cast of the light within a room has a call on our attention. "The rays which stream through the shutter will be no longer remembered when the shutter is wholly removed." These rays do not necessarily point beyond themselves, or "mean" anything, but they are part of the fabric of reality that constitutes our experience. Thoreau was attempting to learn to understand himself, his body, his senses, his thoughts, as part of that fabric, to realize the "necessity of being forever on the alert" (Wa 111).

Immersion in the present is antithetical to the conventional rules of daily scheduling and the usual clock-oriented methods of timekeeping. "I love a broad margin to my life" (Wa 111), Thoreau declared, and one of the pleasures of life at Walden was his liberation from artificial measurements of time. But the chapter on "Sounds" is in fact a description of the passage of the day, marked by the characteristic sounds that set its pattern. Thoreau's immersion in the present is not, then, an erasure of time, as he shows, but a more complete and effectual recognition of time's movements and cycles.

These markers of the day are, for the most part, the sounds of the creatures who inhabit the pond and its environs, the background sounds of nature that Thoreau teaches himself to bring to the foreground. "Regularly at half past seven . . . the whippoorwills chanted their vespers for half an hour" (Wa 123), the screech owls ushered in nightfall with "their wailing, their doleful responses" (Wa 124), and the bullfrogs passed the night with their drunken-sounding bellows of "*tr-r-r-oonk*" (Wa 126). Attention to sound meant attention to the varied life around the pond, making Thoreau a member of a new community.

Complicating this easy absorption into his surroundings, however, was the most dominant sound in the area, that of the Fitchburg Railroad, whose tracks ran past the pond some five hundred yards from Thoreau's cabin. "I watch the passage of the morning cars," he says, "with the same feeling that I do the rising of the sun, which is hardly more regular" (Wa 116). There is irony in this association of the locomotive with the morning, that sacred time of full awakening that Thoreau had consecrated to meditation and study. The train's presence dramatizes the limits of his idyllic setting, constantly reminding him of the presence of the commercial world that he is to some extent hoping to escape. "I usually go to the village along its causeway," he tells us, "and am, as it were, related to society by this link" (Wa 115). While he would no doubt have preferred not to have the train's intrusion, he also recognized that its presence was an important test of his ability to maintain his focus on recovering a natural life in the face of technological modernity and the expansion of commerce.

In describing his reaction to the train (Wa 115–22; see also JP 2:358–59), Thoreau acknowledges the admirable qualities of those who operate it, and of commerce in general, but he cannot dismiss the flawed and limited ends to which their skills are put: "If the enterprise were as innocent as it is early . . . as heroic and commanding as it is protracted and unwearied!" (Wa 117). The challenge of living with this new technology is one of discrimination, of learning to formulate and follow one's own sense of purpose despite the false opportunity that such technological advance seems to offer. "We do not ride on the railroad; it rides upon us" (Wa 92), an inversion of ends and means that Thoreau deplores. The rails, he writes mordantly, are laid over the human "sleepers," laborers who have sacrificed themselves through their extraordinary toil to build it. Their sacrifice seems pointlessly tragic. "They are sound sleepers, I assure you" (Wa 92).

He extends this consideration of technology with his punning admonition to "keep on your own track." While we may feel compelled "to do things 'railroad fashion,'" keeping schedules not of our own making and moving without fail to predetermined destinations, Thoreau argues that we should instead adopt the "enterprise and bravery" (Wa 118) of commerce for our own work of self-development. Finding commerce to be "unexpectedly confident and serene, alert, adventurous, and unwearied" and "very natural in its methods" (Wa 119), he responds by seeing in it the promise of accomplishment that can be translated to the work of self-formation.

Although the railroad is at first an alien and threatening presence, a "travelling demigod" and "cloud-compeller," or an "iron horse" with a "snort like thunder, shaking the earth with his feet, and breathing fire and smoke from his nostrils" (Wa 116), Thoreau revises this initial impression to argue that however alien or non-human the railroad may seem, it is in fact the most human of inventions because of its central role in human commerce. By offering a detailed description of its amazingly varied cargo—palm leaves, rusty nails, torn sails, lumber, Spanish hides, cattle (Wa 119–22; see also JP 2:237–38)—he links it to all forms of human economic activity, and shows it to be a force that was created, and can be controlled, by human decisions. This is a subtle reminder of the potentially enslaving nature of the economics of consumption, and a declaration that, noise and smoke notwithstanding, no one need necessarily be the captive of this new technological invention. "What's the railroad to me?" he asks in a verse that summarizes his sense of freedom from its demands. "I never go to see / Where it ends" (Wa 122).

Absorbed into the larger rhythm of the natural world, the train cannot alter Thoreau's sense of the pace of his life. He is too far immersed in the pattern of the natural day to be disturbed by this artificial interruption. The train becomes instead another of the creatures to whose habits he is able to adapt as he learns a new way to make each day. He does, however, remark on the absence of one creature usually closely associated with time: "I am not sure that I ever heard the sound of cockcrowing from my clearing" (Wa 127). Thoreau praises the song of "this once wild Indian pheasant" and imagines "a winter morning in a wood where these birds abounded, their native woods," their calls "clear and shrill for miles over the resounding earth . . . think of it! It would put nations on the alert" (Wa 127). But even in its domestic state, the still resonant call of the bird is a forceful symbol. "All climates agree with brave Chanticleer. He is more indigenous even than the natives. His health is good, his lungs are sound, his spirits never flag" (Wa 127). Like Chanticleer, Thoreau has been domesticated, but his experiment at the pond returns him to a natural home, and makes him again an essential part of it.

FACE TO FACE TO A FACT

To insist that written words are living utterances and that the sounds of nature are a language was a crucial step in Thoreau's attempt to make his literary endeavors part of a larger quest for enlightenment and personal reform at Walden. Reading and writing became an essential part of a spiritual practice, woven into the daily texture of activity of an awakened, fully conscious self.[6] Exploratory walking ("sauntering," as he would later label it in "Walking"), work in the field or on the house, detailed observation of the parts and processes of the natural world, meditative thought, and even daydream and reverie were also strands of this new fabric of experience. This life could be most easily distinguished for its growing process of awareness, of being fully "awake."

Thoreau's principal vehicle for representing this achievement of perception is an event in which he experiences ("observes" is too limited a word) some aspect of the natural world as an instance of a more comprehensive, even infinitely expanding pattern of interconnections. I have already noted one such interpretive encounter, his hoeing of the beans, which expands into a portrait of the varied and abundant life and the layers of time and culture in his one small field of endeavor. Several other significant moments offer a similar pattern of narrated activity layered with observation and expansive interpretation.

These interpretive encounters include most prominently the personification of Walden in "The Ponds" and its measurement in "The Pond in Winter," the account of animal life in "Brute Neighbors," and the sand foliage passage in "Spring." They are marked by Thoreau's keen observational eye and his usually vivid account of the process by which he comes into fuller recognition of the world around him, a world to which, he implies, we should all be more attentive. But they display not only an arresting sense of detail but also a concomitant desire to reach for a more comprehensive category of explanation for the particular phenomenon. Thoreau consistently tries to see a particular fact or event not as a random or unique occurrence but as indicative of a more comprehensive idea or law. "Men esteem truth remote," he writes, "in the outskirts of the system, behind the farthest star, before Adam and after the last man. In eternity there is indeed something true and sublime. But all these times and places and occasions are now and here. God himself culminates in the present moment, and will never be more divine in the lapse of all the ages" (Wa 96–97).

Such a conception neither denigrates nor subordinates "facts" and their study, nor does it refuse the intellectual task of categorization, generalization, and system building. The intellectual ferment of *Walden*, the element that communicates so vividly a sense of philosophical breakthrough, is Thoreau's growing recognition that "fact" and "theory" are inextricably fused, that the observation or close reading of detail is the entry point of comprehensive and ordered knowledge. A "fact" is always a bundle of relations, the product of a convergence of many entities and events. To "know" a particular fact, he saw with increasing clarity and excitement, is to be given a glimpse into a much wider array of processes and circumstances, an event that is revelatory in every sense.

"If you stand right fronting and face to face to a fact, you will see the sun glimmer on both of its surfaces, as if it were a cimeter, and feel its sweet edge dividing you through the heart and marrow, so you will happily conclude your mortal career" (Wa 98). Thoreau's strange celebration of death by fact suggests the dual quality of such moments of insight. The "fact" is the dividing edge, on either side of which we see the sun, here the representation of both illumination and power. Those two surfaces, coordinate aspects of the same fact or object, are the particular detail and the inclusive law that constitute such revelations. We are indeed "divided" by this edge, asked to look in two directions simultaneously, toward the unique specificity of things and to the larger frames of reference that make them discernible. We are permitted to achieve this seemingly impossible feat in that single moment when fact opens itself to us, or, as Thoreau would have it, opens *us* in its presence.

In light of the recent critical emphasis on Thoreau's increasing engagement with the fact-gathering processes of empirical studies of plant and animal life, it is crucial to see Thoreau's praise of "fact" and his increasing attention to the concrete detail of the material world of nature as one side of a complex attempt to move toward larger projects of categorization and explanatory theorizing about the unifying laws and structures of the universe. He struggled to keep his empirical studies within a larger purposive framework that included philosophical speculation and the search for a unifying theory of the nature and structure of the universe. "Facts should only be as the frame to my pictures," he wrote in 1851. "They should be material to the mythology which I am writing" (JP 4:170).

Thoreau's skill and dedication in empirical study, signaled by his closely observed field notes and his collecting of botanical and even zoological specimens, set him apart from Emerson temperamentally, and most readers of Emerson and Thoreau have recognized Thoreau as a more "physical" or embodied thinker, closer in a practical way to the natural world than Emerson, and somewhat less ethereal in his imagination and forms of expression. The year after Thoreau's death, Emerson praised, with a touch of envy, his gift for concrete metaphor and vivid description, attributing it to "the vigor of his constitution."

> That oaken strength which I noted whenever he walked or worked or surveyed wood lots, the same unhesitating hand with which a field-laborer accosts a piece of work which I should shun as a waste of strength, Henry shows in his literary task. He has muscle, & ventures on & performs feats which I am forced to decline. In reading him, I find the same thought, the same spirit that is in me, but he takes a step beyond, & illustrates by excellent images that which I should have conveyed in a sleepy generality. (JMN 15:352–53)

Robert Kuhn McGregor has described this difference as more than a question of temperament or style, identifying Emerson's philosophical idealism as a major point of distinction between them, and a significant obstruction to Thoreau's intellectual development.[7] In developing a portrait of Thoreau as one of the first ecologists, McGregor depicts Emerson's idealism as a subordination of the material world, a theory that reduced "Nature to the point of possible nonexistence" and also devalued Thoreau's real scientific expertise: "By devaluing the importance of the facts of natural history, Emerson reduced to a mere symbol a portion of the world where Henry possessed some real knowledge." For McGregor, Thoreau's development was a struggle to throw off Emersonian idealism in order to become a naturalist.[8]

At issue here is the complex question of Emerson's influence (and Thoreau's "originality"), an influence that is unquestionably significant but very hard to measure and assess. There was a deep bond between the two men and a shared vision and sense of purpose, but also, as we have come to see more clearly, a tension and a growing sense of betrayal and failed intimacy in their relationship. But McGregor also raises a question that is vital to our understanding of the motives and methods with which Thoreau perceived the natural world. In what ways, and with what impact, did Emerson's idealistic theorizing affect the impressionable and intellectually hungry Thoreau? Did an idealism that seemed to subordinate the material world philosophically become a cumbersome hindrance to Thoreau's perceptual engagement with nature?

Emerson's "noble doubt . . . whether nature outwardly exists" (CW 1:29) is one of the more striking and controversial aspects of *Nature*. But his vivid account of idealism was not a novel or unique philosophical theory for Thoreau but rather one articulation among several of the problem of reconciling the singularity of things with their equally compelling similarities and relations. Emerson's seemingly ethereal dismissal of nature seems strange and even somewhat sinister to many readers today, who react to it as a dismissal of the reality of bodily experience. Those same readers are likely to feel an ardent sense of kinship with Thoreau because of his compelling descriptions of his experience in the natural world and his implicit advocacy of the preservation of the wild. Emerson's idealism thus strikes the modern reader as alien to Thoreau's central message and purpose.

Thoreau, however, found in *Nature* less a denial of the reality and specificity of the material world than a theory that gave facts significance because of their interrelations. Thoreau brought to his reading of *Nature* an already well-developed sense of the Platonic tradition, of eighteenth-century idealism, and of the emerging philosophies that were attempting to synthesize idealism and empiricism. As I noted earlier, both *Nature* and Brownson's *New Views* were published during Thoreau's senior year at Harvard, and we have every reason to believe that he found in them a new and liberating philosophy of experience. His earlier tutelage under Brownson, with whom he shared an interest in German idealism and Victor Cousin's philosophical "eclecticism," had shown him that philosophy and religious thought were on the verge of a major shift. Idealism had to be transcribed into a larger philosophical synthesis, an "eclectic" philosophy that would preserve the values of both empiricism and idealism. This discourse, coming at a moment when he was formulating his own sense of an intellectual mission, taught Thoreau that the task of philosophy is both to observe and to speculate, to collect facts and synthesize them into larger categories and explanatory systems.

Thoreau's interest in idealism was thus more than a deferential imitation of Emerson. He shared Emerson's concern with a set of questions that idealist philosophy was attempting to answer: How can we understand the many particulars of experience as constituting coherent patterns or categories, or of providing discernible similarities among themselves? How can we think of the things of the world as related, or of our own relation to the world? How can the mind comprehend matter? These are among the oldest of philosophical questions, but they posed a fresh challenge to Thoreau, who was introspective, inclined to philosophical speculation, and keenly observant of the natural world. In the last issue of the *Dial* in 1844, James E. Cabot wrote an essay that emphasized how idealism had framed the epistemological basis of modern thought: "Modern speculation, therefore, has returned to the fundamental problem of human science; and asks, first of all, 'Can we know anything?'"[9] *Nature* had been Emerson's attempt to address this question, and his conclusion—that a particular fact can be known completely only as one part of a much larger web of relations and interconnections—proved to be a dynamic and energizing principle for Thoreau. Idealism remained at the center of the continuing discourse among the Transcendentalists, who kept these issues alive for him through the 1840s and 1850s as he was becoming more committed to his field studies in natural history.

A close examination of Emerson's discussion of idealism in *Nature*, moreover, suggests another reason for its appeal to Thoreau, one that continued well into his Walden experiment and beyond. Emerson was proposing not an idealism that made nature disappear, but an idealism that made nature dynamic. He presented idealism as a theory that undermined the common view of matter as inert, and of nature as fixed or static. Idealism was for Emerson, as it was for Thoreau, a way to confirm the ever-mutating energy of the material world. Thoreau was an attentive reader who would not have missed Emerson's nuanced discussion of the paradox of disappearing nature.

To begin with, Emerson rejected the naïve idea that idealism should alter our behavior in relation to material things. Most telling is the ironic humor of Emerson's guilty confession that there is "something ungrateful" about his theorizing, and his resulting declaration of his innocent devotion to nature. "I have no hostility to nature but a child's love to it. I expand and live in the warm day like corn and melons. Let us speak her fair. I do not wish to fling stones at my beautiful mother, nor soil my gentle nest" (CW 1:35–36). This disarming rhetoric responds to our instinctive mistrust of idealism by allowing Emerson to explain how idealism is both misperceived and unacknowledged in daily life, a part of the fabric of our ordinary experience even while we reject it on the grounds of common sense. Our capacity to interact with and use the material world, and our obligation to respect its laws and operations, are not open to question or alteration. "Whether nature enjoy a substantial existence without, or is only in the apocalypse of the mind," he argued, "it is alike useful and alike venerable to me" (CW 1:29). The "permanence of laws" remained inviolable whatever the ontological constitution of nature, and only "the frivolous make themselves merry with the Ideal theory, as if its consequences were burlesque" (CW 1:29).

This quality of permanence did not mean that the material world was dead or inert, or that there was no essential relation between it and our consciousness. One of Emerson's most amusing illustrations of the theory of idealism is his recommendation that we view the world through our legs, one of several examples of optical distortions that serve to undermine the settled familiarity and solidity of the world. "Turn the eyes upside down, by looking at the landscape through your legs, and how agreeable is the picture, though you have seen it any time these twenty years!" (CW 1:31). The appeal is that the familiar is made new, the fixed is made indeterminate. Our sense of the variety and richness of things is reconfirmed, and the possibilities of experience are vastly expanded.[10]

The fundamental perceptual shift that he describes as idealism is to replace a static world with a dynamic one, a detached or isolated world with one that shares with us a fundamental identity. Thus, even when he refers to nature as "an accident and an effect," his actual purpose is to reinvest it with a significance that will pull us into closer relation. "It is the uniform effect of culture on the human mind, not to shake our faith in the stability of particular phenomena, as of heat, water, azote; but to lead us to regard nature as a phenomenon, not a substance; to attribute necessary existence to spirit; to esteem nature as an accident and an effect" (CW 1:30). The distinction between "substance" and "phenomenon" is critical, the first indicating a fixed and inert entity, and the second a convergence of energies or forces. A phenomenon is both in process and in relation, and represents nature's openness and mutability, and the affinity of all its constituent parts. As H. Daniel Peck has observed, "the term that Thoreau most often uses to reconcile the power of the creative eye with the independent status of the world is 'phenomenon.'"[11]

Emerson speaks of idealism less in terms of its absolute truth than of its relative advantage, its pragmatic effect on the human ability to respond to and reshape experience. "It is essential to a true theory of nature and of man, that it contain somewhat progressive" (CW 1:36), he argued. The phenomenal quality of nature implies its mobile and pliant quality as well, and suggests a progressive dynamism that mirrors human nature. "Nature is not fixed but fluid. Spirit alters, moulds, makes it" (CW 1:44). To understand the fluidity of nature is to recognize a correspondent energy within that is the basis of constructive and purposive action. "Know then, that the world exists for you. For you is the phenomenon perfect" (CW 1:44). This is less a justification for the subordination of nature, as many modern readers might at first suspect, than a declaration of the unperceived harmony between nature and the soul, making men and women an essential component of the "phenomenon" of nature that Emerson has been describing. This recognition begins "when the fact is seen under the light of an idea," making us understand that "a fact is true poetry, and the most beautiful of fables" (CW 1:44).

The recognition of nature as a changing, multifarious "phenomenon" of manifold relations takes us more deeply and securely into the world of facts rather than divorcing us from that world. "The invariable mark of wisdom is to see the miraculous in the common," Emerson wrote. "What is a day? What is a year? What is summer? What is woman? What is a child? What is sleep?" (CW 1:44). These questions about the nature of ordinary experience are the most profound, and open the interconnected fabric of phenomena that we call nature. To face a fact, then, is to face the world, to see the particular thing or event clearly and directly, but not in isolation. The most crucial lessons of *Walden* are Thoreau's repeated enactments of the intimate connection between observation and synthesis. The larger identities and relationships of things, their ideal qualities, yield the specific, factual identities to Thoreau, just as the specific identities of things and events inevitably suggest their relationships and their partaking of larger categories of identity.

THE SHADOW OF THE WHOLE

Thoreau's celebration of "fact" and his demonstration of the fruits of detailed observation in *Walden*, however insightful and philosophically significant, betray a growing self-doubt about the course of his intellectual development and the state of his philosophical and speculative powers. At times he felt himself to be drying up intellectually, and though drawn temperamentally toward more intensive projects of field observation and data collection, he distrusted his own tendency to become a collector of information. In August 1851, after his stay at Walden but before he had finally revised and reshaped his manuscript, he confessed his struggle to rein in the increasingly dominant empirical side of his personality: "I fear that the character of my knowledge is from year to year becoming more distinct & scientific— That in exchange for views as wide as heaven's cope I am being narrowed down to the field of the microscope— I see details not wholes nor the shadow of the whole. I count some parts, & say 'I know'. The cricket's chirp now fills the air in dry fields near pine woods" (JP 3:380). Thoreau senses a certain dishonesty in claiming to "know" when that knowledge excludes the larger frame of reference which invests details with their significance. But this worried self-analysis leads to an observation of the "cricket's chirp," the kind of detail that he has just labeled problematic. While Thoreau's fascination with the details of the natural world grows, he continues to doubt that such details can in themselves be fulfilling. He fears that he is gaining the particulars of the world but losing his soul.

This tension between the close observation of the particular and the more expansive pursuit of the whole sharpened for Thoreau in the late 1840s and early 1850s, as he was drawn more directly into the growth of scientific study at Harvard. In 1847 Louis Agassiz began a major effort to build Harvard's presence in science. Committed to a theory of the "special creation" of particular species, as opposed to a developmental theory that would later be articulated by Darwin, Agassiz began an extensive effort to gather and preserve large numbers of animal specimens and developed a network of field naturalists to collect them. Thoreau was one of his coop-erating colleagues in this endeavor, enlisted by Agassiz's assistant, and *Dial* contributor, James E. Cabot. Laura Dassow Walls has noted that Thoreau devoted a month or more to such hunting and capturing in 1847, his second spring at Walden, a detail that he does not include in his narrative of his life at the pond. "What are we to make," Walls asks, "of a Thoreau who so cheerfully trapped, packed, and shipped so many of his Walden 'friends' and neighbors to Harvard's halls of science?" Although he "seems to have lost interest quickly" in such collection, and returned to his more literary proj-ects while at the pond, the experience had a definite impact on him. Even though Agassiz's scientific theories had at best a limited appeal to Thoreau, participating in such collecting provided him with the opportunity to ob-serve and participate in the systematic fieldwork of scientific observation and collection. Even though his misgivings about the activity surfaced quickly, the work had, as Walls argues, reinforced his penchant for vigilant alertness and observational acuity in the field as well as what he felt were his growing tendencies to move "away from a grand and abstract transcenden-talism toward a detailed observation of the specifics of nature, in all its un-accountable diversity."[12]

That Thoreau excelled in this work of field observation, data collec-tion and recording, and specimen gathering is unquestionable, but his continuing uneasiness about the ends of such work is suggested in his reaction to a questionnaire sent him by the Association for the Advance-ment of Science asking him "to fill the blanks against certain ques-tions—among which the most important one was—what branch of science I was specially interested in." Unable to answer the questions as he felt he should—"I felt that it would be to make myself the laughing stock of the scientific community"—he was "obliged to speak to their condition and describe to them that poor part of me which alone they can understand." The questionnaire could not get at the vital truth about him. "The fact is I am a mystic—a transcendentalist—& a natural philosopher to boot. Now I think—of it—I should have told them at once I was a transcendentalist—that would have been the shortest way of telling them that they would not understand my explanations" (JP 5:469–70). Thoreau's insistence on his dual identity as a "transcendentalist" and a "natural philosopher" and his derisive discomfort with the narrow categories that the fields of "sci-ence" offered him are important reminders of a tension that sharpened for him through the 1850s, years that were marked by his struggle to bal-ance, and finally to reconcile, this seemingly dual identity.

Even as his interest in gathering the facts that now dominated the study of "natural history" was growing, it is perhaps somewhat surprising to find that his interest in Hinduism was rekindled by an 1848 article by James E. Cabot, an essay that, as Robert D. Richardson Jr. argues, "gave Thoreau an added impetus to explore Hinduism as a powerful independent corroboration of the central concept of Idealism," and initiated an extensive reading project on Hinduism. The impact of Thoreau's immersion in Hinduism can be seen in *Walden*, with its extensive network of allusions to Hindu texts.[13]

Cabot's article was less an essay than a compilation of passages from recent translations of the Vishnu Purana, the Bhagavad Gita, and other Hindu texts, providing a brief anthology of Hindu wisdom and philosophical precepts. Cabot explained that he had gathered "fragments of a speculative character" from "the theogonies and myths of the Hindoos." These fragments did not "properly [amount] to a system," but they did represent "an attempt to theorize on the Universe." Although Cabot kept his own explication and theorizing to a minimum, the selection and arrangement of his compilation did have a controlling thesis, one of particular relevance to Thoreau's own philosophical concerns in the late 1840s and early 1850s. Cabot describes the development of "three very distinct epochs" in Hindu literature, beginning with "the age of the Vedas," which shows "little trace of reflection, or of intense religious consciousness." The succeeding era, "the age of the Puranas and the Bhagavat Gita, is a meditative, mystical period, during which speculation among the Hindoos reached its highest point." That high point has been followed by a long "age of commentators, of subtle distinctions, and of polemics," a "Scholastic Age" secondary to the creative age that preceded it.[14] Cabot argued that the meditative and mystical era of the Bhagavad Gita, "the essence of the Hindoo metaphysics," could be expressed in one fundamental precept: "the reduction of all Reality to pure, abstract Thought." Although this idea cannot be illustrated by "a methodical arrangement of propositions," it is nevertheless a "constant theme," expressed metaphorically in "often sublime imagery." "The main principle of Hindoo Idealism—that Reality is equivalent to pure abstract Soul or Thought, unexistent, and thus simple and unformed; in a word, pure Negation,—is presented especially under the aspect of the unity and identity of all things in the Deity."[15]

Thoreau read Cabot's essay with care, copying out a number of quotations, including this passage from the Vishnu Purana:

Liberation, which is the object to be effected, being accomplished, discriminative knowledge ceases. When endowed with the apprehension of the nature of the object of inquiry, then there is no difference between it and supreme spirit; difference is the consequence of the absence of true knowledge. When that ignorance which is the cause of the difference between individual and universal spirit is destroyed, finally and for ever, who shall make that distinction between them which does not exist?[16]

Perception is described here as a process of unification, in which the isolated part is reunited with its original whole through the act of perception. "Difference," the result of an initial act of discriminating perception, is the condition that complete knowledge hopes eventually to overcome.

The idea that "difference is the consequence of the absence of true knowledge" had important implications for Thoreau's conception of his work as a naturalist, especially as he took up the more detailed activities of data and specimen collection. The empirical accumulation of facts could be justified only as one stage of a process that ultimately aimed at an explanation of the inclusive whole of nature. Thoreau's immersion in the world of "fact" in the late 1840s and early 1850s was accompanied, then, by a continuing, indeed renewed, interest in idealism, significantly reinforced by his interest in Hinduism.

It seems clear from this seemingly incongruent pattern of study and reading that the intensity with which Thoreau engaged in empirical science in the late 1840s and early 1850s did not undermine his interest in and broad adherence to idealism, if we give that term the comprehensive characterization that Thoreau did. One view of Thoreau's intellectual development, based largely on the increasingly factual character of his journal entries through the 1850s, is that for better or worse, he increasingly surrendered to his passion for fact and detail, and became progressively distanced from the kind of philosophical speculation that Emerson had shown him. But Thoreau's persistent efforts in *Walden* and beyond to push specific observations toward more encompassing theories were a response to his fear of losing his capacity to see "wholes." This fear is also related to a worried sense of personal declension and inadequacy that haunted him in the early 1850s as he revised and augmented the *Walden* manuscript.[17]

Thoreau's struggle to reconcile the particularized empiricism of Agassiz and others with the quest for unified wholes that were represented by the traditions of both Western idealism and Hindu mythology was intensified by a more personal crisis of confidence in his own perceptual capabilities. On July 16, 1851, Thoreau confessed, "Methinks my present experience is nothing my past experience is all in all." He fears the fading of his perceptual power, of a present whose intensity is dwarfed by a remembered past. "I think that no experience which I have today comes up to or is comparable with the experiences of my boyhood– And not only this is true–but as far back as I can remember I have unconsciously referred to the experience of a previous state of experience. 'Our life is a forgetting' &c" (JP 3:305). Underlying this Wordsworthian lament is a wish for a liminal experience in which the boundaries of self and nature evaporate, and we experience an unusual sense of both harmony and elevation. "Formerly methought nature developed as I developed and grew up with me. My life was extacy. In youth before I lost any of my senses–I can remember that I was all alive–and inhabited my body with inexpressible satisfaction, both its weariness & its refreshment were sweet to me. This earth was the most glorious musical instrument, and I was audience to its strains" (JP 3:305–6). Thoreau associates the health and vigor of youth with a bond with the natural world, and expresses some alarm at the progressive diminishment of that bond.[18]

But what of Thoreau's project both to live and describe the "natural life" under these conditions? The "simple and sincere account of his own life" (Wa 3) that he had set out to provide had become deeply problematic. Thoreau's ultimate completion of *Walden*, made possible around 1852 by a breakthrough in his sense of the work's structure and a corresponding recovery of purpose and vision, was in part a response to this sense of intellectual and experiential slippage. Shaping an account of his experience in *Walden* thus became one part of Thoreau's answer to a disappearing capacity to envision enlarged and unifying categories. The *Walden* manuscript, beginning with his journal entries and lectures while he was living at the pond, and evolving through its seven stages of composition in the late 1840s and early 1850s, became the repository of his struggle to maintain his capacity for philosophical reflection on the natural world and the place of the self within it.[19]

Thoreau's chapter "The Ponds," which includes his intricate analysis of the richly symbolic identity of Walden Pond, is indicative of his strategy of portraying perception as factual and sensuous yet also productive of ever-enlarging frames of reference.[20] Walden is a character who is absolutely pure and "perennially young" (Wa 193). Thoreau attributes such human characteristics as eyelids and lips to Walden, and dramatizes his relationship with the pond as that of friendship. Such tactics infuse an imaginative life into material nature and contribute to Thoreau's attempt to re-mythologize the natural world. The humanization of the pond helps to quicken and vitalize it, and stands as the culmination of a series of depictions of an animated natural world which include the besotted, "aldermanic" bullfrogs who "*tr-r-r-oonk*" (Wa 126) at the pond shore in the evening in "Sounds," and the visits from the "old settler and original proprietor, who is reported to have dug Walden Pond," and the "ruddy and lusty old dame, who delights in all weathers and seasons" (Wa 137–38).

Personification is the most easily recognizable strategy through which Thoreau attempts to use the pond and its landscape to enlarge our commonplace perception. It is supplemented by the more extensive passages of description in which Thoreau strives to produce a mental image of the scenery of Walden, which, though "on a humble scale" (Wa 175), becomes impressive through his careful verbal reconstructions. His close observations of the pond's shoreline and the shifting color of its water help us to locate ourselves and begin to see the world with him. But perhaps the most subtle and telling of these passages, rich in descriptive power and resonant with suggestiveness about the pond's unifying qualities, is his observation of the pond's still surface, the very blankness of which is shown to be its secret of association.

Thoreau describes the unusual optical impression of the pond surface on "a calm September afternoon, when a slight haze makes the opposite shoreline indistinct." In a comment that recalls Emerson's looking through his legs at the world in "Idealism," Thoreau writes, "When you invert your head, it looks like a thread of finest gossamer stretched across the valley, separating one stratum of the atmosphere from another." Whereas Emerson altered his usual perspective to make the solid world seem unfixed and malleable, Thoreau likes to think of the surface of the pond as solid, a perfectly integrated extension of the shoreline. "You would think that you could walk dry under it to the opposite hills, and that the swallows which skim over might perch on it" (Wa 186). This shift in perspective discloses the pond as the point of union among the disparate elements of nature, connecting land, water, and sky to suggest that each of these is a version of all the others, and that each part or aspect of nature contains all of nature if seen completely.

Thoreau's descriptive argument extends to his portrait of the remarkable power of the pond's surface to record all the life and energy around it, its even, smooth plane a medium that can disclose the smallest presence and the finest movements above and below it.

> It is literally as smooth as glass, except where the skater insects, at equal intervals scattered over its whole extent, by their motions in the sun produce the finest imaginable sparkle on it, or, perchance, a duck plumes itself, or, as I have said, a swallow skims so low as to touch it. It may be that in the distance a fish describes an arc of three or four feet in the air, and there is one bright flash where it emerges, and another where it strikes the water; sometimes the whole silvery arc is revealed; or here and there, perhaps, is a thistle-down floating on its surface, which the fishes dart at and so dimple it again. (Wa 186–87)

This closely observed and poetically expressive prose is of course one of Thoreau's great achievements in *Walden*, but aside from the compelling visual image that he creates, the description re-creates the pond surface as a medium of cognition, an ideal analogue for the completely perceptive mind. The line of demarcation between two different realms, water and sky, the surface is also the place where these realms meet and merge, recording and thus comprehending each such event. Perception, as represented by Thoreau through the perfectly impressionable pond surface, is thus a process of merger or unification.

Thoreau confirms the metaphoric reach of his description of the pond's surface by concluding that "a field of water betrays the spirit that is in the air. It is continually receiving new life and motion from above" (Wa 188). The spirit above the lake's surface is of course the wind, but Thoreau's choice of words here is significant. "*Spirit* primarily means *wind*," Emerson had written in *Nature*, using this etymological connection as one of his illustrations of how language reveals the connection between the ideal and material realms. "Every word which is used to express a moral or intellectual fact, if traced to its root, is found to be borrowed from some material appearance" (CW 1:18). Thoreau uses "spirit" with this same sense of the identity of the material and the ideal, suggesting that the act of perception unifies the material and the ideal, that the physical discernment of a phenomenon in nature suggests more intangible "moral or intellectual" facts.

Thoreau's account of his return to the frozen surface of the pond in "The Pond in Winter" adds new emphasis on the pond as an embodiment of an enlarged perception that encompasses both material and ideal, fact and law.[21] His morning work of cutting through the ice to obtain fresh water, one of the most memorable lyric moments in the narrative, confirms the eternal presence and inevitable return of the pond's natural life, and also represents the importance and availability of the inner life, perhaps buried or not immediately apparent, but always available. He cuts through the ice and looks down "into the quiet parlor of the fishes, pervaded by a soft light as through a window of ground glass, with its bright sanded floor the same as in summer." The "perennial waveless serenity" of the scene, the inner possession of the pond and of every individual who can delve deeply enough within, leads Thoreau to declare that "heaven is under our feet as well as over our heads" (Wa 283). The pond reveals a further lesson when Thoreau sets about measuring it, intending both to satisfy his curiosity and to dispel the lore that it is bottomless. He finds and records its depth, using measurable fact to counter superstition, but also concludes that fact will open into law if fully examined.

Discovering "that the line of greatest length intersected the line of greatest breadth *exactly* at the point of greatest depth" (Wa 289), Thoreau believed that he may have discovered a law for determining the deepest point in any lake.[22] Although such is not, in fact, the case, the immediacy of Thoreau's reach for the larger implications of his experiment, his eagerness to make Walden a representative entity, is indicative of his need to see his work of observation as a search for more inclusive categories. In this sense, detail can become transformative insight. "If we knew all the laws of Nature, we should need only one fact, or the description of one actual phenomenon, to infer all the particular results at that point" (Wa 290). This is an assertion about the nature of knowledge but also, perhaps more significantly, about the unity of what the mind perceives:

> Our notions of law and harmony are commonly confined to those instances which we detect; but the harmony which results from a far greater number of seemingly conflicting, but really concurring, laws, which we have not detected, is still more wonderful. The particular laws are as our points of view, as, to the traveller, a mountain outline varies with every step, and it has an infinite number of profiles, though absolutely but one form. (Wa 290–91)

This faith that no matter how various it may seem, nature is "absolutely but one form" was Thoreau's justification for his attention to the particulars of nature, an assurance that no act of observation or recognition ended in itself.

The most dramatic and far-reaching of these incidents of observation is the well-known description of the "sand foliage," in which Thoreau recognizes that the forms of melting sand and clay manifest the workings of the laws that control and shape all natural processes of growth and change, including those of the body. One small and seemingly insignificant occurrence becomes revelatory of the entire system of nature. Generally recognized as the climactic scene of *Walden*, the passage has been accorded both intense scrutiny and illuminating explication in recent criticism. Gordon V. Boudreau has shown in impressive detail that the sand foliage passage was a culminating statement of a "resurrection myth" toward which Thoreau had striven in *A Week* and his Journal, in which the thawing of the earth becomes an act of both birth and utterance. Thoreau's observation and description of it links mental perception and linguistic expression to this archetypal moment in the creative process. Robert D. Richardson Jr. calls attention to Thoreau's exclamation that "there is nothing inorganic" (Wa 308) as the recognition that the unifying processes of law invigorate and explain all physical phenomena. Noting that the expansion of the sand foliage description was the most important revision in the final drafts of the *Walden* manuscript, Richardson connects this late expansion with Thoreau's sighting of the thawing sand flow on February 2, 1854, a signal to him of the end of winter. This climactic insight of the triumph of life is part of Thoreau's own emergence from a period of disorientation and despondency in the early 1850s in which his emotional resiliency was keyed to seasonal change. The completion of the *Walden* manuscript, after its long postponement and repeated revision, thus seems to have represented a personal and spiritual achievement as well as a literary one. As Richardson writes, "The 'Spring' chapter of *Walden*, with its exhilarating description of the flowing clay bank at its center, is finally an affirmation of foliage over fossil, natural fact over historical relic, life over death."[23]

Thoreau's detailed and intricate description of the sand foliage phenomenon, coupled with the reach of his interpretive insight, make this one of the most telling examples of the "reading" that was the cornerstone of his natural life at Walden. Confessing the "delight" (Wa 304) that the sand foliage gave him, the loving detail with which he unfolds his description and interpretation dramatizes his enraptured witness to life's origin. The earth's "living poetry" (Wa 309) was a vivid expression of the merging of fact with law, a process that required language as an essential element. The earth itself became a poem, and Thoreau its reader. His toil over Homer and his devotion to his Journal were thus as natural and necessary as the seasonal cycle, and a part of that larger process. "You find thus in the very sands an anticipation of the vegetable leaf. No wonder that the earth expresses itself outwardly in leaves, it so labors with the idea inwardly. The atoms have already learned this law, and are pregnant by it" (Wa 306). Thoreau thus recognized his own efforts to understand and express the work of thinking and writing as consonant with the very process of creation itself. The natural life around him corresponded to the natural life within.

CHAPTER SIX

The Actual World

SUBSISTING ON WILD FLOWERS

Thoreau's descriptions of the changing natural landscape in *Walden* have a quality of immediacy and engagement that makes it all the more surprising that much of the book was written in retrospect. One of the elements that made it a classic of nature writing, its seasonal structure, was in fact a relatively late addition. Studies of the manuscript have suggested that the focus of *Walden* gradually changed over its long process of composition and revision, moving from social criticism to the celebration of nature's revelatory qualities. This change reflects the deepening of Thoreau's environmentally informed, biocentric orientation in the late 1840s and early 1850s. He gained both subject matter and momentum as a writer, while simultaneously insulating himself from the kind of vocational entrapment by the literary market that his brief experience in New York had taught him to fear. Thus the argument for simplicity and self-reliance that he pursued in the opening chapter, "Economy," is crucial to his developing sense of purpose both at the pond and in the years that followed.

Thoreau did not break stride in his literary endeavors after leaving Walden Pond and returning to Concord, and if anything, he seems to have intensified his efforts. In late 1847 and 1848 he sought a publisher for *A*

Week while he continued to expand and revise it. He had begun lecturing on his life at Walden while still living at the pond and continued writing and presenting those lectures in 1848 and 1849, formulating in them the nucleus of *Walden*. By 1849 he had drafted what Robert Sattelmeyer has described as the first stage of that book. After a transformative journey to the summit of Mount Ktaadn in the Maine wilderness, he published "Ktaadn" in a serialized version in the summer and fall of 1848, and also published what would become his most influential essay, "Civil Disobedience," in the spring of 1849.[1]

Even in his absence, however, Emerson continued to exert a pressure on Thoreau, and though Thoreau's literary ambitions were genuine and self-originating, it is also clear that Emerson was hoping to mold Thoreau's literary career through his own experience. Emerson had put much of his professional energy into lecturing, and while he traveled and lectured in England, he looked for opportunities to arrange a similar lecture tour for Thoreau as well. Recognizing that his books were the key to his recognition in England, he felt that Thoreau must get *A Week* in print in order to open doors on the lecture circuit. "My reception here is really a premium often on authorship," he wrote to Lidian in February, 1848, "& if Henry Thoreau means one day to come to England let him not delay another day to print his book" (ELet 4:16). After Thoreau published *A Week* in May 1849 with Emerson's publisher James Munroe and Company, Emerson wrote Theodore Parker, among others, to try to arrange reviews for it. "The book has rare claims," he wrote, "& we must have an American claim & ensign marked on it before it goes abroad for English opinions" (ELet 4:151).

Meanwhile, however, Thoreau was finding some difficulty separating his identity from Emerson's on the New England lyceum circuit. He lectured in Salem in late November 1848, only to have the reviewer in the *Salem Observer* observe that "we were reminded of Emerson continually." The reviewer saw a similarity not only of ideas but of "tone of voice" and "personal appearance" as well, and added that "the close likeness between the two would almost justify a charge of plagiarism, were it not that Mr. Thoreau's lecture furnished ample proof of being a native product, by affording all the charm of an original."[2]

Thoreau's literary apprenticeship to Emerson was further complicated by the economic failure of *A Week*, an outcome that was a severe blow to Thoreau emotionally and financially, and also strained his relationship with Emerson, whom he held in some ways responsible for the failure.[3] The publisher seemed to do very little to promote it, making it, as Steven Fink observes, "virtually inaccessible to the public unless they applied for it directly," conditions that "made failure virtually inevitable."[4] While Emerson's encouragement, influence, and example were invaluable, and his help enormously generous, Thoreau had begun to see that to follow in Emerson's footsteps too closely was to doom himself to failure. Although he had continued his literary endeavors much in Emerson's mold after returning to Concord, he had also brought back from Walden the lesson of self-reliance, one that he would begin to translate into a new conception of his literary career and of his life in Concord after Emerson's return.

Thoreau's developing state of mind at this period can be discerned from several remarkable letters to H. G. O. Blake, an admirer of his work who began a correspondence with him in 1848.[5] Blake shared with Thoreau a suspicion of the conventional paths of vocation, having himself left the ministry. In Blake, Thoreau seems to have felt that he had found an ear for the searching questions about vocation and identity that he could not discuss with Emerson. "Be not anxious to avoid poverty," he wrote Blake in August 1849 (Corr 247), and he expanded more personally on this theme the next November:

> At present I am subsisting on certain wild flowers which Nature wafts to me, which unaccountably sustain me, and make my apparently poor life rich. Within a year my walks have extended themselves, and almost every afternoon, (I read, or write, or make pencils, in the forenoon, and by the last means get a living for my body.) I visit some new hill or pond many miles distant. I am astonished at the wonderful retirement through which I move, rarely meeting a man in these excursions, never seeing one similarly engaged, unless it be my companion, when I have one. (Corr 250–51)

The way of life that Thoreau describes, delicately balanced between the literary and domestic duties of the morning and afternoons of nature exploration, had supplanted the more dramatic withdrawal of his life at Walden Pond.

Thoreau's new way of life also included the resumption of his place in his own family, and, though he minimizes their importance to Blake, his contributions to his family's expanding business. After he had returned from New York in 1843, Thoreau had made improvements in his family's pencil manufacturing process and in the quality of the mixture that constituted the pencil lead.[6] These improvements paid off more handsomely than anyone expected several years later when printers found that the superior Thoreau lead was ideal for use in the process of electrotyping. The Thoreau family's income improved considerably as they abandoned pencil making and sold their ground lead directly to printing companies. One result of their rising economic fortunes was the purchase and renovation of a larger house on Main Street in Concord in late 1849 and early 1850. Once the house was renovated, Thoreau was able to occupy the large finished attic, which afforded him both privacy for study and space for his books and collections of artifacts and natural objects.[7] The irony, for those who know Thoreau principally through *Walden*, is that he seems eventually to have realized that his pursuit of natural life might be conducted most effectively from Main Street in Concord.

Thoreau's search for vocational alternatives that would preserve his independence from the literary market and from a nine-to-five routine is also confirmed by his decision in the fall of 1848 to train himself as a surveyor, a direction that he undertook even while he was actively pursuing both lecturing and magazine publishing, and continuing to revise *A Week*. This new source of potential income, when seen in the context of his contributions to the family business and his decision to continue living in the family home, suggests that Thoreau was beginning to develop a quite different intellectual career from the one that Emerson had envisioned for his protégé. Thoreau was growing more willing to eschew the potential recognition and rewards that might have been open to him as a lecturer and magazine writer in order to secure the greater freedom of subject matter, and the greater freedom of daily life, that he might create for himself in Concord. This strategy of "subsisting on certain wild flowers which Nature wafts to me" began as a response to the seeming drift in his life since the death of John, but it eventually became a firm resolution by the middle 1850s. "Will you live? or will you be embalmed?" he wrote Blake in 1850 (Corr 257), and this sense of starkly differing alternatives helped define the new freedom that he seems to have brought back with him from Walden Pond.

Emerson could not but be disappointed at the way Thoreau appeared to be turning his back on his potential as a lecturer and author, and as Thoreau set his new direction, the closeness of their relationship diminished. The tension between them was greatly exacerbated by Emerson's rising literary stature, and the success, professional and social, of his English lecture tour in the late 1840s. "The Emerson who returned had changed," Robert Sattelmeyer writes, having "picked up some of the habits of a London clubman (even to the extent of smoking after-dinner cigars)." This clash of manners and ambitions added to the already existing emotional complexities of their relationship, driving a wedge between them that was painful to both.[8]

Feeling in some sense that Thoreau was slipping away from him, and perhaps squandering his opportunities to make a trip to England, Emerson continued to admire him but was forced to recognize their differences. He described them in quite dramatic terms after a conversation with Thoreau in 1848: "Henry Thoreau is like the woodgod who solicits the wandering poet & draws him into antres vast & desarts idle, & bereaves him of his memory, & leaves him naked, plaiting vines & with twigs in his hand. Very seductive are the first steps from the town to the woods, but the End is want & madness" (JMN 10:344).[9] This did not, of course, mean the end of their friendship or their regard for each other, and they did make efforts to regain the closeness they once had. But it was clear that they were now headed in different directions, and that Emerson's role as a mentor and model was over. Emerson records a "rambling talk" with Thoreau in October 1850, "in accordance with my proposal to hold a session, the first for a long time, with malice prepense, & take the bull by the horns." England was a major topic of the talk, and one on which they could not agree. Thoreau decisively rejected Emerson's claim that England "ripened" its people more fully than America. "Henry thought, 'the English all train,' are mere soldiers, as it were, in the world. And that their business is winding up, whilst our pioneer is unwinding his lines" (JMN 11:283–84). Emerson was looking to Europe while Thoreau was looking to the western frontier, and this divergence signified the differences in intellectual orientation that would persist between them.

The cumulative impact of Thoreau's repeated excursions into the woods and fields in these years also heavily influenced this change, but two aspects of his nature studies deserve particular attention. In the fall of 1846, after he had been living at the pond for a little over a year, Thoreau took his first excursion into the Maine wilderness, and climbed to the top of Mount Ktaadn, an experience that became the subject of one of his most memorable essays. In the early 1850s, as he began the second phase of his revision of the *Walden* manuscript, he began to incorporate night walks into his pattern of life, exploring the landscape around Concord under moonlight. He recorded impressions of these nocturnal walks in his Journal and developed some of the experiences into a lecture. As different as these two forms of natural experience were, they had an important quality in common: they showed Thoreau the natural world from a new prospect, making the familiar seem strange. The wilderness around Mount Ktaadn, as he would observe, could not easily be described through the assumptions and expectations that he had developed in his life in Concord, or even at Walden Pond. Similarly, the "familiar" landscape of Concord seemed transformed under the varying conditions of the night, becoming a new and constantly changing world that was at once unsettling and exhilarating. In both experiences, Thoreau glimpsed a natural world that was uninhabited, undomesticated, and wild.

THE VERGE OF A PRIMITIVE FOREST

"Ktaadn" provides an indication of these changes, both in its intense engagement with wilderness "experience" and in its surprising report of the source and nature of "revelation." As in his account of his ascent of Saddleback in *A Week*, Thoreau makes the ascent of "Ktaadn" into a journey of revelation, but the process and nature of that revelation seem instructively different. At Mount Ktaadn, Thoreau not only encountered wild nature but also recognized a force that was less pliable to his imagination. This deep nature would not yield its revelations by ordinary or expected means. We can read "Ktaadn" as Thoreau's recognition that the natural world was both richer and more problematic than he had heretofore known. It provided no easy model for either knowing or living.

While "Ktaadn" is primarily the narrative of a spiritual quest in which the ascent of the mountain represents the path to enlightenment, it also carries a secondary and in some ways competing narrative: Thoreau's reportage of the life of backwoods settlers and of the lumber industry, then engaged in clearing the virgin white pine forest of the region. Thoreau progresses from encounters with village life into observations of settlements of an ever sparser kind, the isolated cabins of the settlers, and the primitive seasonal logging camps. He is fascinated with the ways of life he encounters and keen to observe how the "natural" and the "human" interact and interpenetrate. These settlements map Thoreau's advance into the wilderness, and are of particular importance to an author who was making his own life "a mile from any neighbor, in a house which I had built myself" (Wa 3). He cannot help but regard the thinning settlements north of Bangor as versions of the life-text that he himself has been writing at Walden for the past year.

Thoreau had been about the business of re-creating the rudiments of human civilization at his Walden retreat. So too, he found, were the back-country settlers in Maine, whose farms and cabins continually pushed at the border of the wilderness. The most vivid dramatization of this realization, a kind of mirroring or self-discovery, is his investigation of the only farm on the seven-mile road from Houlton to Molunkus—a spot that seems to impress even Thoreau with its isolation. He cannot contain his curiosity about this frontier dwelling which represents a much more serious attempt at permanently settling the wilderness than does his Walden experiment. He climbs the fence to inspect "a new field, planted with potatoes," and his thorough investigation leaves him impressed: "Pulling up the vines, [we] found good-sized potatoes, nearly ripe, growing like weeds, and turnips mixed with them." But he also observes the unusual agricultural practice that yielded the crop. The potatoes were growing "where the logs were still burning between the hills [of potatoes]," a phenomenon that he explains with the eye of a farmer:

> The mode of clearing and planting, is, to fell the trees, and burn once what will burn, then cut them up into suitable lengths, roll into heaps, and burn again; then, with a hoe, plant potatoes where you can come at the ground between the stumps and charred logs, for a first crop, the ashes sufficing for manure, and no hoeing being necessary the first year. In the fall, cut, roll, and burn again, and so on, till the land is cleared; and soon it is ready for grain, and to be laid down. (MW 14)

The modern reader may be shocked by this destruction and waste, and Thoreau, as we shall see, is not undisturbed by it. But he is also impressed; his sojourn at Walden, we should remember, was at least in part an agricultural experiment. He finds in these flourishing hills of potatoes amid the burning logs an omen of future social progress: "Let those talk of poverty and hard times who will, in the towns and cities; cannot the emigrant, who can pay his fare to New-York or Boston, pay five dollars more to get here . . . and be as rich as he pleases, where land virtually costs nothing, and houses only the labor of building, and he may begin life as Adam did?" (MW 14). Thoreau here interposes the conventional view of American western expansion and manifest destiny into a manuscript that also seems oriented to the unique, even sacred, claims of wilderness. Is this a journey to escape civilization or to expand its orbit?[10]

This contradiction is more dramatically evident when Thoreau describes coming upon a large tract of heavily forested land "which had just been felled and burnt over, and was still smoking." The scene he describes is something akin to a massacre: "The trees lay at full length, four or five feet deep, and crossing each other in all directions, all black as charcoal, but perfectly sound within, still good for fuel or for timber; soon they would be cut into lengths and burnt again." While Thoreau laments the destructive waste of the scene, he sees wasted firewood, not destroyed trees or a ravaged landscape: "Here were thousands of cords, enough to keep the poor of Boston and New-York amply warm for a winter, which only cumbered the ground, and were in the settler's way. And the whole of that solid and interminable forest is doomed to be gradually devoured thus by fire, like shavings, and no man be warmed by it" (MW 17). Thoreau can neither countenance the disappearance of the "interminable forest" nor fail to see its potential commodity value. But he does foresee its inevitable destruction.[11]

Thoreau's dual allegiance to nature and civilization has been built into the narrative from the beginning. He is not hiking alone, and though we are sometimes prone to forget it, part of his agenda, and certainly many of his perceptions, are molded by his companions. The trip was initiated by his cousin George Thatcher of Bangor, a lumberman who wanted to inspect a dam on property he owned on the Penobscot River, and included others involved in one way or another with lumbering.[12] The "new" country that Thoreau sees is already marked for economic purposes, and his act of exploration and discovery is inevitably entangled with the possession and settlement of the land that constitute its denial as a wild landscape.

Thoreau's conflicting attitudes about the Maine landscape are particularly notable in the early part of the essay, when he describes the fading of settlement into wilderness, or, as he increasingly understands, the replacement of the wild with the civilized. The lumber mills along the Penobscot River are the means by which "the arrowy Maine forest" is "relentlessly sifted, till it comes out boards, clapboards, laths, and shingles" (MW 5). This reduction of the forest to a commodity is one of the ominous signs of the course of modern life, making his praise of the Adamic heroism of the frontier farmers more sharply contradictory. Thoreau's observations of the logging of the forest, offered with a mixture of despair and intense interest, culminate in his descriptions of the logging camps, the last human habitations that he sees. He is clearly fascinated with the way these makeshift but picturesque huts represent a human accommodation with wild nature:

They are very proper forest houses, the stems of the trees collected together and piled up around a man to keep out wind and rain: made of living green logs, hanging with moss and lichen, and with the curls and fringes of the yellow-birch bark, and dripping with resin, fresh and moist, and redolent of swampy odors, with that sort of vigor and perennialness even about them that toad-stools suggest. (MW 20)

The huts are the very stuff of nature, domesticated to human use in such a way that those who used them would be in some senses be "naturalized."[13] They represent a meeting point between the human and the natural, answering in their own unique way the question of living in nature that Thoreau was attempting to answer in his Walden cabin.

But they answer that question satisfactorily only if viewed very narrowly. The presence of these huts is dictated by the lumber trade, and they are as much a sign of the human incursion into the forest as of an accommodation of the human and the natural. "Every log is marked with the owner's name, cut in the sapwood with an axe, or bored with an auger" (MW 42). The forest is owned, the fate of each tree written on its bark.

Thoreau is curious about the human incursion on the forest, and in some ways moved by what he sees of frontier life, but these observations do not entirely displace the essay's larger hope. He reminds us of his real subject when he describes his first view of Ktaadn's summit, "veiled in clouds, like a dark isthmus in that quarter, connecting the heavens with the earth" (MW 33), a description that looms over the narrative as it continues. As he approaches the mountain, the anticipation that had motivated his journey resurfaces in his description of a moonlight walk from his campground at North Twin Lake, not long after he had attained the first glimpse of the mountain.[14] The poetic intensity with which he describes this moonlight walk is a significant departure from the prevailing tone of factual observation and occasional ironic comment that have prevailed thus far: "The little rill tinkled the louder, and peopled all the wilderness for me; and the glassy smoothness of the sleeping lake, laving the shores of a new world, with the dark, fantastic rocks rising here and there from the surface, made a scene not easily described. It has left such an impression of stern yet gentle wildness on my memory as will not soon be effaced" (MW 40).

Thoreau builds this intensity further in describing the fishing at the Aboljacknagesic River, twelve miles below the summit of Ktaadn, where trout "swallowed the bait as fast as we could throw in." These fish ("the finest specimens . . . that I have ever seen") fell "in a perfect shower" on the shore, and "glistened like the fairest flowers, the product of primitive rivers . . . these bright fluviatile flowers, seen of Indians only, made beautiful, the Lord knows why, to swim there!" (MW 53–54). We have to make allowances for fisherman's brag here, but Thoreau does seem moved as the beauty as the wilderness opens to him.[15] Later that night, he reports, "I dreamed: of trout-fishing; and, when at length I awoke, it seemed a fable, that this painted fish swam so near my couch, and rose to our hooks the last evening—and I doubted if I had not dreamed it all" (MW 55).

Thoreau knows what to do to test the reality of his dream: he gets up before dawn to try his luck again, and the resulting scene is one of the moments of highest visual and emotional intensity in the narrative. "There stood Ktaadn with distinct and cloudless outline in the moonlight; and the rippling of the rapids was the only sound to break the stillness" (55). It is a painterly scene whose visual components are also symbolically potent—the mountain, object of Thoreau's spiritual quest, framed in the richly evocative light of the moon, and the answering stream. It is a moment of transcendent beauty, in which Thoreau's imagination seems to be fulfilled by the scene before him.

Thoreau makes his first attempt to ascend the summit later that day, abandoning the other members of his party who are looking for a camping spot. His blood is up for the ascent. His way leads through a "scraggy country" of dwarfed trees, "their tops flat and spreading, and their foliage blue and nipt with cold," which had formed a uniform covering over the boulder-strewn area, "a mass of coarse basket-work" that marked the upper limit of organic growth on the mountain. It was a path "scarcely less arduous than Satan's anciently through Chaos." "Here," Thoreau remarked wryly, "the principle of vegetation was hard put to it." Emerging finally into an area of pure rock nearer the summit, he is stopped by a visually impenetrable covering of clouds which denies him the achievement of Ktaadn's summit (MW 60–62).

This aborted attempt at ascent increases his appetite for the climb the next day, and although the party sets out as a group, Thoreau soon outdistances them and finds himself alone in the ascent, advancing toward a summit that is still "concealed by mist" (MW 63). Even if we assume that this is factual reporting of the actual details of the trip, it is difficult to overlook the significance of the mist-shrouded summit as a denial of "vision," and a profound challenge to Thoreau's expectations about the interconnection of nature and human perception.[16] "I was deep within the hostile ranks of clouds, and all objects were obscured by them" (MW 63). This obscurity gives rise to a feeling of personal enervation, a loss of the capacity to respond. "Some part of the beholder, even some vital part, seems to escape through the loose grating of his ribs as he ascends. He is more lone than you can imagine" (MW 64). Thoreau is thus forced to revise his earlier characterization of nature's "stern yet gentle wildness" (MW 40). "Vast, Titanic, inhuman Nature has got him at disadvantage, caught him alone, and pilfers him of some of his divine faculty. She does not smile on him as in the plains." He dramatizes his crisis of perception as Ktaadn's maternal rejection of him: "I cannot pity nor fondle thee here, but forever relentlessly drive thee hence to where I *am* kind" (MW 64). Thoreau's spirit quest seems to end in failure.

OUR LIFE IN NATURE

"Ktaadn" persistently records the undermining of the expectations that Thoreau has brought to his excursion. His narrative has yielded as many observations of logging techniques as vistas of scenery, and the Maine forests, magnificent in many respects, have been filled with the troubling reminders of human ownership and exploitation. Moreover, Thoreau's hoped-for achievement of transcendent vision at the summit of Ktaadn has been thwarted by the unconditional fulfillment of what he had been seeking all along—wilderness. The essay yields one more such turn, a revelation from the blind side which forces a reconsideration of all that has come before it. As Thoreau and his party are descending Ktaadn, they cross an area of "Burnt Lands," cleared by a lightning-caused fire, which "looked rather like a natural pasture for the moose and deer, exceedingly wild and desolate, with occasional strips of timber crossing them, and low poplars springing up, and patches of blueberries here and there" (MW 70). The clearing reminds Thoreau of a Concord pasture, hardly the deep wilderness that he had been seeking in Maine; this feeling of prosaic normalcy carries a shock.[17] "I found myself traversing them familiarly, like some pasture run to waste, or partially reclaimed by man," he says, but that odd sense of familiarity heightens his realization that he is in an utterly non-human place. "It is difficult to conceive of a region uninhabited by man. We habitually presume his presence and influence everywhere" (MW 70).[18] He can describe the scene before him only in terms of its denial of human categories: "Here was no man's garden, but the unhandselled globe. It was not lawn, nor pasture, nor mead, nor woodland, nor lea, nor arable, nor waste-land" (MW

70). He speaks with a kind of awe, as if he recognizes the actual earth for the first time.

Thoreau's response to the Burnt Lands can be placed in an Emersonian context, but one quite different from the high Transcendentalism of *Nature*. "Where do we find ourselves?" Emerson asked in "Experience," an essay published some two years before Thoreau's Ktaadn expedition. Emerson's searching question had signaled the limit of the high Romantic aspirations of Transcendentalism. He spoke as a leader who had lost his own way, and his friendship must have given this question particular weight for Thoreau.[19] Emerson's opening image of balked ascent, of waking to find oneself halfway up a stairway with no sense of its beginning or end, resonates well with Thoreau's account of his own thwarted achievement in ascending Ktaadn. That resonance is amplified in Emerson's depiction of the resulting state of emotional and psychic dislocation that he attempts to address in "Experience." "Was it Boscovich who found out that bodies never come in contact? Well, souls never touch their objects. An innavigable sea washes with silent waves between us and the things we aim at and converse with" (CW 3:29). In *Nature*, Emerson envisioned the attainment of a cosmic harmony that would reveal the self to be a part of everything around it. In "Experience" he wrestles with the opposite problem: the inability to bring the self out of a harrowing perceptual isolation. "I take this evanescence and lubricity of all objects, which lets them slip through our fingers when we clutch hardest, to be the most unhandsome part of our condition. Nature does not like to be observed, and likes that we should be her fools and playmates" (CW 3:29). Thoreau has indeed clutched hard at nature in "Ktaadn," and has been made nature's fool as a result. His failure to achieve a holistic and transcendent vision of nature on Ktaadn's summit has dramatically confirmed Emerson's new skepticism.

Emerson is frank in admitting that we have only limited means for addressing the terrifying loss of contact with the world beyond the self. His strategy is to remind us that even though our perception is limited, this blindness need not be paralyzing; action is possible even in the face of epistemological uncertainty. "I am very content with knowing, if only I could know" (CW 3:48), he confesses, but to recognize the limits of our ability is the beginning of a usable, pragmatic wisdom.[20]

Emerson also shows that the limit of our willed knowledge is not necessarily the limit of knowledge itself. "Power keeps quite another road than the turnpikes of choice and will, namely, the subterranean and invisible tunnels and channels of life." The desire for control signified by our thirst for knowledge is sure to be thwarted, and the advances that we are most likely to make will be gifts to us, moments of insight that are unsought and unwilled and that possess us. "Life is a series of surprises, and would not be worth taking or keeping, if it were not" (CW 3:39). It is in these unexpected perceptual leaps that our isolation from the world is broken and contact is reestablished, though this happens on the world's terms, not our own. "It turns out somewhat new," Emerson observes, "and very unlike what [the individual] promised himself" (CW 3:40).

Emerson's confession helps explain Thoreau's surprise at the alien and inhuman quality of the Burnt Lands. "Man was not to be associated with it. It was Matter, vast, terrific,—not his Mother Earth that we have heard of, not for him to tread on, or be buried in,—no, it were being too familiar even to let his bones lie there—the home this of Necessity and Fate" (MW 70). This clear repudiation of his earlier anthropomorphic representations of nature is emphasized by the concentration on the earth as "Matter," and the implication that this matter is beyond the power of mind to project or control it. The implications of this recognition are the substance of one of the most compelling, and difficult, moments in Thoreau's work:

> What is it to be admitted to a museum, to see a myriad of particular things, compared with being shown some star's surface, some hard matter in its home! I stand in awe of my body, this matter to which I am bound has become so strange to me. I fear not spirits, ghosts, of which I am one,—*that* my body might,—but I fear bodies, I tremble to meet them. What is this Titan that has possession of me? Talk of mysteries!—Think of our life in nature,— daily to be shown matter, to come in contact with it,—rocks, trees, wind on our cheeks! the *solid* earth! the *actual* world! the *common sense! Contact! Contact! Who* are we? *where* are we? (MW 71)

Where, indeed, do we find ourselves? There are two contradictory strands in Thoreau's reaction—his indication of an apparent alienation from matter, and thus from the earth itself, and his almost simultaneous claim of contact with the world. The alienation is represented most strikingly in his confession of estrangement from his own body, which he calls "matter to which I am bound," but of which he stands "in awe." This extreme dualism is reinforced with his characterization of himself as something apparently other than his body, a "ghost" or "spirit," which is possessed by a "Titan."[21] The emotional manifestation of this dualism is Thoreau's confession that "I fear not spirits, . . . but I fear bodies, I tremble to meet them." There is certainly more than enough evidence to suggest that Thoreau did indeed have his troubles with bodily contact, but before taking the statement as a simple confession of his resistance to touch, we must note the duality embedded in his phrasing: "I fear bodies, I tremble to meet them." The trembling is in part a sign of fear, but also a sign of awe and expectancy, even of desire, a plea not to abandon bodily experience but to realize it fully. At this moment of trembling the passage moves from confusion and fear to reception and affirmation. "Think of our life in nature." Our life in nature, as Thoreau goes on to make clear, is our life in the senses and the body—"daily to be shown matter, to come in contact with it,—rocks, trees, wind on our cheeks!"

We can feel relatively sure that Thoreau had read with great attention Emerson's remarks on the inability of souls to come into contact with their objects. "Experience," an essay with numerous allusions to friendship and its difficulties, would have had a great personal significance for Thoreau. Moreover, it is the essay in which Emerson attempted to deal with his grief over the loss of his son Waldo, who died in 1842, some two weeks after the death of John Thoreau. Thoreau and Emerson had suffered profound losses almost simultaneously. Emerson's explanation of the soul's isolation had therefore made itself part of Thoreau's agenda of intellectual inquiry, and had colored his own thinking about perception, relations, and the isolated nature of the self. Thus he speaks of the "mystery" of coming "in contact" with nature, a form of unwilled and unplanned knowing, born of the surprise that Emerson had argued was the only possible basis of such knowing.

The impact of his discovery is rhetorically indicated by the progression of the passage into bursts of exclamation, which, when we look at them closely, are in reality acts of naming, a cataloguing of elements of the external world—"rocks, trees, wind on our cheeks! the *solid* earth! the *actual* world! the *common sense!*" The odd member of this list is "the *common sense*," a term that Thoreau uses here to indicate the bridge between consciousness and matter, the vehicle through which contact is made. These outbursts of naming culminate in celebratory exclamations, "*Contact! Contact!*" which indicate that Emerson's "innavigable sea" has somehow been navigated.[22] Revelation comes not on Ktaadn's summit but in Thoreau's descent of the mountain, with his back turned to the expected source.

Any reading that stresses the revelatory and affirmative nature of this complex passage must consider its concluding questions, "*Who* are we? *where* are we?" These appear to be confessions of bewilderment which echo the feeling of thwarted inspiration at the summit. These questions indicate the extent to which Thoreau's experience at the Burnt Lands has unsettled him, separating him from his sense of secured identity ("*Who* are we?") and his certain knowledge of place ("*where* are we?"). Moreover, if we put them in the context of Emerson's "Experience," their similarity to his opening question, "Where do we find ourselves?" is striking. But Thoreau has actually answered Emerson's question with these others, using them as signs of attainment rather than loss. The "contact" that Thoreau celebrates has been a pouring forth of the self beyond its limited boundaries into a merger with the larger world. Thoreau's questions are therefore celebratory as well, extending the implications of his lyric proclamations of contact by emphasizing a liberating humility that is its result. The question "*Who* are we?" is a particularly important sign of the momentary unburdening of the self, and can be linked to what Alan D. Hodder has termed "moments of transparency and acute sensory sensitivity" that were the essential components of Thoreau's religious sensibility.[23] Who we are and where we are constitute the deepest "mysteries" of nature that his experience in the Burnt Lands has revivified for him, making the self and the place that surrounds it entirely new propositions for the inquiring consciousness. "At the same time that we are earnest to explore and learn all things," he would write in *Walden*, "we require that all things be mysterious and unexplorable" (Wa 317). His questions assert the simultaneous bewilderment and exhilaration of unexplored territory, both within and without.

Thoreau's final questions thus enact a rediscovery of the world, the restoration of an innocence that is expressed in his exclamations of bewilderment. Suddenly everything is new. He has not transcended "the solid earth" or "the actual world" but has found or discovered it. "I am reminded by my journey how exceedingly new this country still is. You have only to travel for a few days into the interior and back parts even of many of the old states, to come to that very America which the Northmen, and Cabot, and Gosnold, and Smith and Raleigh visited" (MW 81). The new country that Thoreau has discovered signals his renewed hold on life and his more open acceptance of death. "What a place to live, what a place to die and be buried in!" (MW 81). Thoughts of death and burial may seem surprising in this affirmation of nature, but they suggest that Thoreau has begun to find the restoration that he had been seeking since John's death. Mount Ktaadn has shown him death and life, and their indisputable connection.

Nothing in Thoreau's work matches the dramatic intensity of the "Contact" passage in "Ktaadn," and even with its internal tensions and the extreme modulations of tone, the "Burnt Lands" episode leaves the unmistakable impression of a profound and mysterious encounter with the sources of being. Much of the energy of the moment, as we have seen, arises from Thoreau's sudden recognition of the strangeness of a presumably familiar landscape. The Concord-like clearing in the Maine wilderness reveals itself as an utterly unknown and unexplored place, and his own presence there is made both frightening and exhilarating. This alienation from the familiar, and the corresponding effort to gain power from it, links the experience on Ktaadn to a series of exploratory and often revelatory experiences in the early 1850s, occasioned by Thoreau's nocturnal walks in the woods and fields around Concord. Recorded in his Journal with a reverent sense that they carried a heightened imaginative intensity, these walks disclosed a sometimes unsettling strangeness in Concord's familiar and habitable countryside.[24] Although Thoreau never fully completed his work on these experiences for publication, in October 1854, some two months after *Walden* was published, he lectured on "Moonlight," part of a lecture series on "Walking, or the Wild" that had begun to take shape as a sequel to *Walden*. Much of what we now understand of Thoreau's last decade derives from this significant but only partially completed series of lectures.[25]

The revelatory impact of the moonlight walks differed markedly from the experience descending Mount Ktaadn, which Thoreau described as sudden, unexpected, and enormously disconcerting, but also illuminating and invigorating. Walking by night provided instead a calmer, more slowly unfolding experience, lacking any particular center of attention or turning point except for the modulations in the light that bathed the scene. Part of his account of one such walk, under a waning moon in September 1852, suggests the decidedly non-dramatic quality of many of these excursions:

> To Conantum– A warm night– A thin coat sufficient. I hear an apple fall. as I go along the road. Meet a man going to market thus early. There are no mists to diversify the night–its features are very simple. I hear no whipporwill or other bird– See no fire flies– Saw a whipporwill? flutter across the road. Hear the dumping sound of frogs on the river meadow, and occasionally a kind of croak as from a bittern there. It is very dewy & I bring home much mud on my shoes. (JP 5:335)

The apple's fall and the fluttering of the bird are magnified enormously by the comparative silence and darkness of the night. The stillness and felt absence of many ordinary aspects of the landscape give this scene, and others like it, a remarkable power. This is in part because Thoreau himself is even more alert than usual, having entered into a landscape that is at once recognizable and foreign. These walks lack the high drama of "Ktaadn," but they share with it the sense of a new discovery of the world. In their own quite different way these walks were also moments of revelatory awareness and heightened consciousness, arising from an interaction with landscape in a new and unusual form.

Thoreau's moonlight walks seem different in purpose and in experiential quality from the afternoon walks that became part of the daily pattern of his life after Walden. Even though he often covered the same ground, the daylight walks were devoted to field observations of plants and animals and to specimen gathering. Thoreau's reports of his night walks frequently take on a dreamlike quality, as if the absence of sunlight freed his more imaginative and poetic self.

Finding an unexpected sense of the unknown and the wild in the moonlit countryside around Concord, Thoreau increasingly came to conceive of his nighttime walks as challenging and exotic exercises in exploration and perception. "Is not the midnight like central africa to most?" he asked in 1852. "Are we not tempted to explore it–to penetrate to the shores of its Lake Tchad–to discover the sources of its nile perchance in the Mts of the moon? Who knows what fertility what beauty in the animal & vegetable kingdom are there to be found. What primeval simplicity & reflexion of the truth among its dusky inhabitants" (JP 4:315). This exotic wilderness was also, of course, the same landscape that Thoreau had come to know so well by daylight. The marked differences in experiencing the same place by night and by day intrigued him. He persisted in an effort to see that landscape in a deeper and more revealing way, and relished its strangeness.

Thoreau's association of the mystery of the night with "fertility" and "beauty" hint at the suppressed erotic longing that seems an unspoken undercurrent of these moonlit walks. The excursions were isolated and private, since Thoreau rarely encountered others while out at night, but their very isolation seems an enactment of his loneliness. As I have noted, friendship became one of the key themes of A Week, and expressions of his sense of an oppressive isolation are scattered throughout the Journals of the early 1850s. Although one of the principal causes was his complex relationship with the Emersons, that relationship was part of a larger pattern of personal disappointment that resurfaced periodically as a source of pain. "Here I am 34 years old, and yet my life is almost wholly unexpanded," he wrote in 1851. "How much is in the germ! There is such an interval between my ideal and the actual in many instances that I may say I am unborn. There is the instinct for society–but no society." Such outpourings usually mix self-pity and frustration with self-reproach; Thoreau seems to recognize that his high expectations and exacting standards for others generate persistent problems with his interpersonal relationships, but he is unwilling, or per-haps unable, to conceive of friendship except in the most austerely elevated terms. "I did not *make* this demand for a more thorough sympathy," he de-clares. "This is not my idiosyncrasy or disease. He that made the demand will answer the demand" (JP 3:313–14).[26]

At times his sense of disappointment with others boils up into a dismissive despair: "When I review my list of acquaintances from the most impartial point of view, and consider each ones excesses & defects of character–which are the subject of mutual ridicule astonishment and pity–, and I class myself among them–I cannot help asking myself if this is a sane world, what must a mad–house be?" (JP 4:320). But at other times he questions the rightness of his approach to friendship, berating himself for his failures. "How happens it that I find myself making such an enormous demand on men and so constantly disappointed," he writes in 1852. "Are my friends aware how disappointed I am? Is it all my fault? Have I no heart – Am I incapable of expansion and generosity? I shall accuse myself of everything else sooner." The anguished meditation eventually develops into a more defensive rationalization of his conduct. "Would not men have something to com-municate if they were sincere? Is not my silent expectation an invitation an offer–an opportunity offered?" (JP 5:310).

Such expressions of frustration and disappointment well up periodically in the Journals, but Thoreau was able at times to recognize them as useful. "There is a certain fertile sadness which I would not avoid but rather earnestly seek," he confessed in 1851. "It is positively joyful to me– It saves my life from being trivial" (JP 3:368). Nature therefore became not only a source of physical refreshment and intellectual energy to him, but also a kind of solace for the unity that he did not feel he was capable of achieving in human relationships. "If I am too cold for human friendship–I trust I shall not soon be too cold for natural influences," he wrote in 1852. "It ap-pears to be a law that you cannot have a deep sympathy with both man & nature. Those qualities which bring you near to the one estrange you from the other" (JP 4:435). Thoreau's increasing attentiveness to the details and patterns of natural processes—the growing naturalist's sensibility that readers of his late essays and Journal have noted—is in a certain sense compensatory, a grateful enactment of attentive reverence for a purity and integrity, and even a quality of mystery, that were promised but never achieved in human relationships.

THIS IS MY WORLD NOW

Thoreau's accounts of his night walks are arresting exercises in perception in which his capacity to observe sometimes threatens to outstrip his capacity to categorize imaginatively what he is experiencing. The on-the-edge quality of many of the entries underlines his openness to new experience, which constantly challenged his settled, stable knowledge of his natural surroundings. His account of dusk and twilight gradually giving way to moonlight one summer evening (August 5, 1851) is a good illustration of the way he repeatedly found illumination rather than obscurity in the night: "As the twilight deepens and the moonlight is more & more bright–I begin to distinguish myself who I am & where–as my walls contract I become more collected & composed & sensible of my own existence–as when a lamp is brought into a dark apartment & I see who the company are" (JP 3:353–54). While he is describing the adjustment of his eyes to the darkness and the moon's increasing brightness, his "I begin to distinguish myself who I am & where" is also an existential statement, a gauging of his identity, relationships, and purposes. It answers the questions he posed in his descent of Ktaadn. The moonlight is in this sense doubly revelatory, casting its light both around and within him.

Night thus became a period of inner revelation and self-recovery, which Thoreau contrasted with the day's more superficial concerns. The physical properties of the night, especially the unique qualities of the available light, are the correlatives of mental and emotional states and capacities.[27] "With the coolness & the mild silvery light I recover some sanity–my thoughts are more distinct moderated & tempered." By contrast, the day is full of trivial disruptions that compromise the undistracted and purposeful "sanity" that Thoreau desires. "The intense light of the sun unfits me for meditation makes me wander in my thought–my life is too diffuse & dissipated–routine succeeds & prevails over us–the trivial has greater power then & most at noon day the most trivial hour of the 24" (JP 3:354).

Thoreau is repeatedly pushed back to his experiences of wilderness to find analogies and forms of expression for what he sees under the moon. Fair Haven Pond thus appears as "the wildest scenery imaginable–a Lake of the woods" (JP 3:355), and this impression continues when he observes it a month later from the same place: "Moonlight on Fair Haven Pond seen from the Cliffs. A sheeny lake in the midst of a boundless forest– The windy surf sounding freshly & wildly in the single pine behind you– The silence of hushed wolves in the wilderness & as you fancy moose looking off from the shore of the lake" (JP 4:47). There is obviously more than pure observation here, as the silent wolves and imagined moose suggest. The physical qualities, visual, aural, and tactile, of the moonlit lake release a strong imaginative reaction in Thoreau, one tied to his desire to experience a natural world unaltered by human use and habitation. Thoreau finds in the moonlit lake the same quality of wildness that he found in the Maine wilderness; like the Burnt Lands near the Ktaadn summit, the pond is a familiar landscape revealed to him as alien, but nevertheless somehow allied with some crucial part of him. "The stars of poetry & history–& unexplored nature looking down on the scene. This is my world now–with a dull whitish mark curving northward through the forest marking the outlet to the lake. Fair Haven by moonlight lies there like a lake in the Maine Wilderness in the midst of a primitive forest untrodden by man" (JP 4:47). Poetry, history, and nature converge in the image of the stars that look down to observe the earth. Thoreau is imaginatively merged with those observing stars, entering this network of natural phenomena—the lake, the moonlight, and the observing stars—and finding himself at home.

Such experiences might be read through the terminology of birth or rebirth, or as the recovery of a lost but dimly remembered identity or state of being. They are not, of course, restricted to night or moonlight, but those conditions most effectively enable such moments of recovery. During a nighttime walk on June 11, 1851, Thoreau tells of entering into a field enclosed by woods in which the atmosphere seemed "damp & misty," and finding himself "nearer to the origin of things." Again, a certain physical condition and sensation, the comparative dampness of the air, triggers this feeling, but the report is of far more than his observations and sensations. "There is something creative & primal in the cool mist–this dewy mist does not fail to suggest music to me–unaccountably–fertility the origin of things– An atmosphere which has forgotten the sun–where the ancient principle of moisture prevails" (JP 3:251). These walks provoked some of

Thoreau's sharpest, most intensely aware journal passages, and they released an original and authentic creative energy that he craved.

The central phenomenon of all these walks was the light of the moon—or, perhaps more accurately, the range and variety of lunar light and its effects. Thoreau sees a different world at night because of the light by which he sees it; moonlight is part of the scene that he is observing, and simultaneously the medium of that observation. Moonlight thus becomes very closely intertwined with his own perceptual and imaginative endeavors, a projection of his own transformed psyche.

This transposition of the inner and the outer, of depth and surface, is the subject of an 1852 meditation triggered when Thoreau looks out his window onto a moonlit evening. He reacts to the scene in much that way that he reacted to the Burnt Lands near Mount Ktaadn. "I live so much in my habitual thoughts–a routine of thought–that I forget that there is any outside to the globe.– and am surprised when I behold it as now–yonder hills & river in the moonlight, the monsters." Ordinary and familiar parts of the landscape such as hills and the river become strangely unfamiliar and monstrous under the unusual light of the moon. This surprised sense of rediscovering the ordinary is again connected closely both to the appearance of a scene bathed in moonlight and to other sensory experiences associated with that appearance. "There is something invigorating in this air which I am peculiarly sensible is a real wind blowing from over the surface of the planet– I look out at my eyes, I come to my window, & I feel & breathe the fresh air." It is as if the feel of the wind ("wind on our cheeks! the *solid* earth! the *actual* world!") provides a reassurance or confirmation that the scene he beholds in the moonlight is real. This sensuous awakening also carries with it an imperative for an intellectual revaluation. "Where are these rivers and hills–these hieroglyphics which my eyes behold?" he wonders. The blowing wind "is a fact equally glorious with the most inward experience. Why have we ever slandered the outward? The perception of surfaces will always have the effect of miracle to a sane sense" (JP 5:309).

Thoreau's refusal to "slander the outward" originates in the moon's revelation of the novelty of a familiar scene, a sign that the surface of things is alive rather than inert, that even as "surface" it contains many identities. The surface of things is "there" for him, its physical reality undeniable. But this particular moment of experience cannot exhaust its revelatory potential. It is as if some barrier between himself and the scene he witnesses has been broken. He has been taken into that scene, as the "real wind blowing from over the surface of the planet" has confirmed for him. The moonlight shows him a different face for the world, making him recognize not only its immediacy but also its inexhaustibility.

Thoreau made a similar discovery when examining by night the "sand-foliage," the melting clay and sand running down the banks of hillside that he described in *Walden*. "I saw by the shadows cast by the inequalities of the clayey sand-bank in the Deep Cut, that it was necessary to see objects by moon light–as well as sunlight–to get a complete notion of them." The novel quality of the moonlight and its shadowy reflections, different light on the same surface, suggested dimensions and relationships that he was not able to perceive by the brighter and more direct light of the sun. "This bank had looked much more flat by day when the light was stronger, but now the heavy shadows revealed it prominences" (JP 3:249). In reacting to the different qualities of objects under the moon, Thoreau is confirming his sense of the seemingly endless referential capacities of the material phenomena of nature. The moon reveals ever-enlarging dimensions of meaning in what was once only blank "surface."

The comparative darkness of the night was not, Thoreau found, a diminishment but an enrichment. In July 1851 he described "the silent spiritual–contemplative moonlight shedding the softest imaginable light on the western slopes of the hills–as if after a thousand years of polishing their surfaces were just beginning to be bright." The image itself is arresting, and Thoreau amplifies the scene's evocative power by linking the unusual quality of the light to his desire for some lost, or never really found, place of fulfillment. "Moonlight like day-light is more valuable for what it suggests than for what it actually is. It is a long past season of which I dream." Nature's endless capacity to generate new meaning, its inexhaustible power of reference, was forcefully returned to him at such moments, and in the moon he saw "the mysterious light which for some hours has illustrated Asia and the scene of Alexander's victories" and which has now "come to shine on America." What it illuminates here, significantly, is "that illustrated sandbank" that is older than all human endeavors (JP 3:286). The emphasis on the moonlight as the medium for the natural events occurring on the sandbank is significant, since Thoreau recognized the thawing bank and its sand foliage as the great hieroglyphic of the creation, the illustration of nature's perennial process of renewal. Moonlight is an essential element in that process, the means by which it becomes comprehensible and intelligible. Both outside and within, the revealer of surface and the medium of imagination, moonlight comes to represent those moments in which human perception is in absolute harmony with the structure and the continuing creative energy of the natural world.

Thoreau came to look to the night as the time in which nature became newly infused with life, a companionable place that took him out of himself in a way that was healing and revivifying. "If night is the mere negation of day I hear nothing but my own steps in it— Death is with me & life far away," he wrote in 1853. "If the elements are not human–if the winds do not sing or sigh–as the stars twinkle–my life runs shallow." What is most haunting here is the brief image of an empty earth in which Thoreau hears only his own steps. This is the antithesis of the moment of perception represented by the sand foliage, in which all parts of the natural world, organic and inorganic, are alive and animated by the same laws and the same energy. As he recognizes, his own hold on life is fundamentally connected to his capacity to perceive the renewing life of nature. "I measure the depth of my own being," he writes, "I walk with vast alliances" (JP 5:449). The study of nature was thus also self-study, a continuing attempt to confirm and deepen his own connection with the energy of life, and to confirm his faith in the existence and continuance of that life. Even as Thoreau's studies became more "scientific" or "factual" in the 1850s, he was pushed ahead in them by a powerful spiritual need. His fieldwork was a continual testing of his faith in a vital, harmonious, and evolving cosmos, and a persistent attempt to reclaim his own place in it. The moon, with its "world of poetry–its weird teachings–its oracular suggestions" (JP 4:52), became for him a central scripture.

CHAPTER SEVEN

Life with Principle

AFTER WALDEN

The enduring authority of *Walden*, at once a literary masterpiece, a compelling document of political dissent, and a guide to the revitalization of ethical and spiritual experience, has made the interpretation of the last decade of Thoreau's life problematic. Even though he was enormously productive throughout the 1850s, Thoreau completed no text comparable to *Walden* except for the continuance of his remarkable Journal, a work that presents complicated problems of accessibility, intended audience, and interpretation. The power of *Walden*, combined with Thoreau's early death in 1862, has thus left a somewhat distorted picture of his accomplishments and aspirations after the middle 1850s.

The most common form of this distortion, an assumption broadly shared among literary critics until fairly recently, was the impression that Thoreau's later years were marked by intellectual contraction and imaginative decline. The increasingly empirical nature of several of Thoreau's important later projects, the concern with scientific detail in his Journal, and his own periodic worries about shrinking intellectual and poetic power helped to produce a narrative of declension in which the imaginative seer and accomplished poet of nature was displaced by a dry and unimaginative fact collector. In this reading of Thoreau's last decade, his Journal became engulfed in mere notations on natural phenomena with no attempt to make them referential or philosophically significant.

More recent scholarship has forced a revision of these views. Laura Dassow Walls and William Rossi have shown how this narrative of Thoreau's later declension was in part the result of the hostility of literary scholars to the discourse of science, and Bradley P. Dean's editorial work has shown how conceptually ambitious Thoreau's late unfinished projects were. This reassessment has also been advanced by new constructions of Thoreau as a pioneering ecologist and environmental activist, activities in which a thorough and detailed understanding of natural processes and systems is fundamentally important. This shift of perspective has brought a new sense of significance to Thoreau's later work, and a recognition that the discourses of science and environmental preservation are central to a full comprehension of the direction of his later writing.

This last decade of Thoreau's career is complex, however, and resists any linear description. Taking the origins of this period as the early 1850s, after Thoreau had returned from Walden and completed his initial drafts of that work, it is clear that the next decade was a time of both great intellectual expansion and literary experimentation, in which he was striving to find a literary form that would be sufficient to express his ever-growing comprehension of the processes of natural history. The sheer magnitude of his undertakings, his conceptual changes of course as his projects evolved and his data expanded, and his inability to complete his work as his health failed after 1861 all combine to render inadequate any simplified account of this decade.

The best single guide to this period, arguably Thoreau's greatest achievement, is his Journal; recent scholars have both recognized its significance and shown that it can be regarded as an integral work, not a compilation secondary to some larger literary end. But the Journal existed during these years in a complex relationship with several other writing projects. These included lectures, the magazine publications that often grew out of these lectures, the partially completed manuscripts of two major works of natural history, *Wild Fruits* and *The Dispersion of Seeds*, and manuscript materials for a comprehensive "Kalendar" of natural processes in Concord, a project of daunting magnitude, but one whose general conception seems to have been a very fertile source of productive energy and intellectual order. Moreover, Thoreau responded memorably to the challenge of slavery during the 1850s, taking a particular interest in the character and fate of John Brown as an activist and moral exemplar. Thoreau's political and antislavery addresses constitute one of his most important legacies.

These various projects are illuminated by Thoreau's aspiration both to comprehend and to live what he had termed "natural life." He had articulated the ethical challenge of such a life in *Walden*; that challenge deepened as he returned to live with his family in Concord, where he attempted to retain his independence and protect his opportunities for study while fulfilling his duties as a member of a family and a community. His natural history studies, both in a disciplined program of reading and in the Concord fields, were yielding ever deeper insights into the interactions among natural processes, and in both factual detail and broad conception, his comprehension of the methods of organic life and development was expanding dramatically. Natural life had become both his consuming intellectual subject and the ethical standard of his personal behavior.

After his return from Walden, Thoreau was, as we have seen, also continuing his attempt to establish his reputation as a lecturer and author, a task that he undertook with Emerson's encouragement, but also with the pressure that accompanied that support. His life at Walden had provided a new and appealing range of subject matter for lectures, and *Walden* itself took shape in the early lectures through which Thoreau explained and justified his life at the pond. But as he continued to deliver these lectures, the disparity between the solitary life he described and his life in town became more obvious. If his lectures on Walden were his defense of his experiment of two years, he needed a new and somewhat different apologia for the life he was fashioning at his family home in Concord. He offered the first version of this reconstruction of his life and purpose in a lecture on April 23, 1851, which he called "Walking, or the Wild."[1] It was in this lecture that Thoreau first explored the nature of the "border life" that he was beginning to live after returning from Walden, a life in which one remains a social being and a citizen, but retains through a continuous effort and a rigorous discipline a connection to the phenomena and processes of the natural world.

Thoreau delivered "Walking, or the Wild" twice in 1851, then expanded it and broke it into two lectures, "Walking" and "The Wild" in 1852. As Bradley P. Dean explains, Thoreau expected that the publication of *Walden* in 1854 would create a wider demand for his lectures, and in anticipation of that demand, he began to think of expanding this material into a series of talks. "Walking, or the Wild" thus became the ancestor not only to the essay that we now know as "Walking," which Thoreau prepared for publication near the end of his life, but also to his uncompleted lecture "Moonlight," delivered in 1854, and a lecture titled "What Shall It Profit," which after much evolution was eventually published posthumously as "Life without Principle."[2] "Walking" and "Life without Principle," the essays that Thoreau eventually salvaged from this projected series of lectures, constitute his most sustained description of what he had come to see as the art of a life that was ethically engaged, spiritually disciplined, and in close and constant contact with the processes of wild nature. These works are the successors to *Walden*, representing Thoreau's continuing efforts to define the dynamic connection between the life of nature and our spiritual and ethical condition.

THE SPIRIT OF UNDYING ADVENTURE

Both "Walking" and "Life Without Principle" reach back to the struggle with vocation and self-definition that had preoccupied Thoreau since the early 1840s, and, like the opening chapters of *Walden*, they subject the American work ethic to a withering critical scrutiny. Although a reformulated conception of work is not the central subject of "Walking," it is the implied and necessary context for Thoreau's celebration of "sauntering" in the "wild." The essay centers on a radical change in the pattern of day-to-day life, a change that implies a complete reassessment of values. "I think that I cannot preserve my health and spirits," Thoreau declares, "unless I spend four hours a day at least—and it is commonly more than that—sauntering through the woods and over the hills and fields, absolutely free from all worldly engagements" (CEP 227). By the time we read this declaration, Thoreau has already offered us his engaging etymology of "sauntering," a walking to the holy land, or "*Sainte Terre*," in which the walker becomes a kind of knightly crusader in quest of the Grail. These excursions have less to do, of course, with the religious or political liberation of any particular territory than with the inward liberation of the saunterer, who finds that being "without land or a home" (*sans terre*) is less a deprivation than an enrichment. Having lost a particular home, the saunterer gains instead the whole earth, and becomes "equally at home everywhere" (CEP 225).

The possession of the whole earth, Thoreau tells us, comes with one unbending condition, the willingness to make oneself "absolutely free," for a portion of each day, "from all worldly engagements." Unlike the comparative isolation of his life at Walden Pond, this practice of a daily withdrawal is based on a life that is in other ways engaged with society and its demands.

But Thoreau describes a certain imaginative requirement that makes this divided life an effective alternative. The saunterer must regard a daily walk less as a temporary escape from social pressure and responsibility than as a complete restructuring of values and priorities. His tone is one of humorous and mildly ironic exaggeration, but his underlying point is decidedly serious:

> We should go forth on the shortest walk, perchance, in the spirit of undying adventure, never to return,—prepared to send back our embalmed hearts only as relics to our desolate kingdoms. If you are ready to leave father and mother, and brother and sister, and wife and child and friends, and never see them again,—if you have paid your debts, and made your will, and settled your affairs, and are a free man, then you are ready for a walk. (CEP 226)

Thoreau's allusion to the heroic and chivalric crusade is augmented in this remarkable passage by his allusion to Jesus' demand that his followers forsake all others to follow him. The exercise of this extreme spiritual devotion must be placed ahead of what is closest and dearest to us—the family, the force that also ties us most securely to the social world. He is proposing, then, an unsettling and divisive activity, one whose demands must not be regarded too lightly. He sees it as a transformative practice, but understands that to be successful, the art of sauntering requires both commitment and preparation.

This urgency is emphasized by his darkly comical linking of "sauntering" and death. That we may send back only "our embalmed hearts" from this crusade, that we must make our wills and settle our affairs before embarking, is a humorous but nevertheless real indication of the radical nature of what Thoreau is proposing. Nothing can create significant change in our lives, he implies, unless it reminds us of the tenuous nature of what we regard as established or settled; unless it threatens what we have come to be. To be "free" is to recognize the impermanence of all that constitutes our presumed selfhood.

That freedom becomes less an abstraction when Thoreau specifies the nature of ordinary social experience against which it is constructed. The world of "work," the daily occupation of the shopkeeper or person of business whose vocations seem to require confinement, is Thoreau's principal target. "I am astonished at the power of endurance, to say nothing of the moral insensibility, of my neighbors who confine themselves to shops and offices the whole day for weeks and months, ay, and years almost together" (CEP 227). This pattern of life is an imprisonment, albeit one that seems both chosen and prolonged by its victims. He ironically salutes their "courage," a trait displayed most clearly in their remarkable ability to endure the monotony of a settled and unchanging identity, and "sit down cheerfully" each afternoon with the same "self whom you have known all morning" (CEP 227).

The walking that he advocates is thus an effort at discovery, but a discovery that includes the repressed or buried aspects of our identities, the parts of our "self" that were denied or never allowed to develop. It provides us the opportunity to see the natural world afresh, but also to recover, or reconstruct, new forms of identity and new forms of experience. Since walking is in part a venture into the unknown, both in the landscape and within the self, Thoreau refers to it as "the enterprise and adventure of the day" (CEP 228). He means not merely that it enlivens ordinary patterns of life and serves as a diversion or form or entertainment, but that it provides the core of what is valuable and potentially transformative in human experience. The risk that the true saunterer takes, leaving all connections and facing the temporary nature of any identity, helps to sustain the openness necessary for a continually dynamic remolding of the self.[3]

Such risk taking is, however, a discipline. The mere presence of nature will not cause a miraculous alteration in us unless we are open and aware. "I am alarmed when it happens that I have walked a mile into the woods bodily, without getting there in spirit" (CEP 229). This inability to "shake off the village," even when he has actually left it, is a troubling condition of dissociation. "I am not where my body is,—I am out of my senses." Thoreau makes clever use of the expression "out of my senses," ordinarily a condition of lunacy or insanity. It is crazy to allow ourselves to become emotionally and psychologically divorced from our own physical presence, he argues, and the solution to this insanity is to regain that lost recognition of our bodily inhabitation. "In my walks I would fain return to my senses. What business have I in the woods, if I am thinking of something out of the woods?" (CEP 229). The walker must regain and maintain the state of alertness or wakefulness that Thoreau had described in *Walden*, the "morning" condition in which the senses, the body, and the intellect are integrated and empowered. This is one of the saunterer's fundamental intentions.

Thoreau's introductory disquisition on the art of walking as a religious quest and a means of intellectual and physical reawakening postpones the more mundane question of where one walks, except in its clear directive that one should leave the village, or civilization, and enter the woods. His own preference for excursions along the Old Marlborough Road provides him with another opportunity to deepen the mythological construction of the walk. An outmoded and little used road "which does not go to Marlborough now" (CEP 231), it represents the bypassed, forgotten, or abandoned path that the saunterer must take in order to achieve the kind of spiritual renewal that true walking promises. "It is a living way" (CEP 232), he wryly comments, literally an overgrown road, but also a path of life. The road carries him west, and that fact of geography is more than coincidence when Thoreau considers the historical connotations of western exploration to the history of modern European civilization.

The westward push of "civilization" raises for a modern reader a host of troubling issues, making this pivotal discussion in "Walking" a complex but historically enlightening task.[4] Thoreau represented the West as a place of freedom and natural wildness, an unspoiled area beyond the border, and thus beyond the control, of the eastern or civilized world. This symbolic geography was rooted both in the European exploration of the Americas and in the expanding western frontier in nineteenth-century America. As Thoreau also knew, and as his discussion here in some sense implies, the "discovery" and exploration of the West was also linked with its colonization and "civilization," events that carried with them systems of exploitation and widespread destruction. Thoreau does not directly justify this history, and in fact he speaks as one much at odds with the values of Western civilization. But he also speaks from within the framework of this system of expansion, seeing in the beckoning West the perennial promise of freedom, and in its pursuit the guarantee of an ever-renewing energy. "We go westward as into the future, with a spirit of enterprise and adventure" (CEP 235), he writes, echoing his earlier description of the mood or stance of the saunterer.

Linking the western migration to the natural cycle of the day, he declares that "every sunset which I witness inspires me with the desire to go to a West as distant and as fair as that into which the sun goes down" (CEP 235). This instinct for the distant and unexplored, in its confrontation with the barriers to movement, helped to produce the modern world. "From this western impulse coming in contact with the barrier of the Atlantic sprang the commerce and enterprise of modern times" (CEP 237), he writes, and even though the problematic effect of the culture of "commerce" is precisely the condition that he is addressing in "Walking," he makes it clear through his language and tone that he is drawn to the resourcefulness and raw energy that fuels modern enterprise.

Having himself felt the pull of the American frontier on more than one occasion, and writing for a lecture audience that would have responded readily to the cultural definition of the West as a place of new social beginnings and economic opportunity, Thoreau hopes to link the dynamics of this larger social movement to the more individual and internalized process of self-renewal. But he enters into the celebration of the promise of an American empire in the West and, in a statement with profound implications for American cultural self-conception, declares, "As a true patriot, I should be ashamed to think that Adam in paradise was more favorably situated on the whole than the backwoodsman in this country" (CEP 238). Even though Thoreau's deep interest in and sympathy with the culture of the American Indians is a matter of record, his implicit endorsement of the ideology of "manifest destiny" here indicates the limits of his critical awareness of the oppressive and destructive nature of America's western imperialism. But Thoreau's discussion of the West poses a particularly difficult interpretive problem, because he seems to describe western expansion as both an advance of civilization and an antidote to it. "The West of which I speak is but another name for the Wild," he explains, "and what I have been preparing to say is, that in Wildness is the preservation of the World" (CEP 239).

The "wild" is a principle of vital energy, equally necessary to natural processes and to human civilization. "Every tree sends its fibres forth in search of the Wild. The cities import it at any price. Men plough and sail for it. From the forest and wilderness come the tonics and barks which brace mankind" (CEP 239). As his hymn to the wild unfolds, it becomes clearer that in spite of his earlier advocacy of American western expansion, Thoreau sees the promise of the West less in terms of "empire" than of natural preservation. Unable to anticipate the dramatic advances in technology and the enormous increases in population that have accompanied the settlement of the American West, Thoreau envisioned an essentially agrarian and wilderness West, and did not consider the possibility that civilization could eventually threaten the very forces of the natural world that sustain it. His credo declares a faith not in the western march of civilization but in those aspects of nature on which human well-being is based, a new natural trinity: "I believe in the forest, and in the meadow, and in the night in which the corn grows" (CEP 239).

This conversion of "west" into "wild" is the most important turn in Thoreau's argument, establishing the different and potentially conflicting identities of nature and civilization. Human civilization draws its vital energies from wildness, and must have access to it, even though the wild represents a completely dissimilar set of processes and values. "Give me a wildness whose glance no civilization can endure" (CEP 240), he proclaims. He then offers praise for that wildest of landscapes, the swamp, a valueless and even threatening place when seen in conventional terms: "Hope and the future for me are not in lawns and cultivated fields, not in towns and cities, but in the impervious and quaking swamps" (CEP 241). The swamp becomes the focus of a set of "wild" values that counter those of civilization, "a sacred place,—a *sanctum sanctorum*" where one can find "the strength, the marrow of Nature" (CEP 242). The fertility embodied in the swamp and in "the virgin mould" of the wild forest is a necessity shared by both humans and trees. "A town is saved," he writes, "not more by the righteous men in it than by the woods and swamps that surround it. . . . In such a soil grew Homer and Confucius and the rest, and out of such a wilderness comes the Reformer eating locusts and wild honey" (CEP 242). Thoreau asks that we consider ourselves as both citizens of a human community and creatures of the wild, arguing that our continuing kinship with nature will support and enrich our public lives. Such a relationship with nature has been, throughout human history, the source of poetry, wisdom, and moral prophecy.

As he brings the concept of the wild closer to actual practice in his own town and culture, Thoreau describes it as a principle of independent dissent and of resistance to established social norms, recasting in more nature-oriented terms the spirit of Emerson's praise of nonconformity. "Give me for my friends and neighbors wild men, not tame ones," he declares. "The wildness of the savage is but a faint symbol of the awful ferity with which good men and lovers meet" (CEP 246). He remembers his delight in the unexpected eruptions of wildness in ordinary life, "as when my neighbor's cow breaks out of her pasture early in the spring and boldly swims the river." The Concord cow becomes in that moment "the buffalo crossing the Mississippi" (CEP 246), still in possession of a nature that generations of human domestication cannot erase. In order to come fully into their own potential, men and women must recover a forgotten capacity for play, and relearn the free expression of a creative chaos. They must recall an ability to resist social strictures that originate in the pressure to maintain a predictable and orderly civilization. Such restraints are divorced from natural energy, creativity, and originality. "Men are in the main alike," he notes, "but they were made several in order that they might be various. If a low use is to be served, one man will do nearly or quite as well as another; if a high one, individual excellence is to be regarded" (CEP 247). Genius, poetry, indeed all forms of high accomplishment arise from difference or individuality; this difference is an expression of the wild.

Our access to this wildness sometimes requires that we resist the process of education and cultivation, a process devoted to rationality, order, and, ultimately, tameness. "I would not have every man nor every part of a man cultivated," Thoreau declares, "any more than I would have every acre of earth cultivated" (CEP 249). His wordplay on the term "cultivation" is both amusing and significant. Thoreau reverses its conventional metaphoric impact by reconnecting the process of cultivation with its agricultural roots, thus bringing the "cultivated" gentleman or lady literally back down to earth. The wild or uncultivated corners of our personalities, what Thoreau terms "meadow and forest," become the important ones, both in what they provide for use now and in "preparing a mould against a distant future" (CEP 249). Not only use but waste also has a place in this larger vision, not only knowledge but ignorance. He satirically calls for the formation of a "Society for the Diffusion of Useful Ignorance," which would spread an ignorance that is in fact a "Beautiful Knowledge, a knowledge useful in a higher sense" (CEP 249). It is that forever untapped potentiality that corresponds to the untilled or untillable soil of the earth.

Knowledge can never provide the sense of experiential mystery, the conviction of infinitude and inexhaustibility, of our ever useful ignorance. "The highest that we can attain to is not Knowledge, but Sympathy with Intelligence," Thoreau states. Such sympathy or "higher knowledge" is best described as "a novel and grand surprise on a sudden revelation of the insufficiency of all we called Knowledge before" (CEP 250). Thoreau's experience at Mount Ktaadn, or any of his many less dramatic but no less mysterious experiences as a night walker around Concord, are important personal reference points for this declaration, and in both these cases it seems that it was less *what* Thoreau learned that was significant than *how* he was overtaken by, and then opened himself to, some previously unrecognized event or condition of perception.[5] These experiences, even though they are fundamentally nonrational, bring with them a fresh sense of the vastness of the world and a strangely empowering recognition of the limits of our capacity to know it. To learn our ignorance, then, is to learn the most vital thing.

BORDER LIFE

Thoreau's bold description of the claims of the natural life are shadowed, however, by his fear that his own life inadequately meets those claims. "For my part, I feel that with regard to Nature I live a sort of border life, on the confines of a world into which I make occasional and transient forays only, and my patriotism and allegiance to the State into whose territories I seem to retreat are those of a moss-trooper" (CEP 251). In this vitally important moment in Thoreau's work, he steps out of the role of the prophet lecturing to a wayward people and explores the gap between his prophetic message and his actual embodiment of it. Thoreau's admission that he is in reality less a knight-errant on a holy quest for nature than a "moss-trooper," a border raider or marauder, is an important gesture of recognition of the limits to the absolute integration of civilization and nature. One enters nature but only to return eventually to the village. Despite the opening declaration that the saunterer must embark on a walk as if never to return, Thoreau recognizes that the return is half the walk. Living as a borderer thus describes the most productive and progressive relationship with nature that a man or woman can achieve. If it falls short of the absolute comprehension of nature and integration into it to which Thoreau aspires, it also encompasses a vital dialectic in which the social lives that we inevitably lead are enriched, invigorated, and given ethical purpose by our intercourse with the natural world.

This hybrid condition acknowledges the inescapable reality that one enters the wild natural world in some respects as a stranger, unable to know it in any complete or all-inclusive way. We know only the fragments and pieces that we are perpetually attempting to fit into a more comprehensive pattern. "Nature is a personality so vast and universal that we have never seen one of her features" (CEP 251). While our inevitable ignorance is valuable, ensuring that we can never intellectually exhaust nature, its price is the recognition that nature always lies beyond us, and that our forays into it, though crucially important, are always partial.

Thoreau's description of his "border life" is a retreat from the hyperbole of his description of sauntering, but it provides "Walking" with a more vivid sense of the actual texture of a "natural life." By accepting his hybrid identity, Thoreau is able to lend an air of greater reality to his quest for relationship as the essay closes. The complex argument of "Walking" has repeatedly led us to value experience over theory as the goal of our relationship with nature. In the final pages of the essay he describes the moments in which he crosses a border to recognize something new and unimagined in nature—liminal and transformative events, but not moments of high drama or tension. Such moments are often small discoveries or ordinary occurrences, but their very ordinariness emphasizes the need for a more constant awareness of the natural world.

In the first of these, Thoreau describes how the beams of a setting sun filtering through a stand of pines transform the Spaulding farm, one of the usual sites of his rambles, into a stately outdoor manor, noble and ethereal, inhabited by a mythical family who live in complete harmony with their surroundings. These fairy people are in one sense the Spauldings themselves, who like all people retain some deeper, perhaps unconscious connection to nature. Or perhaps they are, as John Burroughs suggested, the birds in the trees around the farm.[6] In either case, they are creatures who "seemed to recline on the sunbeams." They lead completely elevated lives, serenely undisturbed by the pressures and demands of civilization. This is of course a world of fantasy, in which daily labor, material limitations, and the pressures and divisions of society are suspended. "They are of no politics. There was no noise of labor. I did not perceive that they were weaving or spinning. Yet I did detect, when the wind lulled and hearing was done away, the finest imaginable sweet musical hum,—as of a distant hive in May, which perchance was the sound of their thinking." It is only in this suspension of the patterns of civilization in the heart of the natural world that thinking becomes possible, Thoreau implies, and this is a vitally important possibility. "Nothing can equal the serenity of their lives" (CEP 252). Thoreau admits that his fanciful vision is fleeting, and that his imagined family "fade[s] irrevocably out of my mind even now while I speak" (CEP 253). He had glimpsed, through the unusual impact of the sunset, a utopian moment in which human life reflected nature completely and without conflict. His border crossing, though impermanent, had left its impression.

A second description of his border life is less ethereal but no less unusual than the first: the discovery of "a few minute and delicate red cone-like blossoms, the fertile flower of the white pine looking heavenward" (CEP 253). He regards his discovery as a reward for the effort and curiosity of venturing to the top of the tree, where he saw not only the flowers that were new to him but also "new mountains in the horizon which I had never seen before." Taking one of the flowers to the village and showing it to "farmers and lumber-dealers and wood-choppers and hunters," men who ought to know about white pines, he found that none of his townsmen "had ever seen the like before, but they wondered as at a star dropped down" (CEP 253–54).

The trope of striving upward for enlightenment and of bringing a vision of heaven back to earth is the conventional symbolic language of the spiritual quest, but Thoreau freshens the narrative with details that anchor it in the real experience of a man who climbs trees, collects botanical specimens, and interacts, albeit in a somewhat unusual way, with the fellow citizens of his town. Thoreau remembers getting himself "well pitched" in the climb, and also tells us that he showed the specimen "to stranger jurymen who walked in the streets" in Concord because court was in session. These bits of remembered history transform his story from a somewhat facile allegory into an authentic account of the nature that is always nearby but seldom recognized. "Nature has from the first expanded the minute blossoms of the forest only toward the heavens, above men's heads and unobserved by them. We see only the flowers that are under our feet in the meadows" (CEP 254).

Part of the significance of this anecdote is its enactment of a form of social witness. It is not enough for Thoreau simply to discover and admire the pine's flowers. He must return to his community with a specimen, inquire about the experiences of others, confirm his own sense of the newness and wonder of the flower, and teach his community about it. In fact, the moment in the passage that reflects the most intense excitement is not the actual discovery of the flower but the description of the surprise and curiosity of his fellow citizens when he showed it to them. Thoreau's border life involves attentiveness not just to nature but to dialogue and social interaction. The immersion in the natural world cannot be complete, since we remain always a social creatures with important connections to the civilized world. But those connections can in the best of circumstances be made consequential and productive, and the crossings between nature and society can thus become the focus of a meaningful pattern of life.

"We had a remarkable sunset one day last November," begins the third of Thoreau's depictions of his border life. This moment, like the others, transpires on one of his walks, his doorways to new experience. As in his moonlight walks, the variation of the light, this time at sunset, transforms the familiar into a new and compelling place.

> I was walking in a meadow, the source of a small brook, when the sun at last, just before setting, after a cold, gray day, reached a clear stratum in the horizon, and the softest, brightest morning sunlight fell on the dry grass and on the stems of the trees in the opposite horizon, and on the leaves of the shrub-oaks on the hill-side, while our shadows stretched long over the meadow eastward, as if we were only motes in its beams. (CEP 254–55)

The end of the day becomes its beginning as the new light stimulates the wakeful attentiveness that Thoreau associates with the dawn. The most ordinary features of the landscape, the dry grass and the shrub oak leaves, are suddenly illuminated, reflecting and amplifying the surprising new out-pouring of light. Though part of the scene, as their reflected shadows indi-cate, the observing humans are minimized, "only motes" in the beams of this new sun.

Thoreau's suggestion of the minimal importance of the human presence in the larger order of nature, revealed in this extraordinary late-afternoon dawn, becomes the concluding note of "Walking." The moment that Thoreau remembers so vividly and describes with such wonder and rever-ence is actually "not a solitary phenomenon, never to happen again," but one that "would happen forever and ever an infinite number of evenings." In most of these events there will be few if any human witnesses; the flood of light will instead gild the wings of "a solitary marsh-hawk," or be seen by "only a musquash" living near "some little black-veined brook in the midst of the marsh" (CEP 255). These prospective moments of beauty, imagined by Thoreau but never to be observed by humans, indicate that men and women do have a place in nature, but not one at its center. The processes and laws of the natural world, including what we know as its beauty, continue quite apart from our needs, our participation, or even our recognition.

To live the border life that Thoreau describes is to be constantly re-minded that human categories do not define nature and human drives can-not confine it. As he wrote in the closing pages of the "Spring" chapter of *Walden*, "we need to witness our own limits transgressed, and some life pas-turing freely where we never wander" (Wa 318).[7]

WHAT SHALL IT PROFIT?

Thoreau argues that his "border life" must be lived in resistance to the con-ventional demands of work and money, and to "this incessant business" that is "opposed to poetry, to philosophy, ay, to life itself" (RP 156). The burden of *Walden* had been to prove that obtaining the necessities of life need not become a process that devours life itself. "Life without Principle" is a fer-vent and sometimes acerbic version of this argument, a jeremiad against not only materialism but also its insidious incarnation in a pervasive allegiance to a deadening ethic of purposeless work.

"Life without Principle" evolved from the projected series of lectures ti-tled "Walking, or the Wild," which extended the key premises of *Walden*.

The essay's withering attack on work, and its demand that life's decisions and actions be dictated by seriously considered purpose, is a necessary complement to the commitment to a life of liberated "sauntering." The nucleus of the lecture, as Bradley P. Dean has shown, was a journal meditation of September 7, 1851 (JP 4:50–55).[8] There Thoreau asserted his principal task as an author as the pursuit of the fundamental ethical question of how life should be lived. The "*Art of life!* Was there ever anything memorable written upon it?" (JP 4:52). Recognizing this as an important message for the American public, Thoreau developed an impassioned justification of his vocation of engaged and purposeful leisure. "How to live— How to get the most of life!" (JP 4:53). This was a searching challenge for a culture that seemed to have lost its way, substituting a frantic pursuit of frivolous material goods and a self-destructive habit of meaningless work for authentic aspiration and actual fulfillment.

Thoreau understood that the art of securing "the most life" (JP 2:52) had to be reduced to a much more direct and concrete concern. "I do not remember any page which will tell me how to spend this afternoon," he declared. Seizing a fundamental economic metaphor and transposing it to his own purposes, he observed that "I do not so much wish to know how to economize time—as how to spend it—by what means to grow rich" (JP 2:52). The hunger that he has expressed for life is thus translated into a concern to master "the art of spending a day" (JP 2:53). "Life Without Principle" and "Walking" share this concern with the freedom to shape and construct the day, and the corresponding recognition that each day and its actions were the units by which the moral life was measured. These essays, whose central purpose is to serve as a guidebook for conducting a natural life, provide the context for Thoreau's later work both as a naturalist and as an engaged political critic.

Thoreau couched his radical formula for rethinking the nature of work and of daily life in ironically traditional terms. His original title for "Life Without Principle" was "What Shall It Profit?"; he called the verse from Mark 8:36 his "text," emphasizing his reliance on the biblical wisdom that was ostensibly embraced by his culture.[9] As the lecture evolved over the last eight years of Thoreau's life, it became a kind of credo, autobiographical and self-referential, but aimed at provoking a dialogue with its audience. Thoreau insisted uncompromisingly that each individual must assume responsibility for his or her moral condition, and must maintain a healthy and vital inner life. As in *Walden*, he presents an exemplary self who both challenges and guides his audience; he makes his own apparent lack of vocation a critique of the narrow and ultimately harmful approach to questions of work and value that are widespread in American culture.[10]

America as he finds it "is nothing but work, work, work," an obsession that ultimately is "opposed . . . to life itself" (RP 156). The pointlessness and waste of much of what is admired as "industry" in his culture is the root of the problem. Work is not always ennobling, he argues, and is in fact often degrading. "To have done anything by which you earned money *merely* is to have been truly idle or worse," making it imperative that the work we do serve some more worthy purpose (RP 158). Simply to argue that the process of work is in itself valuable enough to justify it, regardless of its end, is dangerously misguided: "I do not need the police of meaningless labor to regulate me" (RP 156–57). The crucial consideration is to be sure that such work as we undertake does not enslave us and that it achieve a higher end. The stakes in making such decisions are, he argues, very high. "If I should sell both my forenoons and afternoons to society, as most appear to do, I am sure, that, for me, there would be nothing left worth living for" (RP 160).

To live with principle requires the determination to maintain a degree of freedom from the demands of externally imposed work, and the resolve to assess continually the purposes of the tasks we undertake. Thoreau's conviction that "all great enterprises are self-supporting" (RP 160) is not a passive faith but one that places enormous responsibility on every individual to make each "great enterprise" possible. Society, however, seems to sanction many enterprises that are far from being "great." The "disgrace" of the California gold rush is his prime example of American culture's seriously warped values. "That so many are ready to live by luck, and so get the means of commanding the labor of others less lucky, without contributing any value to society! And that is called enterprise!" (RP 162).

Thoreau's vehement protest against the decoupling of work and value extends in a surprising way his earlier argument that our obsession with work is "opposed . . . to life itself" (RP 156). Work that is valued solely as a means of gaining money is ultimately valueless because its larger purpose or meaning is undermined. Prospecting for gold is a telling analogy for the base grubbing that characterizes most socially sanctioned forms of work. "The hog that gets his living by rooting, stirring up the soil so, would be ashamed of such company" (RP 162). Calling the prospector "as much a gambler as his fellow in the saloons of San Francisco," Thoreau argues that such avenues to wealth detach work from any social utility, and increase the arbitrary and chaotic distribution of wealth and power within the social structure. "What difference does it make, whether you shake dirt or shake dice? If you win, society is the loser. The gold-digger is the enemy of the honest laborer, whatever checks and compensations there may be" (RP 163). The rewards of such valueless work as digging for gold undermine the worth of productive work, thus exacerbating the already profound confusion over the nature and meaning of work in American culture.

Gold fever exemplifies the pervading superficiality that is the deeper object of Thoreau's disdain. "The best men that I know are not serene, a world in themselves," but live instead for validation from others. "They dwell in forms, and flatter and study effect only more finely than the rest" (RP 168). This superficiality affects "ordinary conversation," making it "hollow and ineffectual" as "surface meets surface" (RP 169).

Such incessant hollow conversation gradually wears away our ability to live inwardly, as the frivolous and inconsequential gradually crowd out the vital and the essential. The principled life depends on a strict economy of attention which conserves the necessary energy for sustaining an inward life. "Shall the mind be a public arena, where the affairs of the street and the gossip of the tea-table chiefly are discussed? Or shall it be a quarter of heaven itself,—an hypaethral temple, consecrated to the service of the gods? . . . It is important to preserve the mind's chastity in this respect" (RP 171). Superficial conversation and superficial thinking are damaging precisely because they squander the opportunities for deeper and more genuine dialogue and thought.

Triviality and superficiality are thus a greater threat to our moral constitution than impurity or vice because more subtle. Thoreau calls for vigilance in recognizing the threat of what may seem merely dull or insipid. "I believe that the mind can be permanently profaned by the habit of attending to trivial things, so that all our thoughts shall be tinged with triviality" (RP 173). Routine and convention can therefore become the vehicles through which the spiritual life is squandered. "Read not the times. Read the Eternities. Conventionalities are at length as bad as impurities" (RP 173). As Thoreau's aphorisms remind us, alertness, an elevation of our focus of attention, and a constant effort at fresh experience of the moment are critical to a life with principle.

The alternative to life based on the hollowness of convention and superficiality is a natural life, which assumes the cultivation of the spiritual resources that allow one to "read the eternities." This self-development was one of the principal concerns of *Walden*, and one of the core assumptions of the Transcendentalists. It was also, Thoreau believed, a lesson that the era's political reformers badly needed to hear. What disturbed him the most about the reform circles in which he played a peripheral role was the complacent tendency to accept the sufficiency of external change. Although reformed institutions and social arrangements were clearly essential to him, reform was incomplete if it did not address life in its fullest sense. One essential element of social reform was the removal of external barriers to the pursuit of a more complete, because deeper and more inner-directed, way of living. "Have we no culture, no refinement,—but skill only to live coarsely and serve the Devil?" Coarse and devilish living is superficial living, the desire "to acquire a little worldly wealth, or fame, or liberty," achievements that, by themselves, can only suggest that "we were all husk and shell, with no tender and living kernel to us" (RP 173–74). Thoreau's lumping of "liberty" with "wealth" and "fame" as examples of this hollowness is of particular importance. "Liberty" was more than a patriotic slogan in this context; it embodied the central aspiration of most aspects of the reform movement, from associationism to women's rights to antislavery. Thoreau's bold suggestion is that the purpose of many reform efforts is suspect because they are limited to essentially the same superficial goals that characterize conventional life in America. "Liberty" is an empty goal unless it is grounded in a deeper purpose, unless it signifies a freedom to engage life more profoundly than convention and habitual practice suggest.

Thoreau's insistence on a deeper purpose for liberty shakes the foundation of the American sense of a national mission and identity. "America is said to be the arena on which the battle of freedom is to be fought," he writes, "but surely it cannot be freedom in a merely political sense that is meant." The "merely political" conception of freedom arises from the same deficient set of values that sanctions purposeless work or the "enterprise" of hunting for gold. Such illusory "freedom" simply transfers the source of our bondage. "Even if we grant that the American has freed himself from a political tyrant," Thoreau remarks, "he is still the slave of an economical and moral tyrant" (RP 174). We should not, of course, miss the conditional quality of Thoreau's hypothesis that "the American has freed himself from a political tyrant," a proposition that would be opened to further critical inquiry as the slavery crisis deepened. But the sermon that Thoreau wanted to preach to the reformers had less to do with the conditions of American politics than it did with the limits of their own aspirations. To gain the whole political world would be profitless if one's aspirations ended there.

Freedom must be real, Thoreau argues, not theoretical or symbolic. It must be lived. "What is it to be born free and not to live free? What is the value of any political freedom, but as a means to moral freedom?" (RP 174). The weight that Thoreau gives to the concept of "moral freedom" encapsulates his portrayal of the principled life; it is not a complacent autonomy but a condition that implies both engagement and accountability. Thoreau wants to reclaim the concepts of "liberty" and "freedom" from the lexicon of American patriotic symbolism, and give them new vitality as the essence of each individual's moral and spiritual reawakening. This is an awakening of the whole self in both its inward thoughts and its daily acts, and it is only in the ability to translate thought into real and consequential acts that the term "freedom" takes on any meaning. For Thoreau this moral freedom must be centered on the reclamation of each day, day by day; that effort requires the strict economy described in *Walden* and the close scrutiny of the value of work that is the focus of "Life Without Principle." His pursuit of the natural life is, in this decisive essay, envisioned as the pursuit of a life of moral freedom, one in which each choice in our daily life is a reaffirmation of our constructive agency in the world.

WHAT I HAD LOST

Near the end of "Life without Principle," Thoreau emphasized his low opinion of conventional politics: "What is called politics is something so superficial and inhuman, that, practically, I have never fairly recognized that it concerns me at all" (RP 177). Thoreau's dismissal of politics here is belied by his record of involvement in the antislavery movement and the enduring importance of his writings on politics and reform. But his dismissal of the superficiality of politics is of considerable importance in his definition of the principled life. Thoreau believed that one entered the arena of politics only when "political" questions rose to the stature of "moral" issues. The disdain that he expresses for superficial politics is consistent with his well-known refusal to pay his poll tax, an act of protest that resulted in his night in the Middlesex County Jail. "I was seized and put into jail," he writes in *Walden*, "because, as I have elsewhere related, I did not pay a tax to, or recognize the authority of, the state which buys and sells men, women, and children, like cattle at the door of its senate-house" (Wa 171). This act of nonviolent political resistance has become one of the most influential acts in the history of modern democracy, largely because of Thoreau's vivid defense of it in "Civil Disobedience."[11] But Thoreau insisted that his refusal to pay his tax should be taken not as political agitation but rather as an act of conscience. This distinction was fundamental to the larger question of defining the extent of his, or any individual's, moral responsibility. "It is true, I might have resisted forcibly with more or less effect," he continues in *Walden*, "might have run 'amok' against society; but I preferred that society should run 'amok' against me, it being the desperate party" (Wa 171).

"Desperate" is a crucial word for Thoreau, who had described the "quiet desperation" that characterized the lives of "the mass of men." Desperation signified a loss of control, a condition in which men and women were no longer able to direct the path of their lives. "It is a characteristic of wisdom," he had concluded, "not to do desperate things" (Wa 8), and he felt that taking his protest against the state further than he did, turning it into a direct political action, would have been "desperate." Desperation signified a loss of control over one's life, a condition in which external forces dictated one's plans and acts. Although these forces were ordinarily economic ones, reinforced by the unwillingness of most people to forgo unnecessary luxuries, they might also take the form of an aspiration to affect an unjust or corrupt political or social system for the better. Politics could in this way become a form of "doing good" that Thoreau attacks in *Walden* as a diversion from principle and from genuine duty.

Always sensitive to the charge that his pursuit of an ideal life was irresponsible or self-indulgent, Thoreau fought hard to justify the idea that our primary responsibility must be to live our own lives well, a task that could demand all our purpose and all our resources. "It is not a man's duty, as a matter of course, to devote himself to the eradication of any, even the most enormous wrong; he may still properly have other concerns to engage him," he wrote in "Civil Disobedience." Nevertheless, he recognized that such wrongs could have a corrupting influence on anyone too closely enmeshed in them, a worrying complicity that remained a central problem in his moral outlook. Even though Thoreau believed that the individual may not be compelled to try to eradicate social wrong, "it is his duty, at least, to wash his hands of it, and, if he gives it no thought longer, not to give it practically his support" (CEP 209). By making society run amok against him through his arrest, Thoreau felt that he had retained control of formulating the conditions of his life, and had also to some extent diminished the moral complicity inherent in citizenship of a slaveholding nation.[12]

Events in the early 1850s would force him to amend his position. The Fugitive Slave Law of 1850, requiring local authorities to assist in the capture and return of runaway slaves to the South, set in motion a series of political and legal events that changed the tone of the antislavery struggle, making it increasingly difficult for Northerners to deny any role in the maintenance of slavery. In New England the moral stakes of this new phase of the slavery crisis were played out in three dramatic cases: the arrest and rescue of Shadrach Minkins in 1851, the arrest and return of Thomas Sims in 1851, and the arrest, trial, and return of Anthony Burns in 1854.[13] Each of these cases affected Thoreau deeply, and he devoted much energy in his Journal to castigating both the government and his fellow citizens for their assistance or complicity in the return of Sims and Burns. The Burns case, which dramatically intensified New England's antislavery movement in the summer of 1854, provoked "Slavery in Massachusetts," a forceful and impassioned public statement from Thoreau that signaled a revision of his earlier belief that he could distance himself from his government and its laws. Political issues had now undeniably become moral ones, as he saw it, and any conception of a principled life had to take into account the problem of establishing a right relation to this larger social ill.[13] His confession that the Burns affair had in fact changed his world, first recorded in his Journal, comes near the end of "Slavery in Massachusetts": "I have lived for the last month,—and I think that every man in Massachusetts capable of the sentiment of patriotism must have had a similar experience,—with the sense of having suffered a vast and indefinite loss" (RP 106). Thoreau's sense of loss, at first unspecified, is linked with "the sentiment of patriotism," a somewhat surprising turn, given the fact that he has spent most of the preceding address in a withering attack on his government and its key officers, the legal system, the institution of the press, and even the United States Constitution, "an agreement to serve the devil" (RP 103). But Thoreau's "sense of patriotism" has been awakened by its betrayal. A largely unspoken assumption of harmony between the individual and the country has now been breached. Thoreau searches his mood until he can recognize and articulate its cause: "I did not know at first what ailed me. At last it occurred to me that what I had lost was a country" (RP 106).

"Slavery in Massachusetts" explores this condition of life without a country, mixing scorn for America's incomprehensible and outrageous moral obtuseness with a lament for the loss of order, comity, and purpose that accompanies such an alienation from one's political home. Thoreau's recognition of his own naïveté seems in part a comment on his earlier assumption in "Civil Disobedience" that one might live a self-contained life, undisturbed by the surrounding political climate: "I had never respected the Government near to which I had lived, but I had foolishly thought that I might manage to live here, minding my private affairs, and forget it" (RP

106). He discovers instead that the political failure of the Massachusetts government corrupts the entire atmosphere in which he lives and makes it impossible for him to lead the life he wants. Even though he is not directly prevented from choosing and undertaking his own tasks, he finds their value undermined because they are woven into a national fabric that also includes the protection of legalized slavery:

> For my part, my old and worthiest pursuits have lost I cannot say how much of their attraction, and I feel that my investment in life here is worth many per cent. less since Massachusetts last deliberately sent back an innocent man, Anthony Burns, to slavery. I dwelt before, perhaps, in the illusion that my life passed somewhere only *between* heaven and hell, but now I cannot persuade myself that I do not dwell *wholly within* hell. (RP 106)

The Burns episode has been the destruction of an illusion, a fall from an original innocence into a painful state of experience.

Thoreau's identification of Massachusetts with hell is one of the more extreme of a series of attempts to find strong enough language for his sense of moral indignation and betrayal. Burns, "an innocent man," is the victim of imprisonment, waiting in torment his return to slavery. But all citizens of Massachusetts are constrained to feel his suffering even if they are engaged in their own "innocent" pursuits. Injustice permeates every aspect of ordinary life, devaluing the very activities and accomplishments that once represented the measurement of life's value. "Suppose you have a small library, with pictures to adorn the walls—a garden laid out around—and contemplate scientific and literary pursuits, &c., and discover all at once that your villa, with all its contents, is located in hell, and that the justice of the peace has a cloven foot and a forked tail—do not these things suddenly lose their value in your eyes?" (RP 107). As Barbara Packer has noted, Thoreau was revising the final proofs of *Walden* at the same time that he was writing "Slavery in Massachusetts."[15] Thoreau's remembered Walden cabin had become, in this new crisis, a villa in hell, corrupted by the political crimes of the state and the moral obtuseness of his fellow citizens. Thoreau's central intellectual purpose since the Walden experiment has been to restore value to daily experience; he is now forced to recognize the challenge that the political crisis poses to this very purpose.

At the root of the political problem is a moral failure. The state has devalued the life of one of its citizens, Anthony Burns, and in so doing has devalued the life of every other citizen. Thoreau's feeling that he is living in hell is his way of saying that he is living in a place where lives have a diminished value; it is an acknowledgment that whatever part one played in this decision, one must experience the same feeling of diminishment. Government must thus be judged by a simple criterion: "The effect of a good government is to make life more valuable,—of a bad one, to make it less valuable" (RP 106).

Some of his most stinging criticism is saved for the officials who have had a direct hand in Burns's imprisonment, and have thereby threatened the life of every citizen. Edward G. Loring, who presided over the trial resulting in Burns's return, is one of Thoreau's principal targets, as he was for most of the abolitionists observing the case. "Again it happens that the Boston Court House is full of armed men, holding prisoner and trying a MAN, to find out if he is not really a SLAVE." The very question suggests the depth of moral negligence into which the public institutions have sunk. "Does any one think that Justice or God awaits Mr. Loring's decision?" Thoreau sarcastically asks. "For him to sit there deciding still, when this question is already decided from eternity to eternity, and the unlettered slave himself, and the multitude around, have long since heard and assented to the decision, is simply to make himself ridiculous" (RP 92). There are things that simply cannot be decided in a court, or by a legislature, and the value of a human life is principal among them. Thoreau's declaration that Burns's status "is already decided from eternity to eternity" is a powerful dramatization of the "higher law" argument, central to the abolitionist demand for an immediate end to slavery, and in this case the immediate release of Burns.[16]

The falsity of Loring's position is also, however, an indictment of the entire commonwealth for delegating to him this decision. "Her crime, the most conspicuous and fatal crime of all, was permitting him to be the umpire in such a case," Thoreau argues. This negligence has had the effect of reversing the positions of the accuser and the accused. "It was really the trial of Massachusetts. Every moment that she hesitated to set this man free— every moment that she now hesitates to atone for her crime, she is convicted. The Commissioner on her case is God; not Edward G. God, but simple God" (RP 96). He levels similar criticism against the governor's failure to intervene: "If *he* is not of the least use to prevent my being kidnapped, pray of what important use is he likely to be to me? When freedom is most endangered, he dwells in the deepest obscurity" (RP 92). The governor's refusal to act, his failure to use the powers of his office to effect Burns's release, typifies the more general breakdown in the moral order of the society.

Thoreau has not himself been kidnapped, but his imaginative assumption of Burns's condition is the step that every citizen must make. Burns's hell of imprisonment is replicated in the new hell that all people must now recognize as the transformed condition of their homes and communities. The fundamental principle that accounts for this terrifying transformation is the unbreakable link that every individual has to every other individual in a just society. Thoreau thus translates the biblical golden rule of conduct into the basic law of democratic theory: "I wish my countrymen to consider, that whatever the human law may be, neither an individual nor a nation can ever commit the least act of injustice against the obscurest individual, without having to pay the penalty for it" (RP 96).

While Thoreau is deeply disappointed with the behavior of Loring and other officials, his critique runs deeper than any indictment of individuals. At the core of his argument is the insistence that moral judgment must always take precedent over established law. His version of the "higher law" argument emphasizes the act of human moral deliberation in the creation and upholding of the law. It is in a process of constant reconsideration of law that men and women best express, and best develop, their essential moral freedom. "The law will never make men free; it is men who have got to make the law free," he declares. "They are the lovers of law and order, who observe the law when the government breaks it" (RP 98). An unthinking adherence to what has been judged legal, with no attempt to weigh the particular questions raised by each particular case under consideration, is a surrender of conscience and of moral responsibility. Following the law mechanically is not an expression of freedom but a signal of our own bondage.

The Burns case made it plain that individuals had surrendered their moral autonomy to institutions. Thoreau associates this relinquishment of direct moral responsibility with the rise of urbanization and the resulting decline in the direct democratic deliberations that he favors. "I am more and more convinced that, with reference to any public question, it is more important to know what the country thinks of it, than what the city thinks" (RP 98). He contrasts the handling of the political dilemma created by the Burns case with a vision of an agrarian democracy in which citizens confer with one another, consult their own judgments, in response to public questions. "When, in some obscure country town, the farmers come together to a special town meeting, to express their opinion on some subject which is vexing the land, that, I think, is the true Congress, and the most respectable one that is ever assembled in the United States" (RP 99). Thoreau's suspicion of urban corruption betrays his provincial biases, but it also reminds us of the feeling of usurpation that fugitive slave cases created in New England. Decisions with direct moral implications for local citizens and institutions were being made a great distance away, under what they regarded as suspicious or questionable circumstances, thus depriving men and women of their own sense of participation in a larger political community. Thoreau urges his listeners to make themselves a "true Congress" and seize control of their own communities and their own consciences.

At the heart of his message, then, is a call to deny, resist, and disobey the laws that have made Burns a slave, and that would return him to his enslavement in Virginia. Thoreau's invective against the laws and those who were executing them was scathing, and he was prepared to go beyond criticism into direct resistance. As the antislavery advocates had come to realize, the United States Constitution, which gave slavery a protected legal status, was one of the most significant obstacles to any movement toward the elimination of slavery. At the same antislavery meeting where Thoreau delivered "Slavery in Massachusetts," William Lloyd Garrison had dramatically burned a copy of the Constitution, emphasizing the extremes to which his followers must be prepared to go to abolish slavery. Thoreau burned no documents in his address, but his recognition of the necessity to take urgent, radical action, action that went beyond the limits of the presently constituted law, was clear. Arguing that cooperation with the current system of slavery, and with the laws that upheld and enforced it even in Massachusetts, was impossible, he called for the state to break its constitutional ties with the Union: "Let the State dissolve her union with the slaveholder. She may wriggle and hesitate, and ask leave to read the Constitution once more; but she can find no respectable law or precedent which sanctions the continuation of such a Union for an instant" (RP 104). The higher law of justice must take precedence over the law of the Constitution or the appeal to preserve the union of states that it codified.

But this act of nullification by the state must also be accompanied by a similar commitment to a personal nullification: "Let each inhabitant of the State dissolve his union with her, as long as she delays to do her duty" (RP 104). The disbanding of this union between the citizens of Massachusetts and the institutions of their law and government, a moral obligation as Thoreau sees it, is the first and most important step toward purifying the now corrupted state. This is less a declaration of personal independence than an act of "making the law free," as he had earlier described it. It is grounded in the understanding that "policy is not morality—that it never secures any moral right, but considers merely what is expedient" (RP 104). Having lost its moral bearings, the state must now be resisted. "Show me a free State, and a court truly of justice, and I will fight for them, if need be; but show me Massachusetts, and I refuse her my allegiance, and express contempt for her courts" (RP 106).

But what practical form could Thoreau's contempt take? That difficult question haunts the entire address, even as it troubled the entire antislavery movement. "We have used up all our inherited freedom," Thoreau declared. "If we would save our lives, we must fight for them" (RP 108). But how to undertake such a fight, and against what specific enemy? By the time Thoreau delivered his address on July 4, 1854, an attempt to free Burns by force had already failed, as had a complex and prolonged legal battle.[17] In what useful way could one refuse allegiance to the state? Or be of help to Anthony Burns? This particular battle was already lost, as Thoreau's scathing contempt for Massachusetts officials and institutions seems to acknowledge. The purpose of his speech, and the question of its practical aims, are therefore worth considering, given his inclination to engage in philosophy that had decidedly practical implications.

While venting his anger over the Burns affair, Thoreau is also making his support of Burns's freedom and of the larger antislavery struggle publicly known. He is thereby seeking out a community of those who share his views. This search for affirmation and support is a crucial element of citizenship and political development. The embrace of a larger political community which the address signals must be remembered when we consider Thoreau's somewhat surprising turn to the theme of the transcendent power of the continuing cycles of nature at its end.[18]

Thoreau broaches this change by returning to his earlier confession of a sense of loss and alienation, his feeling that the Burns case had altered the atmosphere in which he lived and devalued the things that he had lived for. His principal loss has been the diminishment of his capacity to gain new insight and vitality from the natural world. "I walk toward one of our ponds, but what signifies the beauty of nature when men are base? We walk to lakes to see our serenity reflected in them; when we are not serene, we go not to them" (RP 108). Thoreau has been imprisoned in his own political outrage, unable to find release in nature. "The remembrance of my country spoils my walk," he declares. "My thoughts are murder to the State, and involuntarily go plotting against her" (RP 108).

That sense of order is restored to him quite suddenly, however, in his account of a chance discovery of a "white water-lily" which seems almost magically to alter the tone of the essay. Lawrence Buell has commented on "the essay's abrupt-seeming swerve *from* radicalism" in this incident as part of a larger question about the political character of the pastoral mode and sensibility.[19] This is a potentially troubling moment in its sudden deflation of Thoreau's eloquent political outrage, and the details of Thoreau's language immediately before this shift of tone bear some scrutiny here. He has mentioned the attraction of the ponds and lakes of the Concord area, explaining his desire to see "our serenity reflected." That hoped-for serenity is in contrast to the unwilled or involuntary violence of his own thoughts, the feeling that some alien force has somehow taken control of his will. What these descriptions have in common is the diminishment of the ability to recover through nature a sense of moral order.

It is therefore quite significant that Thoreau portrays his discovery of the lily as an accident: "But it chanced the other day that I scented a white water-lily, and a season I had waited for had arrived. It is the emblem of purity" (RP 108).[20] This unplanned experience is a moment of surprise, like the delayed revelation on the descent from Mount Ktaadn or the shock of the unusual appearance of familiar countryside under moonlight. Thoreau does not reason or calculate toward this experience, he smells it; the perfume of the lily actively overtakes him. He is brought back into his senses, into his body, and in this way is also given a new control over his thoughts.

The unexpected discovery of the perfume of the lily tells him that "a season I had waited for had arrived," and while Thoreau refers principally to the flower as a marker of the change of seasons, his seasonal reference carries political import as well. He also awaits a new "season" for political and legal justice, a change in the American political atmosphere. Thoreau regards the flower as a potent emblem because of its capacity "to show us what purity and sweetness reside in, and can be extracted from, the slime and muck of the earth" (RP 108). Given the harshness and severity of his attack on American political and legal institutions, "slime and muck" seems an apposite symbol for them. But this wry derision explains only part of his implication. The more important truth is that the muck and slime, given time, are eventually productive of something pure. "What a confirmation of our hopes is in the fragrance of this flower! I shall not so soon despair of the world for it, notwithstanding slavery, and the cowardice and want of principle of Northern men" (RP 108). The perfume of the flower has reminded Thoreau that the political morass that has entrapped his nation, and that has entrapped him as well, will not last forever. "Slavery and servility," he concludes, "have no real life." They are instead part of a dead past that weighs human society down, but cannot do so forever. In their destruction will be the energy for new progress. "Let the living bury them; even they are good for manure" (RP 109).

Buell is right to note that the symbol of the lily takes us only partially away from politics and into nature.[21] Although it seems at first a sudden shift of focus, Thoreau's discovery of the flower actually broadens his political reference by underlining the fact that progressive change can emerge from what seems a defeated and hopeless position. Political critique must retain the capacity for hope, or it is futile. Thoreau's lily adds hope, and therefore purpose, to his rage. The perfume of the water lily, the "confirmation of our hopes," signals the unending energy of nature and also the ever present possibility of creating a better nation and community. "If Nature can compound this fragrance still annually, I shall believe her still young and full of vigor, her integrity and genius unimpaired, and that there is virtue even in man, too, who is fitted to perceive and love it" (RP 108).

Thoreau's combination of outrage over slavery and continuing faith in human virtue accounts for his later praise for John Brown, who became for him, as a martyr for moral courage, a sign of the inevitable arrival of a new political season.[22] "It was his peculiar doctrine that a man has a perfect right to interfere by force with the slaveholder, in order to rescue the slave," Thoreau wrote. "I agree with him" (RP 132). And beyond this principle was Brown's sense of his calling to act on it, a calling that made his life "meteor-like, flashing through the darkness in which we live" (RP 145). Extending his earlier description of the way the political turmoil of the Burns case had erased his capacity to experience the natural world, Thoreau describes Brown as a kind of supernatural being or transcendent force, the power of which overwhelmed the ordinary course of the natural world: "I was so absorbed in him as to be surprised whenever I detected the routine of the natural world surviving still, or met persons going about their affairs indifferent" (RP 145). Brown's acts were further confirmation that the moral capacity of men and women had not been finally diminished by the corruption of slavery. His execution could not end his work; it could not diminish his continuing moral impact on his country. "He is more alive than ever he was" (RP 153).

CHAPTER EIGHT

Leaf, Fruit, Seed: Nature's Great Circle

THE MYSTERY OF THE LIFE OF PLANTS

The last phase of Thoreau's literary career presents unusual problems of interpretation, principally because of his early death. In all probability Thoreau was infected with tuberculosis as early as 1836, but he had nevertheless been able to achieve a remarkable physical robustness by his thirties, regularly undertaking long hikes and other outdoor activities that show him to have been a man of great physical vigor. He suffered a period of prolonged weakness in 1855, however, and in December 1860 he contracted a cold that developed into a serious attack of bronchitis. Weakened from this illness, Thoreau became susceptible to his dormant tubercular condition and never fully recovered before his death in 1862.[1] Cut down in mid-stride at the age of forty-four, having undertaken literary and scientific projects of breathtaking ambition and scope, Thoreau spent his last year bringing what lectures and other materials he could into publishable form as essays for the *Atlantic Monthly*.[2] But he left several major projects only partly finished, studies of natural history that indicate the innovative and modern direction of his thinking after *Walden*. After more than a century, the most significant of these unfinished but nevertheless illuminating projects have been edited for publication by Bradley P. Dean. Influenced by new interest in both environmental studies and the history of science, scholars have also begun to reassess the significance of Thoreau's intellectual direction in the last years of his life. What one finds there is not the "late" phase of a literary career, but rather the beginnings of a remarkable work of synthesis between philosophy, literature, and science, in which a commitment to empirical observation and data gathering was the underpinning of a comprehensive theory of the process of nature's variation and development.[3]

As we have seen, Thoreau began a more systematic study of natural history in the early 1850s, and the increasingly factual quality of his Journal reflects that important intellectual reorientation. Thoreau's systematic pursuit of the factual details of his natural surroundings has resulted in two divergent readings of his later work. Literary scholars who measured his achievement by his mastery of a complex symbolic rendering of visionary insight, as exemplified in *Walden*, have tended to see his growing empiricism as a retreat or an imaginative declension, in which Thoreau lost either the requisite faith or the necessary ability to navigate simultaneously the natural and spiritual worlds.[4] He remained attentive to fact, this view holds, but fact no longer seemed to flower into truth for him. Thoreau himself, as we have seen, provides some basis for this view through his own worried comments on the drying up of his philosophical and poetic imagination.

Largely the product of the New Critical celebration of *Walden*'s formal and symbolic achievement, this sense of Thoreau's later imaginative decline is being displaced by a new respect for both the aims and the accomplishments of his work after 1854. Motivated by the availability of new texts and by a deepening interest in Thoreau as a scientific and ecological thinker, more recent readers have been inclined to see this new Thoreau as a proto-modern figure who read Darwin with understanding, and who presciently laid the groundwork for an ecologically informed comprehension of the natural world.[5] For these readers, Thoreau's empiricism is less a declension than a necessary revision and adaptation of Emersonian idealism.

If Thoreau's immersion in scientific study and his contribution to the science of his day must be emphasized, so must his ambivalence about this work, and his insistence that it be seen within a larger framework of philosophical inquiry. "All science is only a makeshift, a means to an end which is never attained" (J 14:117), he remarked in October 1860, comparing "scientific" with "poetic or lively" descriptions of natural objects and events. "What especially motivated him," Lawrence Buell observes, "was not the desire for empirical knowledge alone but also the desire for unifying patterns. The legacy of the Emersonian correspondence project continued to affect Thoreau's work even as he became increasingly committed to the scientific study of nature."[6] As we consider the Journal in conjunction with late natural history projects such as *Wild Fruits* and *The Dispersion of Seeds*, and the finished essays that emerged from them, what is striking is Thoreau's mastery of the concepts and techniques of science, and his simultaneous recognition of its epistemological limits and narrowly circumscribed philosophical foundations. Thoreau apprenticed himself to empirical science, but he was using it for his own ends. Those ends had an impressively grand scope.

Over the last decade of his life, Thoreau devised a set of interlinking projects in which empirical observation and metaphysical conceptualization played vital and complementary roles.[7] The ultimate end of these projects was to investigate and describe what Thoreau understood to be the workings of the law, or, as he sometimes felt, the laws, of nature—the patterns, configurations, and principles through which the energy of nature took recognizable form. These laws or principles explained the material phenomena of nature, but also illuminated consciousness, perception, and the inner life of human experience. Thoreau's later projects were thus continuations by different means of his lifelong process of self-culture. For Thoreau, the *study* of natural life continued to illumine the *living* of a natural life. Although his orientation became more empirical, he did not abandon a working assumption that the understanding of nature's parts both depended on and reinforced a sense of their complementary interaction as a whole. He began to see this unity from the bottom up, however, finding it more productive to assume, as Laura Dassow Walls has written, that "order was not dictated rationally from above but emerged cooperatively from below, from the collective interactions of constituent individuals."[8] His Journal from the early 1850s to the end of his life traces the process by which he came to employ direct and detailed observation of individual parts of nature, observing them fully enough that they eventually ceased to be isolated or separate. He looked at particulars with intensity, believing that a deep perception of them would dissolve their boundaries and their quality of separateness. One could know a thing completely only through the larger network of phenomena in which it played a part. Because that network expanded outward infinitely, the pursuit of the knowledge of a single thing became the unceasing quest to comprehend the encompassing unity of all things.

Thoreau provides an enlightening account of his growing interest in botany in an 1856 journal entry (J 9: 156–58). Having made a false start at learning plant names systematically during his college years, he explains that he began again "half a dozen years ago" by bringing plant specimens home in his hat. "I remember gazing with interest at the swamps about those days and wondering if I could ever attain to such familiarity with plants that I should know the species of every twig and leaf in them, that I should be acquainted with every plant (excepting grasses and cryptogamous ones), summer and winter, that I saw." But Thoreau's attraction to the mastery of the botanical names of his locality was motivated by more than the intellectual challenge that such an undertaking represented. "I wanted to know my neighbors, if possible,—to get a little nearer to them" (J 9:157). Seeing the plants as his "neighbors" and co-inhabitants made his quest consequential, adding a dimension of meaning that the botanical systems in themselves could not supply. He was studying not merely the names of plants but the qualities and distinguishing characteristics of beings who occupied the same place that he did, and were governed by the same laws and conditions to which he himself was subject.

By integrating his botanical studies with the pattern of his daily walks, making the study of plants sometimes the object and sometimes the side effect of his sauntering, Thoreau gained the knowledge he wanted without seeming to have "studied" botany systematically. "I little thought that in a year or two I should have attained to that knowledge without all that labor. Still I never studied botany, and do not to-day systematically, the most natural system is still so artificial" (J 9:157). Yet his desire grew for more exact information about a particular plant's stages of development, or its interaction with its particular environment. "I soon found myself observing when plants first blossomed and leafed, and I followed it up early and late, far and near, several years in succession, running to different sides of the town and into the neighboring towns, often between twenty and thirty miles a day" (J 9:158).

His studies seem to have been driven by a profound curiosity about the patterns of uniformity in the cycles of plant growth and renewal, a curiosity that was both intellectual and emotional in its origins. As he put it, "I soon *found myself* observing" the growth of plants (emphasis added), a form of expression that emphasizes the spontaneous and instinctive nature of his studies. His phrasing—"finding" himself—also subtly suggests the subliminal link between his nature studies and his own effort of self-understanding.

These field observations of the life cycles of plants and the nature of their habitat were closely linked with Thoreau's increasing devotion to his Journal, which became by the middle 1850s the central work of his life, the source from which all his later projects flowed. Don Scheese has carefully analyzed one 1856 journal entry in which Thoreau describes the process of tracking down a rarely seen species of cranberry in Beck Stow's Swamp (J 9:35–46), explaining that such naturalist excursions were "a kind of vision quest," closely related to Thoreau's desire to find the nearby "wildness" that coexists with society and "to live *with* rather than *against* the land."⁹ What we should understand from Scheese and others who have emphasized Thoreau's fascination with both wildness and the work of "inhabiting" his locale is that his search for the laws and patterns of nature was also a determined attempt to learn how to live in nature. His philosophical quest was always, and perhaps essentially, an ethical one, if we understand ethics as the inquiry into how we should live. When Thoreau began to learn the botanical and environmental details of the Concord area in the early 1850s, he was also embarking on a quest to make himself more consciously and fully a part of that world.

In 1853 Thoreau expressed his interest "in each contemporary plant in my vicinity," declaring them "cohabitants with me of this part of the planet." But he tempered his sense of neighborliness with what was for him an equally important recognition: "Yet how essentially wild they are! as wild, really, as those strange fossil plants whose impressions I see on my coal" (J 9:406). Kinship and wildness—these were the polar principles that drove Thoreau's deepening investigation of the workings of nature around his Concord home. Motivated by both a sense of familiarity with plants and a contrasting recognition of their strangeness, he saw his botanical work as a way of approaching a mysterious power that could never finally be penetrated.

Although he understood and used science with increasing sophistication, he remained alert to its potential power to obscure the very thing that it presumably illuminated. "The mystery of the life of plants is kindred with that of our own lives," he wrote in 1859, adding this cautionary proviso: "The physiologists must not presume to explain their growth according to mechanical laws, or as he might explain some machinery of his own making. We must not expect to probe with our fingers the sanctuary of any life, whether animal or vegetable. If we do, we shall discover nothing but surface still" (J 12:23). The imagery of surface and depth of course carries the resonance of two well-known contemporary passages, Emerson's section on "Surface" in "Experience" (1844; CW 3:34–39), which Thoreau knew well, and Ahab's rebuke of Starbuck in the "Quarter-deck" chapter of *Moby-Dick* (which Thoreau probably did not know), in which Ahab declares his desire to "strike, strike through the mask" of the white whale's physical appearance.[10] In both these passages, as in Thoreau's journal entry, surfaces are the limiting boundaries that all thinking must seek to overcome. The mind and perceptions are seemingly imprisoned by the impenetrable material shell of things. Philosophy is the drive to penetrate or break through the surface of nature, the desire to reach its core or its secret. But as Thoreau suggests here, there is a potentially destructive tendency in this urge.

Thoreau advocated instead a form of study centered in fine discrimination and subtle discernment which was essentially reverential in orientation. "The ultimate expression or fruit of any created thing is a fine effluence which only the most ingenuous worshipper perceives at a reverent distance from its surface even." In contrast with this attitude of heightened sensitivity and respectful distance, he depicted the attitude of science in a strikingly negative image: "Science is often like the grub which, though it may have nestled in the germ of a fruit, has merely blighted or consumed it and never truly tasted it" (J 12:23). In the image of the destructive burrowing and feeding of the grub, Thoreau encapsulated his aversion to a form of empirical science to which he was also in many ways strongly attracted. Instead of a knowledge that broke through surfaces in search of the deeper essence of things, he aspired to a recognition of the "effluence" of a thing, a concept that he derived from his practiced attention to the fragrance of fruits and blossoms. The effluence was, in a designation that linked plant with human, "expressed," a form of identifying utterance to which the observer had to be receptive. This attentive openness and receptivity signified a more patient, more humble, and less aggressively destructive way of pursuing a deeper knowledge of nature than the models offered by science. "Only that intellect makes any progress toward conceiving of the essence which at the same time perceives the effluence" (J 12:23).

It must be said of course that what Thoreau is attacking here is not science in the best and most comprehensive sense but science narrowly and ineptly pursued. These statements represent his sense of alienation from detached and narrowly focused fact gathering, and in some respects reflect his dealings with Harvard's Louis Agassiz, the most influential advocate of modern experimental science in America during Thoreau's lifetime.[11] They also reflect an ongoing inner dialogue in which Thoreau constantly attempted to remind himself of larger ends as he pursued his ever-expanding quest for specific data. He understood through experience the overwhelming demands of the detailed observations he was undertaking, and recognized with some alarm how such intensive and demanding work could obliterate the mind's synthetic, intuitive, and speculative capacities. He felt periodically the need to tell himself to stand away and try to sense the "effluence" of a thing rather than blindly probing beneath its surface.

We can also understand Thoreau's resistance to the emerging science of his day as an imperfectly articulated recognition that a scientific "fact" was not necessarily an unmediated perception of a pure phenomenon but an organized and produced result of a particular form of human social practice.[12] While he was intensely interested in the flood of information that the new disciplines of geology, botany, and zoology were producing, his dealings with Agassiz had put a human face on modern science that was not entirely appealing, and had suggested the ways in which scientific information was to some extent shaped by the methods, assumptions, and social identities of those who sought it out. These considerations did not cause Thoreau to abandon his empirical studies, but they did give him an important critical distance from the authority of modern science.

In part because of their vivid and accessible descriptions of plants and animals, Thoreau admired those he called "the old naturalists," the early explorers and natural historians who wrote of their observations and discoveries without the benefit of the modern scientific framework and terminology.[13] "We cannot spare the very lively and lifelike descriptions of some of the old naturalists," he wrote in 1860. "They sympathize with the creatures which they describe." Citing Conrad Gesner's early description of the "delight" that certain antelopes take in drinking the cold water of the Euphrates River, Thoreau acidly observes that "the beasts which most modern naturalists describe do not *delight* in anything, and their water is neither hot nor cold" (J 13:149). The old naturalists were able to bring their subjects to life, a gift that modern naturalists, despite their more systematic knowledge, seemed to have lost.

The "old naturalists" had an advantage that Thoreau himself hoped to retain in his own scientific observations. They described not just their subjects but their subjects in their places, parts of a complex and ever-widening circle of relationships through which identities were formed and sustained. "In science, I should say, all description is postponed till we know the whole, but then science itself will be cast aside." Thoreau insisted that the naturalist's emotions had an essential place in the work of science, and that "unconsidered expressions of our delight which any natural object draws from us are something final and complete in themselves, since all nature is to be regarded as it concerns man" (J 14:117). The study of nature was always an investigation of the processes by which we ourselves live and develop. To deny or obscure this fundamental truth was for Thoreau both disingenuous and harmful, because the emotions and the imagination remained an important means to truths to which the strictly logical and linear mind had no access. "Who knows how near to absolute truth such unconscious affirmations may come?" he asked. Such affirmations derive their energy and insight from the same sources that inspire poets and religious prophets. "Which are the truest, the sublime conceptions of Hebrew poets and *seers*, or the guarded statements of modern geologists, which we must modify or unlearn so fast" (J 14:117). His emphasis on the word "seers" is important, calling attention to the inadequacies of modern science's claims to be able to see the world clearly and completely. Such vision is instead fragmentary and changeable, and further limited by the delusion that it is complete and permanent. Thoreau's avowals of the "old naturalists" and even older poets and seers are reminders of the limits of modern science; they stand as alternative forms of knowing and of expression, enlarging his conception of the purpose of his evolving fieldwork.

Scientific claims to "objectivity" troubled Thoreau especially, since they seemed to interpose an artificial framework of nomenclature and categories between the observer of nature and nature itself. He struggled to achieve what he considered a direct perceptual experience of natural events, unmediated by theory or system, and open to the new, the surprising, or the improbable. This implied a kind of participatory observation in which he remained constantly aware of his own relationship to what he saw. "I think the man of science makes this mistake, and the mass of men along with him: that you should coolly give your chief attention to the phenomenon which excites you as something independent on you, and not as it is related to you. The important fact is its effect on me" (J 10:164–65). Only through such a recognition of one's presence and connection could the act of observation retain its value and authority.[14]

Thoreau described the kind of participatory observation that he aspired to in 1860, in a journal entry that is revealing in its attempt to balance the authority of the scientist with that of the child or what Thoreau calls the "natural" man:

As it is important to consider Nature from the point of view of science, remembering the nomenclature and system of men, and so, if possible, go a step further in that direction, so it is equally important often to ignore or forget all that men presume that they know, and take an original and unprejudiced view of Nature, letting her make what impression she will on you, as the first men, and all children and natural men still do. For our science, so called, is always more barren and mixed up with error than our sympathies are. (J 13:168–69)

The emphasis here is on the achievement of an openness and receptivity to the phenomena of the natural world, a capacity to receive its impression. That capacity, not the claimed objectivity of scientific systems, is the "unprejudiced" approach to nature. For Thoreau this is part of a natural human endowment, lost in the ordinary experience of modern life, which must be recovered.

Thoreau's aspiration toward a participatory observation, his insistence on remaining in relationship to what he was observing and aware of that relationship, was an important aspect of his growing belief that the study of nature was the recognition of an ever-enlarging network of relations, in which natural objects were defined through their part in a larger system, and thus through the process of their interactions. In accord with his long-held faith that the study of nature was intimately connected with the culture of the self, Thoreau believed that this ever-enlarging system of relations also included human consciousness and human agency. This conviction was central to his later natural history projects, and to the evolution of his Journal into a medium of recording observations in the field. Commenting on the patterns of observation and description in the Journal, H. Daniel Peck offered an illuminating description of Thoreau's "'horizontal' framework of perception" and its connection to his larger philosophical goals: "To acquire meaning, [Thoreau] seems to say, every natural object must be seen in relation to another, and then still another. Only in the incremental development of dozens, hundreds, finally thousands, of visual relations does the writer create the full analogical framework—the fully contextualized, composite view—in which an authentic relation to the Ineffable may be achieved."[15] Even with the necessary emphasis on detail that his later projects required, Thoreau worked hard to maintain the larger picture of the interrelation of these details into ever broader categories of relationship and larger systems and networks of meaning.

"Relation" and "process" thus became crucial terms in Thoreau's growing understanding of natural phenomena. As he came to recognize, things in nature were neither separate nor static. The naturalist must always recognize both the cohesion and dynamic energy of the material universe. If Thoreau's assertion that the "important fact" about nature "is its effect on me" (J 10:165) reveals certain anthropomorphic assumptions, it is important to understand that he was not speaking in terms of use value or ownership, nor even in terms of a hierarchy of human privilege or value. His statement does, however, make perception and understanding the means of relationship, providing the observer less with a controlling power than with deeper correlation and attachment to the world. Thoreau's conviction that "the mystery of the life of plants is kindred with that of our own lives" (J 12:23) thus became both the key motivating assumption and the principal inference of his foray into science.

Thoreau's recognition that "relation" and "process" were the fundamentals of a comprehensive theory of nature reflected his growing fascination with the cyclical aspects of nature, in which he saw specific natural objects change and develop predictably in response to their environment. In a memorable description of the experience of walking with Thoreau, Emerson observed his friend's fascination with the regularity of seasonal change: "He drew out of his breast-pocket his diary, and read the names of all the plants that should bloom on this day, whereof he kept account as a banker when his notes fall due" (Trans 662). While his studies remained wide-ranging, they centered increasingly on the life cycles of the flowering and fruiting plants in the Concord area. Bradley P. Dean has noted that the term "Kalendar" emerges in Thoreau's Journal after he read the "old naturalist" John Evelyn's *Kalendarium Hortense* (1664) in 1852. "Apparently," Dean observes, "he intended to write a comprehensive history of the natural phenomena that took place in his hometown each year." The detailed compilation of the patterns of leafing and fruiting in the Journal may have been related to this larger design (WF xi).[16] Thoreau therefore became increasingly fascinated with the circular return of the seasons, seeing in their pattern a sign of the order of nature. He drew on the detailed seasonal observations of his Journal for the calendar-like charts that he made in the last two years of his life.[17] Finding leaf, fruit, and seed to be convincing expressions of the interwoven variety and the evolving permanence of nature, he distilled his late field observations into projects that focused on each of these three elements of the mysterious life of plants.

Thoreau had long been fascinated with the way that natural processes and cycles mirrored artistic and creative impulses, and as we have seen, he had explored the implications of "The Fall of the Leaf" in a series of poems in 1841, also articulating then a hazy vision of "a poem to be called Concord" (JP 1:330), the heart of which would be an account of the local countryside and its changing seasons.[18] *Walden*, with its seasonal structure and close attention to the pond and its surrounding landscape, was a partial fulfillment of this vision, but for Thoreau the movement of the seasons was an inexhaustible subject.[19] Moved by the fall pageant of colors in 1853, he contemplated a book to be titled *October Hues or Autumnal Tints*, which would feature a painted representation of the "brightest characteristic color" of "a specimen leaf from each changing tree and shrub and plant in autumn" (J 5:516). The next spring he compiled a chronologically ordered list of the leafing of local trees and shrubs (JP 8:149–54) and in subsequent falls began to make notations about the sequence and gradations of changing leaf colors. He collected these observations into a lecture first delivered in Worcester on February 22, 1859, the basis of the essay that we now know as "Autumnal Tints."[20] This lecture signaled his conviction that his new mode of more systematic observations in natural history could yield important public results.

While "Autumnal Tints" is a celebratory description of the New England autumn, a phenomenon that Thoreau and many others have found exhilarating and awe-inspiring, it also bears a philosophical burden, but one that, as was typical for Thoreau's post-*Walden* work, was more restrained and suggestive in its expression. The changing leaves in their brilliant colors may point beyond themselves, but they point in several directions, generating less a symbolic meaning than a host of rich emotional and intellectual associations. They become not so much the vehicle for some larger philosophical premise as the occasion for a set of loosely connected meditations and speculations.

At the foundation of his project is the suggestive array of equivalences and associations between the terms "leaf" and "life" which confirm his assumption that the study of nature is in its completeness the study of self.[21] "Do you not feel the fruit of your spring & summer beginning to ripen, to harden its seed within you— Do not your thoughts begin to acquire consistency as well as flavor & ripeness" (JP 8:256). So runs an 1854 journal entry that seems to be both an act of self-reflection and a thrumming on the metaphoric string of the developing and ripening self, the fundamental insight of the Transcendentalist commitment to self-culture. In March of that year he had recorded his observation of ice crystals forming in Nut Meadow Brook, "shaped like feathers or fan-coral,—the most delicate I ever saw." The observation was for Thoreau a clear demonstration of Goethe's theory of the leaf as a universal natural form, whose law or pattern of development he would expound in the sand foliage passage of *Walden* and continue to investigate in his later natural history projects. "Thus even ice begins with crystal leaves–& birds feathers & wings are leaves–& trees & rivers with intervening earth are vast leaves" (JP 8:30). The leaf as the instructive archetype of the examined life became the underlying philosophical principle of "Autumnal Tints."

For Thoreau, the colors of autumn embodied a quality of "ripeness" that is the central concept of the essay. Robert Milder identifies this "evocation of ripeness and impending death" as the key to the essay's expressive power. Thoreau's meditation on the fulfillment and subsequent fall of the leaves is, in this sense, a meditation on his own life, and the life of every creature.[22] The ripeness that Thoreau speaks of allows him to recognize the history of a particular leaf as part of the cycle of the season, and thus an achievement that is both uniquely individual and a single element in a vast, harmonious configuration of reality. "The change to some higher color in a leaf is an evidence that it has arrived at a late and perfect maturity, answering to the maturity of fruits" (W 5:250). The November 1858 journal entry from which he draws this passage adds a phrase that clarifies his sense of "perfect and final maturity" by contrasting the brightly colored leaves with green leaves "which merely serve a purpose" (CEP 367). The green leaves nourish the growth of the tree, but the colored leaves of the fall, having completed that purpose, now seem to be the end for which the tree has lived. The tree now nourishes them. The "maturity" or "ripeness" of the leaves is thus a way of describing their individual fulfillment, their coming into their own as parts of nature which have no subservient function and no purpose except free self-expression. We recognize that self-expression as beauty.

Thoreau's celebration of a leaf's achievement of a fulfillment unique to itself has clear implications for the way that human lives should be recognized and valued, and in this sense the essay subtly reinforces the emphasis on what Thoreau terms "moral freedom" in "Life without Principle." "What is it to be born free and not to live free?" (RP 174), he asked, emphasizing inwardness and self-direction as the means of self-realization and fulfillment. Although before coming to this late ripeness the leaf must move through different stages of development, each of which has its value and importance, this final achievement alters the identity of the tree which the leaf has helped to create. "A single tree becomes thus the crowning beauty of some meadowy vale, and the expression of the whole surrounding forest is at once more spirited for it" (CEP 374).

Even though he is tracing the patterns that define the lives of leaves, and thus demarcate or limit them, Thoreau is fascinated with the way this final ripeness suggests a wild unpredictability, a kind of riotous, beautiful freedom. "I do not see what the Puritans did at this season, when the maples blaze out in scarlet," he wryly remarks, emphasizing that such wild beauty suggests an untamable quality that men and women might do well to imitate. "One wonders that the tithing-men and fathers of the town are not out to see what the trees mean by their high colors and exuberance of spirits, fearing that some mischief is brewing" (CEP 376). In reaching the full measure of their self-expression, the leaves seem to surpass the limits or restraints that may have defined them. Their freedom is in some sense unsettling, a bursting over the boundaries that had heretofore contained their expression. The leaves are drawing a new circle of self-definition.

The leaves achieve this freedom just before they wither and fall, and there is a link between their complete self-realization and their death. Thoreau emphasizes the enrichment of the soil through their decay, observing that "this, more than any mere grain or seed, is the great harvest of the year." In such a cycle of death, decay, and rebirth, "they stoop to rise, to mount higher in coming years" (CEP 381). Their death is then less an occasion for mourning than for celebration. "How beautifully they go to their graves!" he exclaims, pointedly noting that "they teach us how to die" (CEP 381, 382). Yet this strain of melancholy never seems predominant in the essay. While Thoreau acknowledges the obvious truth that winter follows autumn, and that the leaves fall after achieving their richest colors, what seems to impress him most deeply is the always surprising newness of the change that was, after all, quite predictable. His punning observation that a single tree can make a whole landscape more "spirited" captures the simultaneously expressive and ethereal qualities of the vibrant colors, their visual intensity both confirming their presence and casting doubt on their reality. In the same vein he refers to the forest's "burning bushes," and calls the fully "ripe" tree "too fair to be believed." As predictable as this cyclic occurrence is, and Thoreau's essay lays out, to the day, its orderly regularity, it still borders on the incredible. "If such a phenomenon occurred but once, it would be handed down by tradition to posterity, and get into the mythology at last" (CEP 374).

Thoreau's transformation of the leaves into exemplary selves, and his descriptions, both precise and evocative, of the successive waves of color in the New England autumn, carry the essay forward and gain the reader's assent. But within these strands of argumentation and description he also weaves sites of brief but memorable narrative in which he recounts what we might call his own experience of the leaves, unique moments of engagement in which he shares something that could be considered a relationship with them. These moments are enactments of a profound sympathy and openness; they suggest that such experiences of the leaves are an essential avenue of completion for the human personality.

Thoreau goes to his boat at "the acme of the *Fall*," the days in mid-October when a hard frost, rain, or strong winds have dropped "thick beds or carpets" of leaves, and finds it "all covered, bottom and seats, with the leaves of the Golden Willow under which it is moored" (CEP 378, 379). Counting the leaves an adornment, he embarks on a river that is "perfectly calm and full of reflections," which eventually takes him to harbor in "a quiet cove" (CEP 380). The easy drift down the river reinforces the sense of peace and meditative serenity that is one of the emotional rewards of autumn. The river journey is the analogue to an interior journey in which Thoreau recounts the only partly intentional way that he has attained a philosophical calm. One of the distinctive achievements of "Autumnal Tints" and "Wild Apples," Thoreau's most distinctive late essays, is his expression of an attitude of deep acceptance, a mood that occurs in flashes in *A Week* or *Walden* but seems somehow tentative or impermanent there. Thoreau's "quiet cove" embodies a hope for peace and serenity that his earlier works have achieved at certain moments; in "Autumnal Tints" it seems the natural and expected bearing of the essay.

It is less his arrival in the cove that matters so much than what he encounters there and how he responds to it. "I unexpectedly find myself surrounded by myriads of leaves, like fellow-voyagers, which seem to have the same purpose, or want of purpose, with myself" (CEP 380). The leaves have made the same journey that Thoreau has made, and as he recognizes, they share an identity as "fellow-voyagers." The connection is, in the texture of this essay, more than fanciful. Thoreau's ability to read himself in these quite different creations of nature, his recognition that he shares some defining quality with them, is the central claim of "Autumnal Tints."

Their mutual dependence on the water to move them along and the "want of purpose" that this implies become Thoreau's way of entering the world that he has observed, described, and celebrated. No longer only a witness to the fall, he himself has now become part of it. He has gained this new identity not through any intentional act, but through a consciousness of his dependence on the currents of the river, and an unburdening acceptance of that guidance. The leaves are sanctioning companions who confirm his aspiration toward a natural life. As part of "this great fleet of scattered leaf-boats," which includes "Charon's boat probably among the rest" (CEP 380), Thoreau takes his place in the current of life and death.

If this brief strand of narrative has made the leaves close and familiar "fellow-voyagers," a later passage stresses their equally important qualities of mystery and wildness. Thoreau finds this exotic strangeness when he tells of bringing home to his fireside the leaf of a scarlet oak, whose "narrow lobes" and "bold deep scallops" create "a wild and pleasing outline." Contemplating the leaf's "broad, free, open sinuses" and "long, sharp, bristle-pointed lobes," he recognizes that the comparative absence of leaf material created by the scallops actually enlarges its impression, drawing the attention and stimulating the imagination of those who see it. "A simple oval outline would include it all, if you connected the points of the leaf," he remarks; "but how much richer is it than that, with its half-dozen deep scallops, in which the eye and thought of the beholder are embayed!" (CEP 388).[23]

Thoreau's imaginative "embayment" within the deep scallops of the oak leaf links this moment to his arrival at the "quiet cove" of the earlier narrative. In this case, however, the leaf is no "fellow-voyager" but the very map of the territory in which his voyage must be taken. The leaf has become a new world in itself, the site of exploration and discovery. It is a place for new beginnings, "some fair wild island in the ocean, whose extensive coast, alternate rounded bays with smooth strands, and sharp-pointed rocky capes, mark it as fitted for the habitation of man, and destined to become a centre of civilization at last" (CEP 389).[24] The "fellow-voyager" has now become the destination of the voyage.

Thoreau has woven these narratives into the structure of "Autumnal Tints" as examples of a new kind of "seeing," one that not only finds unexpected depths and layers of significance within ordinary events but also enters into and becomes a part of those events. They dramatize Thoreau's directive to become a part of the fall, not merely to observe it. "A man sees only what concerns him," he warns, drawing from his experience as a field botanist to make it clear that such participatory seeing requires both determination and preparation, "a different intention of the eye" (CEP 394). This implies an openness to the world, but an active, not a passive openness. "There is just as much beauty visible to us in the landscape as we are prepared to appreciate,—not a grain more" (CEP 393).

Thoreau has systematically arranged the unfolding of the season not only because he is fascinated with it, but also because he understands that most of those who have lived through this season repeatedly have only the haziest and most incomplete notion of it. "Objects are concealed from our view," he says, "not so much because they are out of the course of our visual ray as because we do not bring our minds and eyes to bear on them." Our seeing is passive and therefore incomplete. "The greater part of the phenomena of Nature are for this reason concealed from us all our lives" (CEP 393), and we live separated both from nature and from ourselves. The only response to this state of separation is to understand our "seeing" as a recognition of our need, a bringing up out of ourselves a sense of the thing that we want to know, so that our discovery of it is an act of self-completion. "The scarlet oak must, in a sense, be in your eye when you go forth," he concludes. "We cannot see anything until we are possessed with the idea of it, take it into our heads,—and then we can hardly see anything else" (CEP 393).

LIVE IN EACH SEASON

Thoreau's calendar of the precise sequence of the changing leaves in "Autumnal Tints" suggests how the cycle of seasonal change that he recorded in his Journal had become a fundamental imaginative principle, guiding his revisions of *Walden* and giving shape to his unfinished *Wild Fruits*. Like "Autumnal Tints," *Wild Fruits* calls on us to be more alert to the world that we sleepily inhabit, and to look at ordinary life as a form of continual exploration. "Most of us are still related to our native fields as the navigator to undiscovered islands in the sea. We can any afternoon discover a new fruit there which will surprise us by its beauty or sweetness" (WF 3). As Thoreau guides us through the unfolding panorama of the fruits of New England, he also teaches us to broaden dramatically our conception of a "fruit," separating it from our tendency to recognize only what we are likely to eat. "How little observed are the fruits which we do not use!" (WF 189), he exclaims, and much of what he details in *Wild Fruits* is intended to widen our ordinary frame of reference, using the fruit as a way of recognizing nature's larger processes of growth, sustenance, and regeneration. Thoreau's expansion of our awareness of the range and variety of local fruits thus carries a subtly biocentric message, reminding us that fruits are important not only to humans but to other animals as well, and to the plants that bear them, and that the processes of nature often continue quite apart from human concerns. He discusses in some detail the varieties of acorns, for example, a major element in the forest's food supply. Even though they are now seldom eaten by humans, they still represent to him a primal food source: "No wonder that the first men lived on acorns. Such as these are no such mean food as they are represented." He speaks, indeed, from experience, describing the "sweet and palatable" taste of the White Oak acorn, which he deems "almost as good as chestnuts" with a "sweetness . . . like the sweetness of bread" (WF 182).

Thoreau's culinary experiment is of course driven by curiosity and by his passion to experience the natural world in as many ways and with as many senses as possible. But it also illustrates the larger lesson that *Wild Fruits* aspires to teach: "And now that I have discovered the palatableness of this neglected nut, life has acquired a new sweetness for me, and I am related to the first men. What if I were to discover also that the grass tasted sweet and nutritious? Nature seems the more friendly to me" (WF 182). Thoreau knows the world more completely now, and has widened his sense of shared experience with other creatures, past and present. Such knowledge has made him more at home in the world, one of its many but essential parts.[25]

Wild Fruits, like "Autumnal Tints," becomes a lesson in perceiving nature, and thus a lesson in living in and with nature. "The value of these wild fruits is not in the mere possession and eating of them," Thoreau insists, "but in the sight and enjoyment of them" (WF 4). The habitual association of fruits with their particular use as food blinds us to other productive ways of perceiving them, in which their place and surroundings add to their beauty. He celebrates the local fruits, but he also celebrates the work of finding and gathering them, counting that activity as the fruit's most enriching part. The search for wild fruits takes us off the ordinary paths and into new and little-explored areas. To get the best blueberries, he explains, you must venture beyond the dry edges of the swamp and into its heart, where you will find "no wilder and richer sight" (WF 32). The most valuable fruits, therefore, are not exotic imports but "those which you have fetched yourself in the hold of a basket from some far hill or swamp." His axiom, "the less you get, the happier and richer you are" (WF 4), makes the difficulty of the search itself the measure of its value.

Such gathering becomes, like the "sauntering" described in "Walking," a spiritual quest in which we "pluck and eat in remembrance" of nature. "It is a sort of sacrament, a communion—the *not* forbidden fruits, which no serpent tempts us to eat" (WF 52). But we must relearn humility and meekness for such a task, recognizing that "the true fruit of Nature can only be plucked with a fluttering heart and a delicate hand" (WF 235). This fruit gathering is a restoration of the fallen self, a return to "some up-country Eden . . . a land flowing with milk and huckleberries" (WF 54).

Thoreau's eruptions into such poetry may at first seem at odds with the more prosaic task of accurately describing the ordered appearance of the area's fruits. His strategy, of course, is to make the ordinary poetic. Even his more strictly factual listings reinforce the sacramental qualities of the fruits by giving them a particular place in the unfolding almanac of the seasons. Using the calendar as a structuring device, Thoreau makes time a central concern of *Wild Fruits*, and of all his later Journal-based works. The seasons mark a time that is both distinctive and always already changing. The implicit message of each listing is to know each day and be alive in it. Thoreau's explicit summation of this wisdom captures the motivating spirit of all his late works, including the Journal: "Live in each season as it passes; breathe the air, drink the drink, taste the fruit, and resign yourself to the influences of each" (WF 238). He refers to the seasons of nature, but he also means, of course, the seasons of our own lives. To experience the particular moment when a fruit is ripe will be to live our own promise fully.

UPWARD WITH JOY

The central character of *Wild Fruits* is the apple, also celebrated by Thoreau in one of his most engaging essays, "Wild Apples."[26] There is an infectiously joyful tone in the essay, which is mellowed and enriched by its vivid narrative detail and a concluding elegiac note, in which Thoreau laments the passing of the very thing that he so enthusiastically describes. His recognition of the end of this era serves as a darker backdrop to an essay otherwise devoted to inventive and high-spirited descriptions of the border lives of apples, and a celebration of a life of carefree rambling, modeled on the wild apple's tart and resilient example. This mix of moods—or, more precisely, this building of elegy and prophecy on the foundation of the celebration of the apple—is one of Thoreau's greatest literary achievements.[27]

Thoreau is of course celebrating more than the apple, for in this fruit he discovers lore, myth, and ceremonial traditions that connect the apple to the fertility of nature and the survival of human communities. "The apple was early so important, and generally distributed, that its name traced to its root in many languages signifies fruit in general" (CEP 444). Offering evidence that ancient peoples used apples as food, and compiling references to them in the Bible and a variety of classical texts, including the account of the fall from Eden, Thoreau argues that "it is remarkable how closely the history of the Apple-tree is connected with that of man" (CEP 444). Although this long and intertwined history has made the apple "the most civilized of all trees" (CEP 445), Thoreau's ultimate goal is to celebrate the apple's inherent and indomitable wildness, a quality that he also hopes can be revived among men and women.

Thoreau links his own celebration of the apple to a line of ancient customs that express humanity's "joy and gratitude" (CEP 449) for the gift of the apple, such as the Devonshire farmers' ceremonially toasting their trees on Christmas Eve to ensure their continued fruitfulness, the kind of practice that bridges myth and history. As his essay shows in abundance, he is interested in the minute particulars of the growth and characteristics of the apple tree, but such particulars by no means obscure the apple's mythical and poetic characteristics.

Those characteristics are best embodied in the "wild apple," which he finds in his rambles in "old orchards of ungrafted apple-trees" (CEP 450) now abandoned, or in other places where they have sprung up as volunteers and found a way to survive and flourish without human cultivation. His account of the growth of these trees is one of his most vivid natural history descriptions, keenly observed and richly imaginative. The description also bears the dual burden of Thoreau's hope for the future and his lament for the past, as the wild apple comes to signal both indomitable endurance and tragic change. Thoreau admits that he speaks "rather from memory than any recent experience" about the "old orchards" he loves, "such ravages have been made!" (CEP 450). In his beloved "Easterbrooks Country," one of Concord's wilder areas, "there are, or were recently, extensive orchards . . . standing without order" (CEP 450–51); his qualification may at first slip past us, but it is important to remember that his vivid descriptions are conditioned by a sense of loss, a recognition that, as he later puts it, "the era of the Wild Apple will soon be past" (CEP 466).[28]

Thoreau's lament for the end of "the era of the Wild Apple" is woven into a larger portrayal of the apple as a paradigm of heroism, whose qualities of independence and tough endurance he admires and hopes to emulate. "*Our* wild apple is wild only like myself," he explains, "who belong not to the aboriginal race here, but have strayed into the woods from the cultivated stock" (CEP 452). Perhaps most important, the wild apple assures him that no life is completely determined or predictable. "Every wild-apple shrub excites our expectation thus, somewhat as every wild child" (CEP 456). The wild apple, once a cultivated fruit, or the ancestor of one, has broken out of its mold and created a new and wholly different form of life for itself. It grows differently and in new places, responding to the particular challenges of its new environment, and bears a fruit that Thoreau finds both unusual and appealing. Its capacity to change, to depart from a determined pattern of life, makes the universe a more diverse and a richer place, a place where "expectation" is still possible.

A paradoxical aspect of Thoreau's later work on natural history is his simultaneous fascination with cyclical regularity, the determining laws of the natural world, and his desire to find and know nature's unusual or extraordinary elements. Although he seems consumed by a passion to know and record the repeating (and unchanging) cycles of life, death, and rebirth in which each individual of a species lives out the script that nature has written for it, he is equally passionate about nature's ability to produce and sustain anomalies, and thus to show itself always new and open. The wild apple spoke to this longing to see the universe as open and capable of change.

Thoreau's wild apple tree is less a static object than a principle through which nature's energy can be expressed; in his descriptions of it he transformed the observation of natural objects such as apples and apple trees into the charting of channels of power, transformation, and dynamic interaction. As we have seen, Thoreau emphasized the importance of the "effluence" of the fruits, flowers, and leaves of plants, their capability of "expression." "There is thus about all natural products a certain volatile and ethereal quality which represents their highest value, and which cannot be vulgarized, or bought and sold" (CEP 447). To see nature fully is to see this volatility; thus, when Thoreau sees a cart of apples going to market, he also sees "the stream of their evanescent and celestial qualities going to heaven" from the cart (CEP 448).

Thoreau's tribute to the wild apple centers on his account of the triumph over adversity that enables it finally to mature and bear fruit. From the "little thickets of apple trees" that spring up "in the pastures where cattle have been," one or two may "survive the drought and other accidents," only to be cut down later by grazing herds. Even if they are cropped off every year, a few manage to survive, each "putting forth two short twigs for every one cut off," and gradually "growing more stout and scrubby, until it forms, not as a tree yet, but a little pyramidal, stiff, twiggy mass, almost as solid and impenetrable as a rock" (CEP 453–54). Through this determined struggle the wild apple tree develops its own shield from its enemies; its low spreading branches grow "so broad that they become their own fence, when some interior shoot, which their foes cannot reach, darts upward with joy." Through this slow and unusual process of development, the tree "has not forgotten its high calling, and bears its own peculiar fruit in triumph" (CEP 455).

This is, in one sense, a very Darwinian narrative, in which only a very few of the hardiest individuals are able to survive and reproduce in a hostile environment.[29] Even though Thoreau understood, as he wrote in *Walden*, that "Nature is so rife with life that myriads can be afforded to be sacrificed and suffered to prey on one another" (Wa 318), he has constructed the wild apple's story as a moral tale, in which endurance and humble persistence eventually produce a joyful fruitfulness. His narrative is grounded in close observation and an understanding of the interaction of plants and animals in a particular locale, but his imagination is transcendental, still inclined to see these processes as expressions of a law that is both "natural" and "moral."

The survival and growth of the wild apple illustrates the survival and growth of the creative mind struggling to prevail in a hostile world. Human beings, in their aspiration to bear "celestial fruit," are also "browsed on by fate," he writes. "Only the most persistent and strongest genius defends itself and prevails, sends a tender scion upward at last, and drops its perfect fruit on the ungrateful earth" (CEP 456). The "pursuit of knowledge" is "an Herculean labor," a dangerous gathering of "celestial fruits . . . ever guarded by a hundred-headed dragon which never sleeps" (CEP 456). The unmentioned but omnipresent fruit of "Wild Apples" is thus Thoreau's essay itself, the product of his endurance and humble persistence as an observer and chronicler of the natural life around him.

The moral example of the wild apple is the philosophical core of Thoreau's essay, and indeed of all Thoreau's interlinked late natural history projects. Yet it must be admitted that neither the essay nor the entire manuscript of *Wild Fruits* leaves the overall impression of an excursion into moral philosophy. The tone of "Wild Apples" is determined much more by Thoreau's devoted descriptions of the varieties of taste and aroma to be found in apples, his amusement at the fanciful names applied to the many cultivated varieties, and his exuberant takeoff on the process of naming the wild apple. These are the aspects of the work that resonate most prominently when we reconsider it, not its identity as a moral essay. But that is the key to its achievement. "Wild Apples" lives in the reader's memory not as a sermon but as a kind of rambler's guide to apples; its praise of the look, smell, and taste of the wild apple is a celebration of a way of life that will allow us to be attentive to such things.

Thoreau makes it clear that he is concerned with molding a way of living when he insists that the wild apple tastes "spirited and racy when eaten in the fields or woods" but "harsh and crabbed" when eaten indoors. Its taste is, in other words, a test of our capacity to rise to the apple's heroic moral example. "To appreciate the wild and sharp flavors of these October fruits," he writes, "it is necessary that you be breathing the sharp October or November air." Taste is in this case more than one of the five senses; it signals a consonance of all the physical and mental powers, and a further consonance of body and mind with the encompassing energies of nature. To taste the fruit is to become a part of its life and expression, and to find a participation and belonging with the elements and conditions that produced it. It requires that we be at the peak of our own powers, fully "awake" as he had advocated in *Walden*. The taste of a wild apple is a grace that we must be prepared to receive. "These apples have hung in the wind and frost and rain till they have absorbed the qualities of the weather or season, and are thus highly *seasoned*, and they *pierce* and *sting* and *permeate* us with their spirit" (CEP 459).

Thoreau's orientation to what we would now call "bioregionalism," a focus on the geography, ecology, and general spirit of a particular place, is much in evidence in his search for new strains and varieties of wild apples that are defined by very particular places, and the mock-fancy names that he invents for them: "the Apple which grows in Dells in the Woods"; "the Apple that grows in an old Cellar-Hole"; "the Hedge-Apple"; "the Railroad-Apple" (CEP 462–63). Such names refer not to the look or even to the taste of the apples but to the places where Thoreau finds them, and the taste of each apple carries a memory that links him to a place and a particular visit; in that way each apple records a ramble or saunter that was his own expression of the tree's branching out and shooting "upward with joy." These accounts of his discoveries and culinary experiments with wild apples are an essential theme of the essay, adding a vivid and humorous counterpoint to his construction of the apple as a moral exemplum. Moral purpose is therefore interfused with the senses of taste and smell, instinctual and embodied experience, and also with the memory of a specific place at a specific season. Thoreau thereby creates a thoroughly worldly perspective in which the referential qualities of apples, while real and significant, are inextricably infused with their material being.

CONSTANT NEW CREATION

The seed begins and then completes nature's ever-continuing circle of leaf, fruit, and seed. It is the culmination of the life cycle and the promise of its perennial renewal. In *The Dispersion of Seeds*, the most nearly complete of

Thoreau's later natural history projects, he studies "nature's way" of dispersing seeds and thus continually renewing plant life on earth. The essence of his study of seed dispersal is presented in "The Succession of Forest Trees," an address that shows how far Thoreau's nature studies had taken him into areas that we now classify as land management and ecology. As Michael Berger has written, Thoreau's observations of the processes of natural forest succession in *The Dispersion of Seeds* describe "the dynamic principles underlying a complex ecosystem," and offer "a vision of nature's fecundity that is compelling both in the comprehensive mass of detail and in the precision with which the examples are presented."[30] The release, diffusion, and germination of seeds provided Thoreau with a window into the multifaceted interaction of plants, animals, landscape, and climate, showing us the "vital force in Nature" and the perpetual work of "constant new creation" (FS 102).

Although Thoreau's observations of the dispersal of seeds were advanced for his day, and, as Laura Dassow Walls shows, can be read in the larger context of the Darwinian reconception of natural processes, he couches his essay as an attempt to elucidate the as yet incompletely understood ways of nature, thereby characterizing nature as a personality that employs intention in working toward a larger design.[31] He was, by the middle 1850s, beginning to move beyond such an anthropomorphic conception, but he had not yet formulated a new language to describe his emerging understanding of natural processes. Thoreau also understood the rhetorical effectiveness of the language of intentionality, an important consideration since he saw his seed studies as having an immediately practical purpose of countering erroneous conceptions about the spontaneous generation of plants and the sources and longevity of seeds which were widespread among farmers and landholders at the time.

After his opening description of the seeding of the pitch pine and white pine, a work accomplished largely by wind and squirrels, Thoreau comments reflectively on nature's somewhat uneconomical but consistent methods, the gradual pace of which tends to make them obscure. "There is no part of this town so remote from a seed-bearing pine but its seed may be blown thither, and so a pine spring up there." The problem is that we are not ordinarily observant enough to recognize this wide diffusion of seeds or to notice the small seedlings that grow as a result. "There is nothing to prevent their springing up all over the village in a few years but our plows and spades and scythes," he notes. The pace of this process is slow by human standards, but that perception only suggests what a comparatively limited perspective humans have on the workings of nature. By showing the vastly different measure of time that must be used in considering nature's self-regeneration, Thoreau forces his reader to take a view from outside the ordinary human frame of reference. While "a great pine wood may drop many millions of seeds in one year," perhaps "only half a dozen of them are conveyed a quarter of a mile and lodge against some fence, and only one of these grows up there" (FS 35–36). Over time, though, that single tree will itself sow a new group of seedlings, and the pine wood will have begun to extend itself.

This process suggests "how persevering Nature is and how much time she has to work in," a method alien to humans but undeniably effective. "In this haphazard manner Nature surely creates you a forest at last, though as if it were the last thing she were thinking of. By seemingly feeble and stealthy steps—by a geologic pace—she gets over the greatest distances and accomplishes her greatest results" (FS 36). The divergent terms "haphazard" and "surely" suggest the distance between our assumptions of orderly procedure and the reality of nature's system. The eventual emphasis has to be placed on "surely," however, as Thoreau presents the considerable evidence of his field observations of seed dispersal. This gradual but inevitable accomplishment of forest regeneration helps confirm a larger order and regularity in nature, a concept that was compromised by popular beliefs in the spontaneous generation or special creation of plants. "It is a vulgar prejudice that such forests are 'spontaneously generated,'" he writes, "but science knows there has not been a sudden new creation in their case but a steady progress according to existing laws." Those "laws" are embodied in the seed, the vehicle through which new life is preserved and extended. New stands of trees, and ultimately new forests, "came from seeds—that is, are the result of causes still in operation, though we may not be aware that they are operating" (FS 36).

One of the barriers to a more complete understanding of the method of nature is the tendency to confine the "purpose" of natural processes to a rather narrow range. Although Thoreau is still inclined to speak anthropomorphically in terms of nature's purpose, he moves toward a more modern understanding of these processes by expanding the range of "purpose" that any particular natural act may embody. A seed, as his text shows, has more than one role to play, and plays its multifarious parts in a complex pattern of organic interactions. "Nature works no faster than need be," he explains. "If she has to produce a bed of cress or radishes, she seems to us swift; but if it is a pine or oak wood, she may seem to us slow or wholly idle, so leisurely

and secure she is. She knows that seeds have many other uses than to reproduce their kind" (FS 37). *The Dispersion of Seeds* is thus more than a description of seed dispersal; it moves toward an account of the varied interactions
among ever larger groups of the elements of nature. Thoreau's text elucidates
both the daunting vastness and the interdependent harmony that nature represents; this depiction of nature undermines the assumptions of supernatural
intervention or human-like intention in the processes of nature, and makes
the human "control" of nature simply impossible. Our only hope is to develop the ability to work in harmony with nature. If we see nature clearly
enough, Thoreau argues, we will understand that misguided interventions
into its workings are futile and self-defeating.

Thoreau uses his observations of the processes of plant diffusion and the
larger theory of nature's "constant new creation" to move *The Dispersion of
Seeds* toward pragmatic advice for the farmers and landowners of Concord.
He condensed the essence of his argument into "The Succession of Forest
Trees," an address for the 1860 meeting of the Middlesex Agricultural Society in which he tried to put his information into the hands of those who
could most use it. Recognizing the somewhat unusual nature of this venue
for a scholar and poet associated with abstract and unconventional theories,
Thoreau began by asserting drolly that "every man is entitled to come to
Cattle-Shows, even a transcendentalist," and reminding his audience that
"in my capacity of surveyor, I have often talked with some of you, my em-
ployers, at your dinner tables," and that as a local naturalist, "I have been in
the habit of going across your lots much oftener than is usual as many of
you, perhaps to your sorrow, are aware" (CEP 429). Thoreau's strategy is to
demystify the process of plant regeneration by describing the agency of
seeds, and thus to make farmers and woodsmen more aware of the chain of
relations and causation of which their own work plays a part. "In the planting of the seeds of most trees, the best gardeners do no more than follow
nature, though they may not know it," he writes, and his analysis makes it
clear that the best method is "doing as Nature does" (CEP 438).[32]

The practical becomes prophetic, however, when Thoreau looks at
longer phases in the change of the landscape, as he does in *The Dispersion of
Seeds*. After describing the role of squirrels in the seeding of "our oak
forests, vast and indispensable as they are," he observes that they are widely
regarded as "vermin" to be eradicated. "The farmer knows only that they
get his seed corn occasionally in the fields adjacent to his woodlot, and perchance encourages his boys to shoot them every May," a practice that is repeated elsewhere on an even more destructive scale: "Up-country they have

squirrel hunts on a large scale every fall and kill many thousands in a few hours, and all the neighborhood rejoices" (FS 130).

Apart from the sad spectacle of this slaughter, such practices have long-term dangers. "The noblest trees, and those which took it the longest to produce, and which are the longest lived—as chestnuts, hickories, and oaks—are the first to become extinct under our present system and are the hardest to reproduce," Thoreau argues. "Their place is taken by pines and birches, of feebler growth than the primitive pines and birches, for want of a change of soil" (FS 130–31). Thoreau recognizes here both the need for conservation and the role that insensitive and misguided human overmanagement and waste play in causing forest damage, themes that would grow in importance as the American conservation movement developed in later decades. When we remember that both *Wild Fruits* and *The Dispersion of Seeds* were incomplete on Thoreau's death and have only recently been published, we are reminded that had Thoreau lived to complete his "broken task," as Emerson referred to these unfinished projects, his impact on American environmental thinking might well have been even larger than it was.

Michael Berger has shown that *The Dispersion of Seeds* should be seen as a central part of Thoreau's intellectual accomplishment, explaining how this increasing mastery of empirical observation merged with a still vibrant philosophical idealism and a continuing appreciation of the poetics of nature. Thoreau had adopted empirical methods while resisting "the positivistic reductions of modern science," and had thus assumed "the role of a cultural mediator" between a scientific and a literary understanding of nature.[33] This mediating role was also beginning to provide him with a new means of both assessing patterns of American cultural practices in nature and intervening into those practices with an influential and authoritative voice. In Thoreau's late works we begin to hear a new voice with a different and in some respects more secure sense of both purpose and audience, a voice with both a practical message and the confidence that factual authority can impart. It profits us still to listen.

Epilogue

In his eulogy for Thoreau, Emerson lamented Thoreau's "broken task," the later projects in natural history that he was unable to complete before his death, and that "none else can finish." Aware that Thoreau's work had entered a new phase, Emerson wrote that "the country knows not yet, or in the least part, how great a son it has lost" (Trans 668). Modern readers have only begun to share Emerson's glimpse of the reach and promise of Thoreau's later projects. But to examine this "broken task" is also to gain a new perspective on all the work that had gone before it. Even the achievement of a masterpiece like *Walden* seems altered when we recognize it as in part the prelude to the saunterer and naturalist of the middle 1850s. *Walden* itself is not diminished in this perspective, but we understand it as a book that was not just a culmination but a point of departure, in some senses only preparatory for the real work to follow.

That work was literary, to be sure, but it was not merely literary. Emerson recognized how deeply Thoreau's literary projects were intertwined with his nature studies, how each made the other significant and, indeed, possible. "The length of his walk uniformly made the length of his writing. If shut up in the house he did not write at all." These later Journal-centered excursions were more than nature studies and essay projects. They were profound forays into self-comprehension, driven by the desire not to know the world but to live its life. "He said he wanted every stride his legs made" (Trans 658–59).

Thoreau's persuasive expression of this desire to live the world's life is his great achievement, the final proof of his recovery from the loss of his brother John and his own near death from grief and guilt. It is the greatest of the many legacies that he left his readers, a message of affirmation, of purpose, of self-discovery and self-acceptance. "Do what you love," he wrote to H. G. O. Blake (Corr 216); "know your own bone; gnaw at it, bury it, unearth it, and gnaw it still."

NOTES

I. AN ORIGINAL RELATION TO THE UNIVERSE

1. Canby, *Thoreau*, 57–62.

2. Brownson, *New Views*, 3.

3. Ibid., 10.

4. Cousin, *Introduction to the History of Philosophy*, 414.

5. Brownson, *New Views*, 42.

6. Ibid., 49.

7. Ibid., 47.

8. Ibid., 49.

9. Ibid., 47.

10. For a discussion of Thoreau's reading of *Nature*, see Sattelmeyer, *Thoreau's Reading*, 22–23 (quote from 22); and Richardson, *Henry Thoreau*, 18–23.

11. On the development of the concept of self-culture, see Robinson, *Apostle of Culture*, 7–29; Neufeldt, *The Economist*, 3–52; and Howe, *Making the American Self*, 235–55 and passim.

12. In *Walden* he transformed this comment into praise for those who hear "a different drummer" (Wa 326).

13. Stevenson, *Familiar Studies of Men and Books*, 102–3.

14. This path of will-less achievement is grounded in a long tradition of Christian mysticism and quietism, one that remained vital in the New England religious tradition, reinforced by the Transcendentalist call to religious renewal. Thoreau saw it rather dramatically enacted in the life and work of another of Emerson's protégés, Jones Very, who claimed that spirituality was a state of will-less existence, and who regarded his intensely dramatic religious sonnets as direct dictations of the Holy Spirit. ("Cannot the Spirit parse and spell?" Emerson had pointedly asked him.) On Very's theory of "will-less existence," see Gittleman, *Jones Very*, 255–352, quote from 337. Such quietism, though not so extreme as Very's, is also expressed

often in both Emerson's journals and essays. Thoreau's mystical quietism would also soon be deepened by his reading of Eastern scriptures, especially Hinduism. As Robert Sattelmeyer notes, Emerson drew Thoreau's attention to *The Institutes of Hindu Law* (or *Laws of Manu*) in late July 1840, and it had an immediate impact on him (*Thoreau's Reading*, 29). For Thoreau's encounters with Hinduism, see Hodder, "'Ex Oriente Lux'" and *Thoreau's Ecstatic Witness*.

15. Melville, *Moby-Dick*, 140.

16. For the development of the Journal, see Neufeldt, *The Economist* and "Thoreau in His Journal"; Cameron, *Writing Nature*; Peck, *Thoreau's Morning Work*; and Scheese, "Thoreau's Journal."

17. On Thoreau's struggles with the literary market and the social role of the author, see Neufeldt, *The Economist*, 23–69; Fink, *Prophet in the Marketplace*, passim; Milder, *Reimagining Thoreau*, 3–28; and Teichgraeber, *Sublime Thoughts/Penny Wisdom*, 44–74.

18. Howarth, *The Book of Concord*, 25–35.

2. THE SCRIPTURE OF ALL NATIONS

1. For Alcott's career as an educational leader, see McCuskey, *Bronson Alcott, Teacher*; and Alcott's "Doctrine and Discipline of Human Culture,'" the introduction to his *Conversations with Children on the Gospels* (1836). Fuller's teaching experience is described in Capper, *Margaret Fuller*, 206–51. For Peabody's lifelong involvement in education, see Ronda, *Elizabeth Palmer Peabody*.

2. See Henry Seidel Canby's informative account of Thoreau's appeal for Brownson's assistance in *Thoreau*, 57–62.

3. For Ellery Channing's brief account, see *Thoreau the Poet Naturalist*, 32–33. Henry Seidel Canby describes Thoreau's attempt to repeat in Concord "the experiment of Alcott in his famous Temple School . . . in which 'the spirit of love, the reverence for childhood, the ideal of home' were the bases for discipline. . . . The feruling of the six, however, was Thoreau's own idea. Since physical punishment has no relation to educational progress, let it be applied, if the deacon insists, to good and poor students alike, to show up its futility, and also the deacon" (*Thoreau*, 67). Walter Harding explains Thoreau's motive as a desire "to keep his side of the bargain" (though, as he also notes, school regulations specified that corporal punishment be minimized) and "to dramatize the preposterousness of Deacon Ball's request" (*The Days of Henry Thoreau*, 53). Robert D. Richardson Jr. attributes the action to Thoreau's being "stung and angered past self-possession" by Ball's reprimand (*Henry Thoreau*, 5–6).

4. O'Connor, "Thoreau in the Town School, 1837."

5. On Thoreau's school, see Harding, *The Days of Henry Thoreau*, 55–59 and 75–88, quote from 88.

6. For discussions of Thoreau's relationship with Emerson, his literary projects, and his role in the Emerson household at this time, see ibid., 113–44; Sattelmeyer, "Thoreau's Projected Work on the English Poets"; Witherell, "Thoreau's Watershed Season as a Poet"; and Richardson, *Henry Thoreau*, 71–113.

7. Harding, *The Days of Henry Thoreau*, 134. See also Myerson, "More Apropos of John Thoreau," and Richard Lebeaux's discussion in *Young Man Thoreau*, 167–204.

8. For the details of Thoreau's illness and recovery, see Harding, *The Days of Henry Thoreau*, 135–37. For important interpretations of Thoreau's reaction to John's death, see Lebeaux, *Young Man Thoreau*, 167–204; and Richardson, *Henry Thoreau*, 113–16. Lebeaux's is the most detailed and psychologically probing analysis, stressing the submerged rivalry between the brothers which had recently surfaced in their romantic pursuit of Ellen Sewall. Lebeaux argues that John's death caused Thoreau acute guilt because of this rivalry,

and also increased his suspicion of the external world of Concord, which he felt might have valued John's life more than his own because of John's more compliant and accommodating personality. But I am most impressed with Lebaux's observation that John's death caused Thoreau to question the purity of his ambitions, which were, at that point, focused on literature. John's death "strongly reinforced his distaste for 'worldly' ambitions" (177), Lebeaux writes, and while it "aggravated and prolonged Thoreau's identity confusion, in the long run it also contributed mightily to the further development of his identity as artist and naturalist" (182). Richardson believes that "the deaths of John and Waldo [Emerson] called out a response in Thoreau that dealt with grief by a powerful willed affirmation of the life principle," but that it was a response that "was not won or maintained easily" (115).

9. See Steven Fink's valuable study of the impact of the limited American literary market on Thoreau's authorial aspirations in *Prophet in the Marketplace*.

10. Witherell, "Thoreau's Watershed Season as a Poet," 50, 57.

11. As Witherell points out, these poems "present the fullest early treatment of an issue central to his philosophy—the place of man in nature—using themes and images that recur later in both his literary and scientific work" (ibid., 52).

12. Ibid., 56. On Thoreau's fascination with Hindu thought, see, in addition to Witherell, Sattelmeyer, *Thoreau's Reading*, 35; Richardson, *Henry Thoreau*, 106–9; and Hodder, "'Ex Oriente Lux'" and *Thoreau's Ecstatic Witness*.

13. This was Thoreau's first extended attempt to represent the leaf as the central natural form. See Robert D. Richardson Jr.'s discussion of the impact of Goethe's theory on *A Week* (*Henry Thoreau*, 153–59). The well-known and extensively interpreted "sand foliage" passage in the "Spring" chapter of *Walden* reflects this continuing focus on the leaf as nature's fundamental unit.

14. See Witherell, "Thoreau's Watershed Season as a Poet," 59–61, on Thoreau's abandonment of his poetic project.

15. Sattelmeyer, "Thoreau's Projected Work on the English Poets," 239–57, quote from 239.

16. As Sattelmeyer points out, "Thoreau's interest in the ballad and particularly in early Scottish poetry seems thus to have presaged a focus of his collection, perhaps for the reason that the 'rough' and 'untutored' qualities of the verse constituted a kind of virtue in some Romantic theory" (ibid., 251).

17. Packer, "The Transcendentalists," 454.

18. Paul, *The Shores of America*, 105. Paul's belief in the importance of this work to Thoreau's emotional and intellectual development has been confirmed by Robert Sattelmeyer, who stressed the essay's emphasis on the importance of experiential knowledge and its avowal of the principle that "no theory of nature or way of representing nature should be mistaken for nature itself" (intro. to *The Natural History Essays*, xv).

19. Paul, *The Shores of America*, 103.

20. Buell, *Literary Transcendentalism*, 188.

21. Several scholars have noted the significance of this essay, finding it to be, in Linck C. Johnson's words, "a vehicle for an inward journey of mind and spirit" (*Thoreau's Complex Weave*, 12). Lawrence Buell has provided a valuable discussion of the essay as illustrative of Thoreau's use of the literary excursion (*Literary Transcendentalism*, 188–207). See also Sherman Paul's discussion of "A Walk to Wachusett" and its relation to the development of Thoreau's later works in *The Shores of America*, 157–65; and Robert Sattelmeyer's discussion of the work in the context of Thoreau's development of the excursion narrative as an effective literary genre for his vision in "A Walk to More than Wachusett."

22. Sherman Paul comments on the significance of Thoreau's destination: "To go to the

mountain, then, was to go westward and heavenward, to experience transcendentally" (*The Shores of America*, 159).

3. NO HIGHER HEAVEN

1. Johnson, *Thoreau's Complex Weave*, 47.

2. For an insightful discussion of the development of the symbol of the leaf in Thoreau's thought, see Richardson, *Henry Thoreau*, 153–59 and 310–13.

3. There is mention of the possibility of Thoreau's moving to New York as early a mid-February 1843 in a letter from Thoreau to Emerson (Corr 89; see also Borst, *Thoreau Log*, 89). It is not clear whether Thoreau had discussed such a plan with Emerson earlier, though it seems likely.

4. Hawthorne, *American Notebooks*, 371. See also Borst, *Thoreau Log*, 91. On Thoreau's complicated role as friend, pupil, and servant in the Emerson household, see Ryan, "Emerson's 'Domestic and Social Experiments.'"

5. As Robert D. Richardson Jr. observes (*Henry Thoreau*, 124–27), Thoreau's letters from New York to his own family and to both Emerson and his wife, Lidian, confirm his deep emotional attachments and reveal his homesickness.

6. For an informative discussion of Emerson's editorship of the *Dial*, see Myerson, *The New England Transcendentalists and the "Dial,"* 77–99.

7. On Greeley's support of Thoreau, see Harding, *The Days of Henry Thoreau*, 151; and Richardson, *Henry Thoreau*, 131–32.

8. Fink, *Prophet in the Marketplace*, 86–121, quote from 95.

9. Harding, *The Days of Henry Thoreau*, 177–78; on Thoreau and his father's work in developing the design of the pencil, see Petroski, *The Pencil*, 104–25.

10. The genesis of *A Week* is complex. For helpful discussions, see Johnson, *Thoreau's Complex Weave*, 41–201; Adams and Ross, *Revising Mythologies*, 35–50; and Richardson, *Henry Thoreau*, 156–59.

11. Harding, *The Days of Henry Thoreau*, 179–80; Borst, *Thoreau Log*, 109; Richardson, *Henry Thoreau*, 146–51.

12. On the reception of *A Week*, see Johnson, *Thoreau's Complex Weave*, 248–60; Myerson, *Emerson and Thoreau;* and Scharnhorst, *Henry David Thoreau*.

13. Parker, *A Discourse of Matters Pertaining to Religion* (1842), 46. For a discussion of Parker's "absolute religion" and his central role in Transcendentalism, see Grodzins, *American Heretic*.

14. Thoreau's remarks reflect his work on the *Dial*'s series of translations of "Ethnical Scriptures," which were intended to open Asian religious texts and other world religious writings to a wider audience.

15. On the rise of the philosophy of "associationism," see Guarneri, *The Utopian Alternative*; and Francis, *Transcendental Utopias*. On Thoreau's complex relationship with the reform movements, see Johnson, "Reforming the Reformers."

16. On Thoreau's interest in Hinduism, see Hodder, "'Ex Oriente Lux'" and *Thoreau's Ecstatic Witness*, 176–217. For a discussion of the impact of Asian religions on Transcendentalism, see Versluis, *American Transcendentalism and Asian Religions*.

17. Paul, *The Shores of America*, 200. Stephen Adams and Donald Ross Jr. see Thoreau as a "poet quester" and emphasize the questing and mythological aspects of this part of *A Week*, writing that "rhetorically, Thoreau transforms the actual vacation trip into a symbolic journey, a quest for paradise" (*Revising Mythologies*, 82, 83). Robert Milder sees the Saddleback narrative as "the ambiguously visionary climax of *A Week*, too inconclusive to serve as the

resolution of the quest, yet rhapsodic enough to make the balance of the narrative seem mundane" (*Reimagining Thoreau*, 38). Henry Golemba notes the rhetorical differences between the descriptions of the Saddleback ascent and of the ascent of Ktaadn (*Thoreau's Wild Rhetoric*, 90–91).

18. Peck, *Thoreau's Morning Work*, 29–30. On the chronological shifts in *A Week* and their significance for the Saddleback episode, see Garber, *Thoreau's Fable of Inscribing*, 116–41; and Peck, *Thoreau's Morning Work*, 22–36. Garber argues that through the episode's placement in the text, "Thoreau skews the regular temporality" of the natural cycles that seem to regulate both his voyage and the structure of the book (140). He notes that "the Saddleback episode is actually a single element in a rich and complex sequence, one of a series of mountain ascents referred to in *A Week*" (126). The effect of the Saddleback digression, Peck writes, is that of a "memory called up from deep in the past," leading us "to understand it as a prior experience" of the "narrator-journeyer" of *A Week* (26).

19. Johnson, *Thoreau's Complex Weave*, 337.

20. As Laura Dassow Walls observes, "From the text of *A Week*, Thoreau can be quoted to sound like the perfect transcendentalist, the mystic of the empyrean, or like a rock-bound realist. The text oscillates from one position to the other" (*Seeing New Worlds*, 49).

21. See also, for a different perspective, Frederick Garber's reading of the episode, which emphasizes the contrast between the "clarity" on the mountain's peak and the fog below it. "That clarity is nagging, ironic, and cruel, eternity's tease upon time" (*Thoreau's Fable of Inscribing*, 190).

22. Linck C. Johnson has provided a definitive account of the process of Thoreau's composition of *A Week*, and of its significance in his early career, in *Thoreau's Complex Weave*. See also Johnson, "*A Week on the Concord and Merrimack Rivers*," in *The Cambridge Companion to Henry David Thoreau*. Johnson believes that "Thoreau's sketchy record suggests that he did not originally plan to write about the trip" (*Thoreau's Complex Weave*, 6), a fact that would place greater stress on his powers of recollection and invention in constructing the narrative.

23. *Thoreau's Complex Weave*, 45.

24. For discussions of the Thoreau brothers' romantic pursuit of Ellen Sewall, see Harding, *The Days of Henry Thoreau*, 94–104; Lebeaux, *Young Man Thoreau*, 114–49; and Richardson, *Henry Thoreau*, 57–62. Lebeaux discusses this incident as an instance of competitive rivalry between the brothers, and a source of guilt for Thoreau after John's death.

25. The claim to these resources is confirmed in Thoreau's poem "The Inward Morning," the most accomplished and significant of the poems included in *A Week*. The poem celebrates the arrival of "some new ray of peace uncalled" that "illumines my inmost mind" (Week 295), an illumination that is compared with the experience of the coming of dawn. Both unsought and empowering, the "new ray of peace" is the metaphorical assurance of life's constantly renewing energy.

26. Johnson, *Thoreau's Complex Weave*, 66–69. Johnson describes the continual expansion and refinement of Thoreau's discussion of friendship as the draft of the book developed. Lawrence Buell calls the discourse on friendship "the thematic climax of the book, the ultimate object of Thoreau's literary quest" (*Literary Transcendentalism*, 225). Richard Bridgman writes that "friendship was the consuming ache at the center of Thoreau's being," and finds the discussion in *A Week* to show Thoreau "at his most emotionally vulnerable" (*Dark Thoreau*, 57, 61).

27. Thoreau read Emerson's *Essays* (later retitled *Essays: First Series*), in which "Friendship" and "Love" were published, on March 12, 1841 (von Frank, *Emerson Chronology*, 160). The volume is listed as number 472 in "Bibliographical Catalogue" in Robert Sattelemeyer's *Thoreau's Reading*. See Buell, *Literary Transcendentalism*, 227–30, on the connection between Emerson's "Friendship" and Thoreau's discourse on friendship in *A Week*. For discussion of

the changing nature of Emerson and Thoreau's friendship, see Sattelmeyer, "'When He Became My Enemy'"; Packer, "The Transcendentalists," 522–24; and Smith, *My Friend, My Friend*.

28. Thoreau's use of the term "affinity" is rooted in part in Goethe's *Elective Affinities*, which made a significant impact on the Transcendentalists.

29. Margaret Fuller, whose influence on the entire Transcendental circle was profound, became Goethe's leading American interpreter and advocate, and pursued and championed friendships that were intense, open, dialogic, and profoundly transformative. For a discussion of Fuller's intellectual development and the impact of Goethe and Emerson, see Robinson, "Margaret Fuller and the Transcendental Ethos." For discussions of Fuller's theorizing of friendship and love, and of her relationships with Emerson and others, see Strauch, "Hatred's Swift Repulsions"; Zwarg, *Feminist Conversations*; Capper, *Margaret Fuller*, 252–350; and Crain, *American Sympathy*.

30. Emerson completed "Friendship" in late June or early July 1840, and it was published in March 1841 in *Essays* (von Frank, *Emerson Chronology*, 154–55, 160).

31. Eric J. Sundquist has commented on the "Edenic mythologizing" that marks Thoreau's digression on Dustan, linking it to the conception of a lost paradise which predominates Thoreau's meditations in the book's final chapters (*Home as Found*, 63).

32. See Sundquist's perceptive discussion of Thoreau's complicity with the New England settlers, and of the way Thoreau's version of the story of Dustan's captivity and escape "places the episode in a more valuable context of American mythology and buttresses its sacramental power" (ibid., 61–66, quote from 63).

33. On the autumnal mood of *A Week*, see Buell, *Literary Transcendentalism*, 232–33.

34. As Alfred I. Tauber observes, Thoreau's description of a "natural life" can be seen as his self-directed "moral agenda" (*Henry David Thoreau and the Moral Agency of Knowing*, 102). Thoreau's resolutions in this section of *A Week* are illumined by Lawrence Buell's discussion of his environmental projects during his Walden experiment (*The Environmental Imagination*, 126–39).

4. DEVOUR YOURSELF ALIVE

1. Charles R. Anderson provides a helpful discussion of Thoreau's leaving Walden Pond in *The Magic Circle of Walden*, 259–71.

2. Steven Fink characterized Thoreau's return to Concord from New York as a "strategic retreat" that did not alter his desire "to engage in a relationship with American society and elicit some response from it" (*Prophet in the Marketplace*, 123, 3). Richard F. Teichgraeber remarked that the Walden cabin "turned out to be less of a home and more of a headquarters" for the aspiring author (*Sublime Thoughts/Penny Wisdom*, 49).

3. See Harding, *The Days of Henry Thoreau*, 153–54; and Richardson, *Henry Thoreau*, 126–27.

4. Robert Sattelmeyer writes: "It seems almost certain that Lidian Emerson was the inspiration for the passage, not only because its date falls shortly after Thoreau's departure from her house and because he had already referred to her as 'a very dear sister' [in a letter to Emerson] but also because the terms of address here are quite similar to those in a passionate letter he had written to Lidian from Staten Island in 1843 after leaving her house for the first time" ("'When He Became My Enemy,'" 200).

5. Canby, *Thoreau*, 163. Sattelmeyer discusses the journal passage in some detail in the context of Thoreau's deteriorating relationship with Emerson in "'When He Became My Enemy.'" For useful discussions of Thoreau's regard for Lidian, see Moller, *Thoreau in the*

Human Community, 24–37; and Smith, *My Friend, My Friend,* 112–28. For dissenting opinions to Canby's assessment that Thoreau was "in love" with Lidian, see Harding and Meyer, *The New Thoreau Handbook,* 21–22; and Richardson, *Henry Thoreau,* 126–27.

6. On the historical contexts and ideological bases of the utopian experiments of the 1840s and 1850s, see Rose, *Transcendentalism as a Social Movement;* Guarneri, *The Utopian Alternative;* and Francis, *Transcendental Utopias.* As Barbara Packer notes, Thoreau "sought to combine the best features" of Brook Farm and Fruitlands in his Walden experiment ("The Transcendentalists," 494).

7. Miller, "Individualism and the New England Tradition," 37. Sacvan Bercovitch has offered an influential critique of the political shortcomings of Emerson and Thoreau in *The Puritan Origins of the American Self* and *The Rites of Assent.*

8. For a perceptive analysis of Thoreau's discussion of philanthropy, see Woodson, "Thoreau on Poverty and Magnanimity."

9. For a discussion of the relationship between Thoreau's advice on economy and his larger spiritual aims while at the pond, see Anderson, *The Magic Circle of Walden,* 19–38.

10. Paul, *The Shores of America,* 294 and 331; and Marx, *The Machine in the Garden,* 242. For a refinement of Marx's approach to *Walden* as an example of pastoralism, see James S. Tillman ("The Transcendental Georgic in *Walden,*" 137), who argues that *Walden* is "a Transcendental version of the georgic." Also important to this inquiry is Lawrence Buell's assessment of the ideology of pastoralism in America, which stresses the "duality" of the pastoral impulse as both "counterinstitutional and institutionally sponsored" ("American Pastoral Ideology Reappraised," 20; see also *The Environmental Imagination*). Thoreau was not alone among his contemporaries in sensing the socially redemptive possibilities of the agrarian life. As Robert D. Richardson Jr. noted (*Henry Thoreau,* 148–51), he established his residence at the pond in the same year that the National Reform Association was founded, an organization led by Horace Greeley which was devoted to the preservation of public lands for the mission of the small farmer. Broadly Jeffersonian in its aims, with a fundamental commitment to both the economic and ethical advantages of the small farm, the organization embodied a cultural ethos of which *Walden* is one reflection. Richardson includes agrarian reform among three "public contexts" for the Walden experiment, including the rise of the utopian communal experiments, and the Mexican War, with the associated building of the slavery crisis.

11. Adams and Ross, *Revising Mythologies,* 54–55; and Dean and Hoag, "Thoreau's Lectures before *Walden,*" 164–65.

12. For an important discussion of Thoreau's complicated attitude toward farm life, see Leonard N. Neufeldt's treatment of his relationship with his boyhood friend Joseph Hosmer, a farmer in the Concord area, in "'We Never Agreed . . . in Hardly Anything.'"

13. Despite these examples, his attitude toward the American work ethic was a complicated one. In "'The True Industry for Poets,'" Robert Sattelmeyer has discussed Thoreau's ambivalence about fishing as an activity that was free from the routines of daily work, but that also garnered "cultural disapproval" (191) for its tendency to flout the standards of responsible hard work.

14. As Sherman Paul notes in discussing Thoreau's reaction to plans for utopian reform, he never relented in his belief that work, both physical and moral, was the necessary means of reform. "The price of virtue still had to be paid in the immemorial way, by the sweat of the brow" (*The Shores of America,* 153).

15. On the origins of the term "ecology," and an amusing account of his mistaken effort to attribute it to Thoreau, see Walter Harding's article "Thoreau's Text and Murphy's Law." Lawrence Buell has provided the fundamental discussion of Thoreau's complex connection to modern environmental thinking in *The Environmental Imagination.* Also helpful on the "Green" Thoreau are the essays in Schneider, *Thoreau's Sense of Place.*

16. The importance of the sand foliage description in "Spring" has long been recognized as a key to understanding Thoreau's vision in *Walden*. Important readings include Paul, *The Shores of America*, 346–49; Anderson, *The Magic Circle of Walden*, 242–57; Gura, *The Wisdom of Words*, 124–41; Richardson, *Henry Thoreau*, 310–13; Milder, *Reimagining Thoreau*, 151–60; Boudreau, *The Roots of Walden and the Tree of Life*, 105–34; and West, *Transcendental Wordplay*, 183–96.

17. Sayre, *Thoreau and the American Indians*, 75; Cavell, *The Senses of Walden*, 25. Thoreau's mindfulness of working in the fields previously inhabited by Indians is one example of his belief that the Indian was important to what Philip F. Gura has called his search for "representative men" ("Thoreau's Maine Woods Indians"). On the metaphoric quality of Thoreau's work, see Sherman Paul, who notes that the work in the bean field "could easily represent the creative process of the romantic artist" (*The Shores of America*, 331); Frederick Garber (*Thoreau's Redemptive Imagination*, 133–34), who discusses the work with the beans in terms of the artist's attempt to work through his material; Dieter Schulz (*Amerikanischer Tranzendentalismus*, 46–54), who discusses the work in the context of self-improvement, and Cavell, who provides a detailed reading in *The Senses of Walden*.

18. As H. Daniel Peck writes, the "urgent work of perception" constitutes Thoreau's most important project in *Walden* and in the Journals (*Thoreau's Morning Work*, 162). The work in the bean field, which opens Thoreau more completely to the life in the field around him, stands as an important means to his achievement of his "morning work."

5. LIVING POETRY

1. Sattelmeyer, "The Remaking of *Walden*." F. O. Matthiessen presented the classic reading of *Walden* as a masterpiece of organic form in his chapter "The Organic Principle" (*American Renaissance*, 133–75). Charles R. Anderson's reading of *Walden* as an extended poem in *The Magic Circle of Walden* was also significant.

2. Harding, *The Days of Henry Thoreau*, 263–66.

3. See Robert Milder's discussion of Thoreau's conception of reading as "a spiritual calisthenics whose effect is to elevate the soul" (*Reimagining Thoreau*, 76).

4. Cavell, *Senses of Walden*, 28. See also Charles R. Anderson's discussion of Thoreau's reading as part of the new patterns of his activities (*The Magic Circle of Walden*, 39–47).

5. On the connection between "Reading" and "Sounds," see Matthiessen, *American Renaissance*, 168–69; and Anderson, *The Magic Circle of Walden*, 39–41.

6. See Cavell, *The Senses of Walden*, 26–35 and passim for a detailed and perceptive discussion of the activity and the motif of reading in *Walden*.

7. McGregor, *A Wider View of the Universe*, 33–86. McGregor also notes, however, the importance of Emerson's influence in encouraging Thoreau to begin his career as a writer. More subtle readings of the complexities of Thoreau's reception of idealism are offered by Charles R. Anderson (*The Magic Circle of Walden*, 93–130), H. Daniel Peck, and Laura Dassow Walls. Peck (*Thoreau's Morning Work*, 66–78) has depicted Thoreau's early work, including *Walden*, as a test of idealism, a theory that Thoreau eventually rejected for a conception of experience that much more closely resembles the phenomenology of Heidegger. "Philosophical idealism was inevitably his legacy," Peck writes. "But what makes him so interesting to us is that he inherited idealism not as a faith but as a problem" (73). Walls (*Seeing New Worlds*, 53–93) describes Thoreau's principal direction of intellectual development as a rejection of "rational holism," one form of idealism that she terms the "dominant paradigm of romanticism" (54) propounded by Coleridge and Emerson, and a movement toward a more fact-oriented "empirical holism" characteristic of the scientific method of Humboldt.

8. McGregor, *A Wider View of the Universe*, 40, 44. Recent critical discourse on two related issues, the history of science and "ecocriticism," have helped to frame this issue. Both seek to present Thoreau as a "naturalist," as opposed to a literary or philosophical figure, and concentrate on his later Journal and the natural history projects of his later career. In addition to the work of Peck, Walls, and McGregor, see also Howarth, *The Book of Concord*; Buell, *The Environmental Imagination*; Rossi, "Education in the Field" and "Thoreau's Transcendental Ecocentrism"; and Berger, *Thoreau's Late Career and "The Dispersion of Seeds."* Also of importance is the recent editorial work on late Thoreau manuscripts by Bradley P. Dean: *Faith in a Seed* (1993) and *Wild Fruits* (2000).

9. Cabot, "Immanuel Kant," 409.

10. See Anderson, *The Magic Circle of Walden*, 112–30, and Dieter Schulz (*Amerikanischer Tranzendentalismus*, 110–45) for further discussion of Emerson's and Thoreau's discussions of the eye and its significance.

11. Peck, *Thoreau's Morning Work*, 67–68.

12. Walls, *Seeing New Worlds*, 113–16, quote from 115. As Robert Sattelmeyer (*Thoreau's Reading*, 82–86) and Robert D. Richardson Jr. (*Henry Thoreau*, 362–68) have shown, Thoreau also read Louis Agassiz and A. A. Gould's *Principles of Zoology* (1848; revised edition 1851) and Agassiz's "Essay on Classification" (1857), learning much from them even as he moved away from Agassiz's larger conception of special creation of each species. For an informative reading of Thoreau's developing reaction to pre-Darwinian ideas of evolution, see Rossi, "Thoreau's Transcendental Ecocentrism."

13. Richardson, *Henry Thoreau*, 205. On the impact of Hindu writings on Thoreau, see Hodder, "'Ex Oriente Lux'" and *Thoreau's Ecstatic Witness*, 139–59.

14. Cabot, "The Philosophy of the Ancient Hindoos," 400–401.

15. Ibid., 403.

16. Ibid., 417; see also Richardson, *Henry Thoreau*, 206–7; Cameron, *Transcendental Apprenticeship*, 222.

17. In *The Senses of Walden* (110), Stanley Cavell has remarked on the problematic quality of "the depth of the book's depressions and the height of its elevations" and "the absence of reconciliation between them." These gaps can be taken as the signs of Thoreau's attempt to use his literary task in *Walden* to address his inner conflicts and fears of slippage and deterioration. Of pertinence on this issue is Robert D. Richardson Jr.'s discussion of *Walden* as "the earned affirmation of a man who had to struggle almost constantly against a sense of loss, desolation, and decline that grew on him age" (*Henry Thoreau*, 256).

18. See John Hildebidle's comments on this passage, which he reads in the context of Thoreau's struggle with the emerging new discourse of Science (*Thoreau*, 102–11).

19. See Sattelmeyer, "The Remaking of *Walden*." For detailed information on the *Walden* manuscript, see Clapper, "The Development of Walden."

20. For perceptive analyses of the profusion of symbolic associations of the pond, see Paul, *The Shores of America*, 332–45; and Lyon, "Walden Pond as Symbol."

21. Robert Milder has provided an informative discussion of the evolution of this chapter in Thoreau's development of the *Walden* manuscript (*Reimagining Thoreau*, 144–51).

22. Paul, *The Shores of America*, 343–45.

23. Boudreau, *The Roots of Walden and the Tree of Life*, 117; Richardson, *Henry Thoreau*, 310–13, quotation from 312. Other important readings of the sand foliage passage include Charles R. Anderson's emphasis on the centrality of the "leaf metaphor" (*The Magic Circle of Walden*, 243) and its connection to Thoreau's reading of Goethe; and Milder, *Reimagining Thoreau*, 151–60. The particular linguistic context of the passage has been helpfully worked out by Philip F. Gura (*The Wisdom of Words*, 124–41) and Michael West (*Transcendental Wordplay*, 183–96).

6. THE ACTUAL WORLD

1. Sattelmeyer, "The Remaking of *Walden*," 58. Building on J. Lyndon Shanley's distinguishing seven different stages of the *Walden* manuscript in *The Making of Walden*, Sattelmeyer discerns two major phases of its composition, one including three drafts written 1846–49, and four more written 1852–54. For further details of Thoreau's activities in these years, see Harding, *The Days of Henry Thoreau*, 261–356; and Borst, *The Thoreau Log*, 110–75.

2. Borst, *The Thoreau Log*, 140.

3. Johnson, *Thoreau's Complex Weave*, 256–58; Fink, *Prophet in the Marketplace*, 241–53.

4. Fink, *Prophet in the Marketplace*, 251.

5. Harding, *The Days of Henry Thoreau*, 231–34. Harding notes that Blake was the recipient of "the longest and most philosophical letters [Thoreau] ever wrote" (213).

6. Harding, *The Days of Henry Thoreau*, 157–59; Petroski, *The Pencil*.

7. Harding, *The Days of Henry Thoreau*, 261–66.

8. Sattelmeyer, " 'When He Became My Enemy,' " 197 and passim.

9. See the discussion of their differences regarding wealth and poverty in Robinson, *Emerson and the Conduct of Life*, 139–46.

10. Thoreau's reference to "Adam" is of particular importance. R. W. B. Lewis has made us aware of the potent cultural implications of the Adamic myth in American culture, and David Shi has more recently reminded us of the persistent power of the ideology of the "simple life" in America. These studies provide helpful frameworks for assessing Thoreau's reactions to the Maine frontier. See in particular Lewis's discussion of Whitman and the "new Adam" (*The American Adam*, 28–53), and Shi's discussion of "Transcendental Simplicity" (*The Simple Life*, 125–53).

11. Bruce Greenfield, reading "Ktaadn" as an example of the genre of "discovery" literature, discusses this contradiction, noting that "Thoreau both admires and deplores what he calls the 'mission' of the lumbermen, with their great energy and appalling greed" ("Thoreau's Discovery of America," 88).

12. For details about the trip, see Cosbey, "Thoreau at Work," 21; and Richardson, *Henry Thoreau*, 179–81.

13. James McIntosh has termed these camps "a symbol of the loggers' immersion in nature" (*Thoreau as Romantic Naturalist*, 193), a comment that is accurate within certain limits. Those limits constitute one of the chief critical problems in the essay.

14. As Robert D. Richardson Jr. has noted, North Twin Lake "was, for Thoreau, the beginning of the real wilderness" (*Henry Thoreau*, 180), and it is here that we begin to see him enact some of his expectations for an experience of the wild.

15. For an engaging discussion of the general importance of fishing to Thoreau's hierarchy of values, with particular reference to the discussions of fishing in Walden, see Sattelmeyer, " 'The True Industry for Poets.' "

16. Sherman Paul wrote that Thoreau had hoped to rediscover the "inspirational powers" of mountains at Ktaadn, "but the ascent of Ktaadn did not work that miracle . . . because he was overcome by a vast, titanic, and inhuman nature" (*The Shores of America*, 360). John C. Blair and Augustus Trowbridge find that the experience on the mountain "threatened [Thoreau's] most basic premise" ("Thoreau on Katahdin," 508) about the interaction of nature and humanity. James McIntosh notes the "deflation of [Thoreau's] adventurous ambition" and finds in his account "an experience of personal and metaphysical shock" (*Thoreau as Romantic Naturalist*, 203). Frederick Garber notes that the summit of Ktaadn is "a land where perception is blocked and therefore the most basic activities of the imagination cannot go to work" (*Thoreau's Redemptive Imagination*, 82). Stephen Adams and Donald Ross Jr. portray Thoreau as "rebellious, defiant, struggling against a hostile environment" (*Revising*

Mythologies, 71). For a persuasive dissent, see Ronald Wesley Hoag ("The Mark on the Wilderness," 30–35), who reads the experience on the summit and "Burnt Lands" in terms of the Burkean sublime.

17. In an important reading of "Ktaadn," Randall Roorda (*Dramas of Solitude*) has noted that the "Burnt Lands" episode was a late addition to the "Ktaadn" draft, and is therefore perhaps in part the result of Thoreau's need to fulfill narrative expectations arising from the motif of "retreat" in nature writing.

18. Thoreau's experience seems to center on a feeling of displacement, a loss of the ordinary human assumption of domination over nature. This recognition can be linked to what contemporary theorists have termed "deep ecology," and "Ktaadn" can, I believe, be very fruitfully read in this context. For a discussion of the emergence of the discourse of "deep ecology" and its reliance on the displacement of the human ego, see Nash, *The Rights of Nature*, 146–51. For an important collection of essays defining this concept, see Devall and Sessions, *Deep Ecology*.

19. "Experience" was an essay that Thoreau knew well, having read proofs of *Essays: Second Series* for Emerson. *Essays: Second Series* is listed as item 473 in Sattelmeyer's "Bibliographical Catalogue" of Thoreau's reading (*Thoreau's Reading*, 173). Robert Milder has connected "Experience" to passages in Thoreau's Journal and to the "Pond in Winter" chapter of *Walden* (*Reimagining Thoreau*, 142–43). See Cavell, *This New Yet Unapproachable America*, 88–91 and 108–9, for an influential analysis of the essay's significance.

20. Linck C. Johnson notes Emerson's enthusiastic reception of "Ktaadn," even at a time in which his friendship with Thoreau was beginning to be complicated by differing expectations, including Emerson's disappointment with *A Week* (*Thoreau's Complex Weave*, 242–43). For further analysis of the difficulties of their friendship in the late 1840s and early 1850s, see Sattelmeyer, "'When He Became My Enemy.'"

21. See the discussion of Thoreau's use of Titan imagery in McIntosh, *Thoreau as Romantic Naturalist*, 201–4.

22. The rhetoric of the passage has been read in quite different terms from those I propose here. John G. Blair and Augustus Trowbridge comment that "the tone is frantic; the mood is one of desperate disturbance. Instead of complete thoughts and sentences, Thoreau uses broken epithets as he grasps for comprehension" ("Thoreau on Katahdin," 511). John Tallmadge argues that "Thoreau's normally pliant syntax becomes brittle and disjointed, finally breaking apart into ejaculatory fragments. We feel, with a twinge of panic, that our narrator is losing control of his material. Language seems to be failing him" ("'Ktaadn,'" 145).

23. Hodder, *Thoreau's Ecstatic Witness*, 299.

24. Robert D. Richardson Jr. characterizes Thoreau's writings about night and moonlight, which were projected at one point as a series of lectures, as "the night piece to balance or complement the sunny moods of *Walden*" (*Henry Thoreau*, 326). For a discussion of the moonlight walks as catalysts of religious perception and experience, see Hodder, *Thoreau's Ecstatic Witness*, 27–29 and 281–84.

25. Dean and Hoag, "Thoreau's Lectures after *Walden*," 254–55. The essay "Night and Moonlight," which drew on these materials, was published posthumously in the *Atlantic Monthly* 12 (November 1863), 579–83, and included in the volume *Excursions*. The final version of this essay apparently was not prepared by Thoreau. William Howarth (*The Literary Manuscripts of Henry David Thoreau*, 335–36) notes that Thoreau worked on the moonlight papers in late 1859 and early 1860, but probably not after that, and concludes that they were edited by either Sophia Thoreau or Ellery Channing. For further discussion of the moonlight papers, see Howarth, "Successor to *Walden*?"; Dean and Hoag, "Thoreau's Lectures after *Walden*"; Hoag, "Thoreau's Later Natural History Writings," 152–53; and Packer, "The Transcendentalists," 588–90.

26. In this context, see Richard Bridgman's discussion of Thoreau's suppressed erotic desire in *Dark Thoreau*, 57–61 and 262–77. Thoreau's sexuality has been discussed in several essays which have explored the psychosexual implications of his passion for nature, his attitude toward women and the feminine, and his sexual orientation. See Gozzi, "Some Aspects of Thoreau's Personality" and "Mother-Nature"; Moller, "Thoreau, Womankind, and Sexuality" and *Thoreau in the Human Community*; Harding, "Thoreau's Sexuality"; Warner, "Thoreau's Bottom"; and Westling, "Thoreau's Ambivalence Toward Mother Nature."

27. Alan D. Hodder observes, "As he reflected more on his moonlight walks later that summer [1851], it seemed to him that sun and moon represented two different states of consciousness, two different orders of reality even" (*Thoreau's Ecstatic Witness*, 28).

7. LIFE WITH PRINCIPLE

1. Dean and Hoag, "Thoreau's Lectures Before *Walden*," 198–200.

2. On the division of "Walking, or the Wild," see ibid., 208–11. For Thoreau's lecture plans in the middle 1850s, and the evolution of "Life Without Principle," see Dean, "Reconstructions of Thoreau's Early 'Life Without Principle' Lectures."

3. Ronald Wesley Hoag explains the essay's stringent demands on the potential disciple: "Simply stated, the principal message of "Walking" is that the boundlessness of nature requires an attempt, however necessarily imperfect, at a corresponding boundlessness on the part of one who would know it, however necessarily imperfectly" ("Thoreau's Later Natural History Writings," 154).

4. For discussions of "Walking" within the context of the larger question of the American westward expansion, see Robinson, "Thoreau's 'Walking' and the Ecological Imperative"; and Schneider, "'Climate Does Thus React on Man.'"

5. As Alan D. Hodder has observed, Thoreau's later Journals record his attempts to open himself completely to the events of nature in a way that transcended his own observing ego. "His greatest ecstasies occurred in moments of sheerest transparency, when nature ran through him like a rushing stream" (*Thoreau's Ecstatic Witness*, 297).

6. Burroughs, "In the Hemlocks," 672.

7. This "ecocentric" perspective, in which the natural world is valued as it is and not as it can be used or even appreciated by humans, is a crucially important Thoreauvian legacy. For a more detailed discussion, see Buell, *The Environmental Imagination*, 115–39.

8. Dean explains that as he began work on the lecture, Thoreau was in part responding to a request for a lecture "of a *reformatory Character*" ("Reconstructions of Thoreau's Early 'Life Without Principle' Lectures," 287).

9. Ibid., 312.

10. For a persuasive case for the overlooked importance of "Life Without Principle" in the Thoreau canon, see Neufeldt, *The Economist*, 70–98. Robert Milder (*Reimagining Thoreau*, 168–70) writes that the lecture suggests Thoreau's lifelong conflict with the values of his fellow townsmen, and also reveals his ambivalence about the purposes and value of lecturing itself.

11. Thoreau's "Civil Disobedience" was first published under the title "Resistance to Civil Government," and that title was restored in the Princeton edition of the *Reform Papers*. I am persuaded, however, by Fritz Oehlschlaeger's argument that that the change in title "from 'Resistance to Civil Government' to 'Civil Disobedience' was part of a pattern of substantive revision by Thoreau himself" ("Another Look at the Text and Title of Thoreau's 'Civil Disobedience,'" 251). See also, in concurrence with this position, Elizabeth Witherell's textual commentary (CEP 659–60). On the early reception of "Civil Disobedience," see

Steven Fink, *Prophet in the Marketplace*, 206–11. For a discussion of Thoreau's later political influence, see Meyer, *Several More Lives to Lead*.

12. On the context and importance of "Civil Disobedience," see Richardson, *Henry Thoreau*, 175–79; Howe, *Making the American Self*, 235–55; Teichgraeber, *Sublime Thoughts/Penny Wisdom*, 113–34; Carton, "The Price of Privilege"; and Rosenwald, "The Theory, Practice, and Influence of Thoreau's 'Civil Disobedience.'"

13. For further details on these cases, see Campbell, *The Slave Catchers*; Collison, *Shadrach Minkins*; and von Frank, *The Trials of Anthony Burns*.

14. For a different reading of "Civil Disobedience" as "a gesture of individual purgation" for Thoreau, see Milder, *Reimagining Thoreau*, 177. As the antislavery and reform movements grew, Thoreau lectured for those interested in reform and wrote for publications for which supporters of reform were the primary audience. For discussion of how his sense of audience shaped "Slavery in Massachusetts," see Fink, "Thoreau and His Audience"; Teichgraeber, *Sublime Thoughts/Penny Wisdom*, 113–34; and Petrulionis, "Editorial Savoir Faire."

15. Packer, "The Transcendentalists," 580–81.

16. For an illuminating discussion of the impact of the Burns affair on Thoreau, and on the New England culture as a whole, see von Frank, *The Trials of Anthony Burns*.

17. For the details of Burns's trial and return, see ibid.

18. My reading of "Slavery in Massachusetts" is in part a response to Lawrence Buell's perceptive analysis of the interpretive problems raised by Thoreau's recourse to the pastoral mode at the end of the essay. See Buell, *The Environmental Imagination*, 36–44.

19. Ibid., 37. On the sign of the lily, see also Albrecht, "Conflict and Resolution," 183–84.

20. See Thoreau's journal entry recounting the discovery of the lily (JP 8:194–96).

21. Buell, *The Environmental Imagination*, 40.

22. On Thoreau's response to John Brown, see Richardson, *Henry Thoreau*, 368–73; Teichgraeber, *Sublime Thoughts/Penny Wisdom*, 135–51; Tauber, *Henry David Thoreau and the Moral Agency of Knowing*, 189–90; and Hyde, "Henry Thoreau, John Brown, and the Problem of Prophetic Action."

8. LEAF, FRUIT, SEED

1. On Thoreau's general health and his tubercular condition, see Harding, *The Days of Henry Thoreau*, 44–45; 357–58, 362–64, and 441–68.

2. Ibid., 457–59.

3. See Bradley P. Dean's edition of Thoreau's *Dispersion of Seeds* in *Faith in a Seed*, and his edition of *Wild Fruits*. For Thoreau's later work as a lecturer and naturalist, see Howarth, *The Book of Concord*; Hildebidle, *Thoreau*, 69–96; Dean and Hoag, "Thoreau's Lectures after Walden"; Rossi, "'The Limits of an Afternoon Walk'" and "Thoreau's Transcendental Ecocentrism"; Milder, *Reimagining Thoreau*, 118–203; Buell, *The Environmental Imagination*; Walls, *Seeing New Worlds* and "Believing in Nature"; McGregor, *A Wider View of the Universe*; Hoag, "Thoreau's Later Natural History Writings"; and Berger, *Thoreau's Late Career*. Berger's book is particularly valuable for making clear the intellectual contexts of Thoreau's work on seed dispersal, and suggesting the unified framework of his later natural history projects. There is a growing body of literature that approaches Thoreau from an "ecocritical" perspective. In addition to the above sources, see the essays in Schneider, *Thoreau's Sense of Place*.

4. See Milder, *Reimagining Thoreau*, 52–56, and Buell, *The Environmental Imagination*, 359–60, for a detailed discussion of the formalist critical assumptions behind the early readings of *Walden*. Milder shows the difficulties that the genesis of the text of *Walden* holds for such a view.

5. See Buell, *The Environmental Imagination*, 362–69, on the "green" Thoreau.

6. Ibid., 131.

7. Michael Benjamin Berger stresses "the interrelatedness of Thoreau's late natural history works," his attempt to create, in reflection of nature itself, "a system of mutually glossing works, establishing various patterns of foregrounding and backgrounding in kaleidoscopic fashion" (*Thoreau's Late Career*, 37–38, 39).

8. Walls, "Believing in Nature," 18.

9. Scheese, "Thoreau's *Journal*," 144. See also Peck, *Thoreau's Morning Work*, 79–114; and Blakemore, "Reading Home." The Journal was capacious and flexible enough to contain notations, meditations, and anything between, and as Alan D. Hodder has noted, it became an important tool in Thoreau's pursuit of a more direct and less mediated relationship with nature. His "efforts to represent his experience journalistically led to a new aesthetic—more concrete, minimalist, and less subjectively reflexive" (*Thoreau's Ecstatic Witness*, 293).

10. Melville, *Moby-Dick*, 144.

11. As Robert D. Richardson Jr. has pointed out, "much of Thoreau's longstanding ambivalence about science—though not about natural history or botany or zoology—can be understood in the context of his long associations with and eventual rejection of the views of Louis Agassiz" (*Henry Thoreau*, 363). Richardson notes in particular Thoreau's rejection of Agassiz's theory of "special creation." For more on Thoreau and Agassiz, and on Thoreau's relationship to modern science, see Walls, *Seeing New Worlds*, 113–16 and 134–47; and Berger, *Thoreau's Late Career*, 48–75.

12. For useful contextual information that sheds light on Thoreau's struggle with the emerging professional disciplines of science, see Jan Golinski's discussion of the "constructivist" approach to the history of science in *Making Natural Knowledge*. As Golinski explains, from the constructivist position, "understandings of 'nature' are products of human labor with the resources that local cultures make available" (47).

13. Thoreau's struggle with the premises of the emerging new science of his day is traced informatively in Baym, "Thoreau's View of Science"; and Hildebidle, *Thoreau*, 69–125.

14. See H. Daniel Peck's discussion of the way Thoreau rejected both the objective scientific view of nature and the "distanced (alienated) 'appreciation' of beauty" common to the aesthetics of his day. As Peck argues, "In his Journal, he is creating, day by day, a new mode of apprehension that mediates between science and art, between 'naturalism' and 'poetry'" (*Thoreau's Morning Work*, 65).

15. Ibid., 54.

16. Dean also points out the Smithsonian Institution's "Registry of Periodical Phenomena," which circulated in 1852, as a possible stimulus for Thoreau's charting of seasonal phenomena. The circular called for observers to record the dates on which each of a list of 127 species flowered in their area.

17. H. Daniel Peck describes this as "an attempt to lay out all of nature's phenomena on a flat plane, that is, to graph their temporality and make a comprehensive picture of time" (*Thoreau's Morning Work*, 47). For a fuller description of Thoreau's "Kalendar" and a reproduction of one of the relevant manuscript pages from the Pierpont Morgan Library, see ibid., 46–48 and 163–66. William Howarth describes the manuscripts in *The Literary Manuscripts of Henry David Thoreau*, 306–31. For additional discussions of Thoreau's conception of a "Kalendar," see Howarth, *The Book of Concord*, 161–89; and Berger, *Thoreau's Late Career*, 34–47.

18. See Witherell, "Thoreau's Watershed Season as a Poet."

19. On the seasonal theme in both *Walden* and the Journal, see Anderson, *The Magic Circle of Walden*, 228–57.

20. "Autumnal Tints" is an integral part of Thoreau's later natural history work, and it

may have been a distillation of his larger project, "The Fall of the Leaf." As Bradley P. Dean and Ronald Wesley Hoag have noted, Thoreau mentioned such a work, but "it is not yet clear if Thoreau kept that project separate or if he subsumed it into one of his other projects, such as the *Wild Fruits* project" ("Thoreau's Lectures after Walden," 296). Lawrence Buell notes that the subject of autumn leaf colors had become a somewhat fashionable topic in the 1850s (*The Environmental Imagination*, 407–8).

21. In a perceptive reading of "Autumnal Tints," Robert Milder observes that the essay's elegiac theme is built on the personification of "falling leaves as falling lives." The essay "operates with the density and symbolic richness of poetry, which it comes nearest to approaching" (*Reimagining Thoreau*, 188, 186).

22. Milder, *Reimagining Thoreau*, 187. For further discussion of Thoreau's philosophical uses of the figure of the leaf, see Sattelmeyer's introduction to Thoreau, *The Natural History Essays*, xxviii–xxx; and Berger, *Thoreau's Late Career*, 107–11.

23. See Michael Benjamin Berger, *Thoreau's Late Career*, 108–116, who sees the scarlet oak leaf as a sign of Thoreau's reconstruction of a holistic symbiosis between empiricism and idealism in his late works.

24. As William Howarth notes, the scarlet oak leaf and the sugar maple serve Thoreau as "emblems of America's future" (*The Book of Concord*, 170).

25. An important recent strand of Thoreau interpretation rooted in the philosophical school of phenomenology has centered on Thoreau's representations of dwelling in and inhabitation of a particular place as fundamental to an understanding of his philosophy and his enactment of it. See Garber, *Thoreau's Fable of Inscribing*; and Peck, *Thoreau's Morning Work*.

26. On the relation of "Wild Apples" to *Wild Fruits* and Thoreau's other late natural history projects, see Howarth, *The Book of Concord*, 165–85; and Berger, *Thoreau's Late Career*, 34–40.

27. Lawrence Buell has called "Wild Apples" "a key naturist work in the Thoreau canon," emphasizing Thoreau's subtle but engaging self-portraiture in the essay (*The Environmental Imagination*, 105–6).

28. For information on Thoreau's relationship to the "Estabrooks" area of Concord, see Ells, "Henry Thoreau and the Estabrook Country"; and Garman et al., " 'This Great Wild Tract.' "

29. For details on Thoreau's connection with Darwin and Darwinian views of nature, see Howarth, *The Book of Concord*, 194–98; Hildebidle, *Thoreau*, 39–51; Richardson, *Henry Thoreau*, 373–84; Buell, *The Environmental Imagination*, 416–23; Walls, *Seeing New Worlds*, 179–99; and Berger, *Thoreau's Late Career*, 48–58. Robert Milder (*Reimagining Thoreau*, 190–203) argues that Thoreau's acceptance of Darwin's theory of natural selection was incomplete.

30. Berger, *Thoreau's Late Career*, 24, 26. Berger discusses the importance of *The Dispersion of Seeds* to Thoreau's later natural history projects, and places the work in the context of mid-nineteenth-century scientific discourse, suggesting that Thoreau was on the cutting edge of research into seed dispersion, a fundamental element in what we now think of as the Darwinian view of natural processes. *The Dispersion of Seeds* has been opened for wider study among literary scholars, ecocritics, and historians of science by Bradley P. Dean's edition of it in *Faith in a Seed*, which has brought much needed attention to Thoreau's later phase.

31. Walls, *Seeing New Worlds*, 179–99.

32. John Hildebidle comments that Thoreau's tone in the essay suggests his recognition of the divergence between the older form of natural history writing and a new form of science (*Thoreau*, 94–96).

33. Berger, *Thoreau's Late Career*, 40.

BIBLIOGRAPHY

Adams, Stephen, and Donald Ross Jr. *Revising Mythologies: The Composition of Thoreau's Major Works*. Charlottesville: University Press of Virginia, 1988.

Agassiz, Louis. "Essay on Classification." In his *Contributions to the Natural History of the United States of America*. 2 vols. Boston: Little, Brown and Company, 1857.

Agassiz, Louis, and Augustus A. Gould. *Principles of Zoology*. Boston: Gould, Kendall and Lincoln, 1848.

Albrecht, Robert C. "Conflict and Resolution: 'Slavery in Massachusetts.'" *ESQ: A Journal of the American Renaissance* 19 (3rd quarter 1973):179–88.

Alcott, Amos Bronson. *Conversations with Children on the Gospels*. Boston: James Munroe and Co., 1836.

Anderson, Charles R. *The Magic Circle of Walden*. New York: Holt, Rinehart and Winston, 1968.

Baym, Nina. "Thoreau's View of Science." *Journal of the History of Ideas* 26 (April–June 1965):221–34.

Bercovitch, Sacvan. *The Puritan Origins of the American Self*. New Haven: Yale University Press, 1975.

———. *The Rites of Assent: Transformations in the Symbolic Construction of America*. New York: Routledge, 1993.

Berger, Michael Benjamin. *Thoreau's Late Career and "The Dispersion of Seeds": The Saunterer's Synoptic Vision*. Rochester, N.Y.: Camden House, 2000.

Blair, John G., and Augustus Trowbridge, "Thoreau on Katahdin." *American Quarterly* 12 (winter 1960):508–17.

Blakemore, Peter. "Reading Home: Thoreau, Literature, and the Phenomenon of In-habitation." In *Thoreau's Sense of Place: Essays in American Environmental Writing*. Ed. Richard J. Schneider. Iowa City: University of Iowa Press, 2000. 115–32.

Borst, Raymond R. *The Thoreau Log: A Documentary Life of Henry David Thoreau, 1817–1862*. New York: G. K. Hall, 1992.

Boudreau, Gordon. *The Roots of Walden and the Tree of Life*. Nashville: Vanderbilt University Press, 1990.

Bridgman, Richard. *Dark Thoreau*. Lincoln: University of Nebraska Press, 1982.

Brownson, Orestes. *New Views of Christianity, Society, and the Church*. 1836. In *The Works of Orestes A. Brownson*. Ed. Henry F. Brownson. Vol. 4. 1882. New York: AMS Press, 1966.

Buell, Lawrence. "American Pastoral Ideology Reappraised." *American Literary History* 1 (spring 1989):1–29.

———. *The Environmental Imagination: Thoreau, Nature Writing, and the Formation of American Culture*. Cambridge: Belknap Press of Harvard University Press, 1995.

———. *Literary Transcendentalism: Style and Vision in the American Renaissance*. Ithaca: Cornell University Press, 1973.

Burroughs, John. "In the Hemlocks." *Atlantic Monthly* 17 (June 1866): 672–84.

Cabot, James E. "Immanuel Kant." *Dial* 4 (April 1844):409–15.

———. "The Philosophy of the Ancient Hindoos." *Massachusetts Quarterly Review* 4 (September 1848): 401–22. Rpt. in Kenneth Walter Cameron, *Transcendental Apprenticeship*. 223–33.

Cameron, Kenneth Walter. *Transcendental Apprenticeship: Notes on Young Henry Thoreau's Reading*. Hartford: Transcendental Books, 1976.

Cameron, Sharon. *Writing Nature: Henry Thoreau's Journal*. New York: Oxford University Press, 1985.

Campbell, Stanley W. *The Slave Catchers: Enforcement of the Fugitive Slave Law, 1850–1860*. Chapel Hill: University of North Carolina Press, 1970.

Canby, Henry Seidel. *Thoreau*. Boston: Beacon, 1939.

Capper, Charles. *Margaret Fuller: An American Romantic Life. The Private Years*. New York: Oxford University Press, 1992.

Carton, Evan. "The Price of Privilege: 'Civil Disobedience' at 150." *American Scholar* 67 (1998):105–12.

Cavell, Stanley. *This New Yet Unapproachable America: Lectures After Emerson After Wittgenstein*. Albuquerque: Living Batch Press, 1989.

———. *The Senses of Walden: An Expanded Edition*. San Francisco: North Point, 1981.

Channing, William Ellery. *Thoreau the Poet-Naturalist*. 1873. New Edition, enl. Ed. F. B. Sanborn. Boston: Charles E. Goodspeed, 1902.

Clapper, Ronald Earl. "The Development of Walden: A Genetic Text." Ph.D Diss., University of California, Los Angeles, 1967.

Collison, Gary. *Shadrach Minkins: From Fugitive Slave to Citizen*. Cambridge: Harvard University Press, 1997.

Cosbey, Robert C. "Thoreau at Work: The Writing of 'Ktaadn.'" *Bulletin of the New York Public Library* 65 (January 1961):21–30.

Cousin, Victor. *Introduction to the History of Philosophy*. Trans. Henning Gotfried Linberg. Boston: Hilliard, Gray, Little, and Wilkins, 1832.

Crain, Caleb. *American Sympathy: Men, Friendship, and Literature in the New Nation*. New Haven: Yale University Press, 2001.

Dean, Bradley P. "Reconstructions of Thoreau's Early 'Life without Principle' Lectures." In *Studies in the American Renaissance 1987*. Ed. Joel Myerson. Charlottesville: University Press of Virginia, 1987. 285–364.

Dean, Bradley P., and Ronald Wesley Hoag. "Thoreau's Lectures after *Walden*: An Annotated Calendar." In *Studies in the American Renaissance 1996*. Ed. Joel Myerson. Charlottesville: The University of Virginia Press, 1996. 241–362.

———. "Thoreau's Lectures before *Walden*: An Annotated Calendar." In *Studies in the American Renaissance 1995*. Ed. Joel Myerson. Charlottesville: The University of Virginia Press 1995. 127–228.

Devall, Bill, and George Sessions, eds. *Deep Ecology: Living as If Nature Mattered*. Salt Lake City: Gibbs M. Smith, 1985.

Ells, Stephen F. "Henry Thoreau and the Estabrook Country: A Historic and Personal Landscape." *Concord Saunterer* 4 (1996):73–148.

Emerson, Ralph Waldo. *The Collected Works of Ralph Waldo Emerson*. Ed. Alfred R. Ferguson et al. 6 vols. to date. Cambridge: Harvard University Press, 1971–. (Abbreviated CW)

———. *The Complete Works of Ralph Waldo Emerson*. Ed. Edward Waldo Emerson [Centenary Edition]. 12 vols. Boston: Houghton Mifflin, 1903–04. (Abbreviated WE).

———. *The Journals and Miscellaneous Notebooks of Ralph Waldo Emerson*. Ed. William H. Gilman, Ralph H. Orth et al. 16 vols. Cambridge: Harvard University Press, 1960–82. (Abbreviated JMN)

———. *The Letters of Ralph Waldo Emerson*. Ed. Ralph L. Rusk (vols. 1–6) and Eleanor Tilton (vols. 7–10). New York: Columbia University Press, 1939–95. (Abbreviated ELet)

Fink, Steven. *Prophet in the Marketplace: Thoreau's Development as a Professional Writer*. Princeton: Princeton University Press, 1992.

———. "Thoreau and His Audience." In *Cambridge Companion to Henry David Thoreau*. Ed. Joel Myerson. Cambridge: Cambridge University Press, 1995. 71–91.

Francis, Richard. *Transcendental Utopias: Individual and Community at Brook Farm, Fruitlands, and Walden*. Ithaca: Cornell University Press, 1997.

Garber, Frederick. *Thoreau's Fable of Inscribing*. Princeton: Princeton University Press, 1991.

———. *Thoreau's Redemptive Imagination*. New York: New York University Press, 1977.

Garman, James C., Paul A. Russo, Stephen A. Mrozowski, and Michael A. Volmar. "'This Great Wild Tract': Henry David Thoreau, Native Americans, and the Archaeology of Estabrook Woods." *Historical Archaeology* 31 (1997):59–80.

Gittleman, Edwin. *Jones Very: The Effective Years, 1833–1840*. New York: Columbia University Press, 1967.

Golemba, Henry. *Thoreau's Wild Rhetoric*. New York: New York University Press, 1990.

Golinski, Jan. *Making Natural Knowledge: Constructivism and the History of Science*. Cambridge: Cambridge University Press, 1998.

Gozzi, Raymond D. "Mother-Nature." In *Henry David Thoreau: A Profile*. Ed. Walter Harding. New York: Hill and Wang, 1971. 172–87.

———. "Some Aspects of Thoreau's Personality." In *Henry David Thoreau: A Profile*. Ed. Walter Harding. New York: Hill and Wang, 1971. 150–71.

Greenfield, Bruce. "Thoreau's Discovery of America: A Nineteenth-Century First Contact." *ESQ: A Journal of the American Renaissance* 32 (2nd quarter 1986): 81–95.

Grodzins, Dean. *American Heretic: Theodore Parker and Transcendentalism*. Chapel Hill: University of North Carolina Press, 2002.

Guarneri, Carl J. *The Utopian Alternative: Fourierism in Nineteenth-Century America*. Ithaca: Cornell University Press, 1991.

Gura, Philip F. "Thoreau's Maine Woods Indians: More Representative Men." *American Literature* 49 (November 1977):366–84.

———. *The Wisdom of Words: Language, Theology, and Literature in the New England Renaissance*. Middletown: Wesleyan University Press, 1981.

Guthrie, James R. *Above Time: Emerson's and Thoreau's Temporal Revolutions*. Columbia: University of Missouri Press, 2001.

Harding, Walter. *The Days of Henry Thoreau: A Biography*. 1962. Princeton: Princeton University Press, 1992.

———. "Thoreau's Sexuality." *Journal of Homosexuality* 23 (1991):23–45.

———. "Thoreau's Text and Murphy's Law." *ESQ: A Journal of the American Renaissance* 33 (4th quarter 1987):207–8.

Harding, Walter, ed. *Henry David Thoreau: A Profile*. New York: Hill and Wang, 1971.

Harding, Walter, and Michael Meyer. *The New Thoreau Handbook*. New York: New York University Press, 1980.

Hawthorne, Nathaniel. *The American Notebooks*. Ed. Claude M. Simpson. In *The Centenary Edition of the Works of Nathaniel Hawthorne*. Vol. 8. Columbus: Ohio State University Press, 1972.

Hildebidle, John. *Thoreau: A Naturalist's Liberty*. Cambridge: Harvard University Press, 1983.

Hoag, Ronald Wesley. "The Mark on the Wilderness: Thoreau's Contact with Ktaadn." *Texas Studies in Literature and Language* 24 (spring 1982):30–35.

———. "Thoreau's Later Natural History Writings." In *Cambridge Companion to Henry David Thoreau*. Ed. Joel Myerson. Cambridge: Cambridge University Press, 1995. 152–70.

Hodder, Alan D. "'Ex Oriente Lux': Thoreau's Ecstasies and the Hindu Texts." *Harvard Theological Review* 86 (1993):403–38.

———. *Thoreau's Ecstatic Witness*. New Haven: Yale University Press, 2001.

Howarth, William. *The Book of Concord: Thoreau's Life as a Writer*. New York: Viking, 1982.

———. *The Literary Manuscripts of Henry David Thoreau*. Columbus: Ohio State University Press, 1974.

———. "Successor to *Walden?* Thoreau's 'Moonlight'—An Intended Course of Lectures." *Proof* 2 (1972): 89–115.

Howe, Daniel Walker. *Making the American Self: Jonathan Edwards to Abraham Lincoln.* Cambridge: Harvard University Press, 1997.

Hyde, Lewis. "Henry Thoreau, John Brown, and the Problem of Prophetic Action." *Raritan* 22, no. 2 (fall 2002): 125–44.

Johnson, Linck C. "Reforming the Reformers: Emerson, Thoreau, and the Sunday Lectures at Amory Hall, Boston." *ESQ: A Journal of the American Renaissance* 37 (4th quarter 1991): 235–89.

———. *Thoreau's Complex Weave: The Writing of "A Week on the Concord and Merrimack Rivers."* Charlottesville: University Press of Virginia, 1986.

———. "*A Week on the Concord and Merrimack Rivers.*" In *The Cambridge Companion to Henry David Thoreau.* Ed. Joel Myerson. New York: Cambridge University Press, 1995. 40–56.

Lebeaux, Richard. *Young Man Thoreau.* Amherst: University of Massachusetts Press, 1977.

Lewis, R. W. B. *The American Adam: Innocence, Tragedy, and Tradition in the Nineteenth Century.* Chicago: University of Chicago Press, 1955.

Lyon, Melvin E. "Walden Pond as Symbol." *PMLA* 82 (May 1967):289–300.

Marx, Leo. *The Machine in the Garden: Technology and the Pastoral Ideal in America.* New York: Oxford University Press, 1964.

Matthiessen, F. O. *American Renaissance: Art and Expression in the Age of Emerson and Whitman.* New York: Oxford University Press, 1941.

McCuskey, Dorothy. *Bronson Alcott, Teacher.* New York: Macmillan, 1940.

McGregor, Robert Kuhn. *A Wider View of the Universe: Henry Thoreau's Study of Nature.* Urbana: University of Illinois Press, 1997.

McIntosh, James. *Thoreau as Romantic Naturalist: His Shifting Stance toward Nature.* Ithaca: Cornell University Press, 1974.

Melville, Herman. *Moby-Dick.* New York: Norton, 1967.

Meyer, Michael. *Several More Lives to Lead: Thoreau's Political Reputation in America.* Westport, Conn.: Greenwood Press, 1977.

Milder, Robert. *Reimagining Thoreau.* New York: Cambridge University Press, 1995.

Miller, Perry. "Individualism and the New England Tradition." 1942. In *The Responsibility of Mind in a Civilization of Machines.* Ed. John Crowell and Sanford J. Searl Jr. Amherst: University of Massachusetts Press, 1979.

Moller, Mary Elkins. *Thoreau in the Human Community.* Amherst: University of Massachusetts Press, 1980.

———. "Thoreau, Womankind, and Sexuality." *ESQ: A Journal of the American Renaissance* 22 (3rd quarter 1976):123–48.

Myerson, Joel. *Emerson and Thoreau: The Contemporary Reviews.* New York: Cambridge University Press, 1992.

———. "More Apropos of John Thoreau." *American Literature* 45 (March 1973): 104–6.

———. *The New England Transcendentalists and the "Dial."* Rutherford: Fairleigh Dickinson University Press, 1980.

Myerson, Joel., ed. *Cambridge Companion to Henry David Thoreau*. New York: Cambridge University Press, 1995.

———. *Transcendentalism: A Reader*. New York: Oxford University Press, 2000. (Abbreviated Trans)

Nash, Roderick Frazier. *The Rights of Nature: A History of Environmental Ethics*. Madison: University of Wisconsin Press, 1989.

Neufeldt, Leonard N. *The Economist: Henry Thoreau and Enterprise*. New York: Oxford University Press, 1989.

———. "Thoreau in His Journal." In *Cambridge Companion to Henry David Thoreau*. Ed. Joel Myerson. New York: Cambridge University Press, 1995. 107–23.

———. "'We Never Agreed . . . in Hardly Anything': Henry Thoreau and Joseph Hosmer." *ESQ: A Journal of the American Renaissance* 35 (2nd quarter 1989):85–107.

O'Connor, Dick. "Thoreau in the Town School, 1837." *Concord Saunterer* 4 (fall 1996):151–72.

Oehlschlaeger, Fritz. "Another Look at the Text and Title of Thoreau's 'Civil Disobedience.'" *ESQ: A Journal of the American Renaissance* 36 (3rd quarter 1990):239–54.

Packer, Barbara. "The Transcendentalists." In *The Cambridge History of American Literature. Vol. 2. Prose Writing, 1820–1865*. Ed. Sacvan Bercovitch. New York: Cambridge University Press, 1995. 329–604.

Parker, Theodore. *A Discourse of Matters Pertaining to Religion*. 1842. New York: Arno Press, 1972.

Paul, Sherman. *The Shores of America: Thoreau's Inward Exploration*. Urbana: University of Illinois Press, 1958.

Peck, H. Daniel. *Thoreau's Morning Work: Memory and Perception in "A Week on the Concord and Merrimack Rivers," the "Journal," and "Walden."* New Haven: Yale University Press, 1990.

Peckham, Morse. *Beyond the Tragic Vision: The Quest for Identity in the Nineteenth Century*. New York: George Braziller, 1962.

Petroski, Henry. *The Pencil: A History of Design and Circumstance*. New York, Alfred A. Knopf, 1999.

Petrulionis, Sandra Harbert. "Editorial Savoir Faire: Thoreau Transforms His Journal into 'Slavery in Massachusetts.'" *Resources for American Literary Study* 25 (1999):206–31.

Richardson, Robert D. Jr. *Henry Thoreau: A Life of the Mind*. Berkeley: University of California Press, 1986.

Robinson, David M. *Apostle of Culture: Emerson as Preacher and Lecturer*. Philadelphia: University of Pennsylvania Press, 1982.

———. *Emerson and the Conduct of Life: Pragmatism and Ethical Purpose in the Later Work*. New York: Cambridge University Press, 1993.

———. "Margaret Fuller and the Transcendental Ethos: *Woman in the Nineteenth Century*." *PMLA* 97 (January 1982):83–98.

———. "Thoreau's 'Walking' and the Ecological Imperative." In *Approaches to Teaching Henry David Thoreau's "Walden."* Ed. Richard Schneider. New York: Modern Language Association, 1996. 167–74.

Ronda, Bruce. *Elizabeth Palmer Peabody: A Reformer on Her Own Terms*. Cambridge: Harvard University Press, 1999.

Roorda, Randall. *Dramas of Solitude: Narratives of Retreat in American Nature Writing*. Albany: State University of New York Press, 1998.

Rose, Anne C. *Transcendentalism as a Social Movement, 1830–1850*. New Haven: Yale University Press, 1981.

Rosenwald, Lawrence A. "The Theory, Practice, and Influence of Thoreau's 'Civil Disobedience.'" In *A Historical Guide to Henry David Thoreau*. Ed. William E. Cain. New York: Oxford University Press, 2000. 153–79.

Rossi, William. "Education in the Field: Recent Thoreau Criticism and Environment." *ESQ: A Journal of the American Renaissance* 42 (2nd quarter 1996): 125–51.

———. "'The Limits of an Afternoon Walk': Coleridgean Polarity in Thoreau's 'Walking.'" *ESQ: A Journal of the American Renaissance* 33 (2nd quarter 1987): 94–109.

———. "Thoreau's Transcendental Ecocentrism." In *Thoreau's Sense of Place: Essays in American Environmental Writing*. Ed. Richard J. Schneider. Iowa City: University of Iowa Press, 2000. 28–43.

Ryan, Barbara. "Emerson's 'Domestic and Social Experiments': Service, Slavery, and the Unhired Man." *American Literature* 66 (1994): 485–508.

Sattelmeyer, Robert. Introduction to Henry David Thoreau, *The Natural History Essays*. Salt Lake City: Peregrine Smith, 1980.

———. "The Remaking of *Walden*." In *Writing the American Classics*. Ed. James Barbour and Tom Quirk. Chapel Hill: University of North Carolina Press, 1990. 53–78.

———. "Thoreau and Emerson." In *The Cambridge Companion to Henry David Thoreau*. Ed. Joel Myerson. New York: Cambridge University Press, 1995. 25–39.

———. "Thoreau's Projected Work on the English Poets." In *Studies in the American Renaissance 1980*. Ed. Joel Myerson. Boston: Twayne, 1980. 239–57.

———. *Thoreau's Reading: A Study in Intellectual History with Bibliographical Catalogue*. Princeton: Princeton University Press, 1988.

———. "'The True Industry for Poets': Fishing with Thoreau." *ESQ: A Journal of the American Renaissance* 33 (4th quarter 1978): 189–201.

———. "A Walk to More than Wachusett." *Thoreau Society Bulletin*, no. 202 (1992):1–4.

———. "'When He Became My Enemy': Emerson and Thoreau, 1948–49." *New England Quarterly* 62 (1989): 187–204.

Sayre, Robert F. *Thoreau and the American Indians*. Princeton: Princeton University Press, 1977.

Scharnhorst, Gary. *Henry David Thoreau: An Annotated Bibliography of Comment and Criticism before 1900*. New York: Garland, 1992.

Scheese, Don. "Thoreau's *Journal*: The Creation of a Sacred Space." In *Mapping American Culture*. Ed. Wayne Franklin and Michael Steiner. Iowa City: University of Iowa Press, 1992). 139–51.

Schneider, Richard J. "'Climate Does Thus React on Man': Wildness and Geographic Determinism in Thoreau's 'Walking.'" In *Thoreau's Sense of Place: Essays in American Environmental Writing*. Ed. Richard J. Schneider. Iowa City: University of Iowa Press, 1999. 44–60.

Schneider, Richard J., ed. *Thoreau's Sense of Place: Essays in American Environmental Writing*. Iowa City: University of Iowa Press, 1999.

Schulz, Dieter, *Amerikanischer Transzendentalismus: Ralph Waldo Emerson, Henry David Thoreau, Margaret Fuller*. Darmstadt: Wissenschaftliche Buchgesellschaft, 1997.

Shanley, J. Lyndon. *The Making of Walden*. Chicago: University of Chicago Press, 1957.

Shi, David. *The Simple Life: Plain Living and High Thinking in American Culture*. New York: Oxford University Press, 1985.

Smith, Harmon. *My Friend, My Friend: The Story of Thoreau's Relationship with Emerson*. Amherst: University of Massachusetts Press, 1999.

Stevenson, Robert Louis. *Familiar Studies of Men and Books*. In *The Works of Robert Louis Stevenson*. Vol. 5. South Seas Edition. New York: Charles Scribner's Sons, 1925.

Strauch, Carl F. "Hatred's Swift Repulsions: Emerson, Margaret Fuller, and Others." *Studies in Romanticism* 7 (winter 1968): 65–103.

Sundquist, Eric J. *Home as Found: Authority and Genealogy in Nineteenth-Century American Literature*. Baltimore: Johns Hopkins University Press, 1979.

Tallmadge, John. "'Ktaadn': Thoreau in the Wilderness of Words." *ESQ: A Journal of the American Renaissance* 31 (3rd quarter 1985): 137–48.

Tauber, Alfred I. *Henry David Thoreau and the Moral Agency of Knowing*. Berkeley: University of California Press, 2001.

Teichgraeber, Richard F. III. *Sublime Thoughts/Penny Wisdom: Situating Emerson and Thoreau in the American Market*. Baltimore: Johns Hopkins University Press, 1995.

Thoreau, Henry David. *Collected Essays and Poems*. Ed. Elizabeth Hall Witherell. New York: Library of America, 2001. (Abbreviated CEP)

———. *Correspondence*. Ed. Walter Harding and Carl Bode. New York: New York University Press, 1958. (Abbreviated Corr)

———. *Early Essays and Miscellanies*. Ed. Joseph J. Moldenhauer and Edwin Moser, with Alexander C. Kern. Princeton: Princeton University Press, 1975. (Abbreviated EEM)

———. *Faith in a Seed: "The Dispersion of Seeds" and Other Late Natural History Writings*. Ed. Bradley P. Dean. Washington, D.C.: Island Press, 1993. (Abbreviated FS)

———. *Journal*. Ed. John C. Broderick, Robert Sattelmeyer, Elizabeth Hall Witherell et al. 7 vols. to date. Princeton: Princeton University Press, 1981–. (Abbreviated JP)

———. *The Journal of Henry D. Thoreau*. Ed. Bradford Torrey and Francis H. Allen. 14 vols. Boston: Houghton Mifflin, 1906. (Abbreviated J)

———. *The Maine Woods*. Ed. Joseph J. Moldenhauer. Princeton: Princeton University Press, 1972. (Abbreviated MW)

———. *The Natural History Essays*. Ed. Robert Sattelmeyer. Salt Lake City: Peregrine Smith Books, 1980.

———. "Night and Moonlight." *Atlantic Monthly* 12 (November 1863):579–83.

———. *Reform Papers*. Ed. Wendell Glick. Princeton: Princeton University Press, 1978. (Abbreviated RP)

———. *Walden*. Ed. J. Lyndon Shanley. Princeton: Princeton University Press, 1971. (Abbreviated Wa)

———. *A Week on the Concord and Merrimack Rivers*. Ed. Carl Hovde et al. Princeton: Princeton University Press, 1980. (Abbreviated Week)

————. *Wild Fruits: Thoreau's Rediscovered Last Manuscript*. Ed. Bradley P. Dean. New York: Norton, 1999. (Abbreviated WF)

Tillman, James S. "The Transcendental Georgic in *Walden*." *ESQ: A Journal of the American Renaissance* 21 (3rd quarter 1975): 137–41.

Versluis, Arthur. *American Transcendentalism and Asian Religions*. New York: Oxford University Press, 1993.

Von Frank, Albert J. *An Emerson Chronology*. New York: G. K. Hall, 1994.

————. *The Trials of Anthony Burns: Freedom and Slavery in Emerson's Boston*. Cambridge: Harvard University Press, 1998.

Walls, Laura Dassow. "Believing in Nature: Wilderness and Wildness in Thoreauvian Science." In *Thoreau's Sense of Place: Essays in American Environmental Writing*. Ed. Richard J. Schneider. Iowa City: University of Iowa Press, 2000. 15–27.

————. *Seeing New Worlds: Henry David Thoreau and Nineteenth-Century Natural Science*. Madison: University of Wisconsin Press, 1995.

Warner, Michael. "Thoreau's Bottom." *Raritan* 11 (winter 1992): 53–79.

West, Michael. *Transcendental Wordplay: America's Romantic Punsters and the Search for the Language of Nature*. Athens: Ohio University Press, 2000.

Westling, Louise. "Thoreau's Ambivalence toward Mother Nature." *ISLE: Interdisciplinary Studies in Literature and Environment* 1 (spring 1993): 145–50.

Witherell, Elizabeth. "Thoreau's Watershed Season as a Poet: The Hidden Fruits of the Summer and Fall of 1841." In *Studies in the American Renaissance, 1990*. Ed. Joel Myerson. Charlottesville: University Press of Virginia, 1990. 49–106.

Woodson, Thomas. "Thoreau on Poverty and Magnanimity." *PMLA* 85 (January 1970): 21–34.

Zwarg, Christina. *Feminist Conversations: Fuller, Emerson, and the Play of Reading*. Ithaca: Cornell University Press, 1995.

INDEX

Adams, Stephen, 208, 211, 214
Aeschylus, 104
Agassiz, Louis, 115–16, 181, 182, 213, 218
Albrecht, Robert C., 217
Alcott, Abigail, 84, 206
Alcott, Amos Bronson, 30, 84–85
Anderson, Charles R., 210, 211, 212, 213, 218
Atlantic Monthly, 176

Ball, Nehemiah, 31, 206
Baym, Nina, 218
Bercovitch, Sacvan, 211
Berger, Michael Benjamin, 198, 201, 213, 217, 218, 219
Blair, John C., 214, 215
Blake, H. G. O., 127, 128, 203, 214
Blakemore, Peter, 218
Borst, Raymond, 208, 214
botany, see Thoreau, scientific studies
Boudreau, Gordon V., 123, 212, 213
Bridgman, Richard, 209, 216
Brook Farm, 30, 84, 211
Brown, John, 149–50, 175, 217
Brownson, Orestes, 12–18, 26, 30–31, 35, 56, 101, 112, 205, 206

Buddhism, 54–57
Buell, Lawrence, 43, 174–75, 177, 207, 209, 210, 211, 213, 216, 217, 218, 219
Burns, Anthony, 6, 168–75, 217
Burroughs, John, 159, 216

Cabot, James E., 112, 116–18, 213
Calvinism, 12
Cameron, Kenneth Walter, 213
Cameron, Sharon, 206
Campbell, Stanley W., 217
Canby, Henry Seidel, 80–81, 205, 206, 210, 211
Capper, Charles, 206, 210
Carton, Evan, 217
Cavell, Stanley, 97, 104, 212, 213, 215
Channing, (William) Ellery (1817–1901), 52, 206
Channing, William Ellery (1780–1842), 12, 18
Chaucer, Geoffrey, 39
Christian Examiner, 13
Christianity, 12–15, 53–57, 205–06
Clapper, Ronald E., 213
Coleridge, Samuel Taylor, 212
Collison, Gary, 217

Cosbey, Robert C., 214
Cousin, Victor, 13–16, 112, 205

Darwin, Charles, 7, 115, 177, 196, 198, 213, 219
Dean, Bradley P., 8, 149, 150, 162, 176, 185, 211, 213, 215, 216, 217, 218, 219
Devall, Bill, 215
Dial, 3, 34, 38, 39, 40, 50, 51, 53, 112, 208
Dustan, Hannah, 73–74, 210

eclecticism, 13, 112; see also Cousin, Victor
ecology, 5–8, 20–28, 34–38, 40–47, 74–76, 89–99, 108–47, 157–61, 176–203, 211, 215, 217, 218, 219
Ells, Stephen F., 219
environment, see ecology
Emerson, Charles, 50
Emerson, Lidian, 33, 80–81, 126, 141, 210–11
Emerson, Ralph Waldo, 3, 10–12, 14–19, 23, 26, 28, 32–35, 38, 40, 48, 50–52, 53, 61, 62, 64–72, 77–81, 84–86, 101, 102, 110–21, 126–29, 136–39, 141, 156, 177, 180–81, 185, 202–03, 205, 206, 209, 210, 212, 215
Emerson, Waldo (son of Ralph Waldo Emerson), 32–33, 138, 207
Emerson, William, 50–51
Evelyn, John, 185

Fink, Steven, 51, 126–27, 206, 207, 208, 210, 214, 217
Fourierism, 84–85
Francis, Richard, 208, 211
Fruitlands, 84–85, 211
Fuller, Margaret, 38, 44, 51, 206, 210
Fuller, Richard, 44

Garber, Frederick, 58, 209, 212, 214, 219
Garman, James C., 219
Garrison, William Lloyd, 172
Gesner, Conrad, 182
Gittleman, Edwin, 205–06
Goethe, Johann Wolfgang von, 14, 42–43, 186–87, 207, 210, 213
Golemba, Henry, 209
Golinski, Jan, 218
Gould, A. A., 213
Gozzi, Raymond, 216

Greeley, Horace, 51, 208, 211
Greenfield, Bruce, 214
Grodzins, Dean, 208
Guarneri, Carl J., 208, 211
Gura, Philip F., 212, 213

Harding, Walter, 32, 206, 208, 209, 210, 211, 212, 214, 216, 217
Harvard College, 11, 12, 15, 28, 38, 39, 44, 115–16, 181
Hawthorne, Nathaniel, 50–51, 208
Heidegger, Martin, 212
higher law, 171–73
Hildebidle, John, 213, 217, 218, 219
Hinduism, 35, 39, 53–57, 101, 117–19, 206, 207, 208, 213
Hoag, Ronald Wesley, 211, 215, 216, 217, 219
Hodder, Alan D., 139, 206, 207, 208, 213, 215, 216, 218
Homer, 39, 44, 103, 104
Hosmer, Joseph, 211
Howarth, William, 206, 215, 217, 218, 219
Howe, Daniel Walker, 205, 217
Humboldt, Alexander von, 44, 212
Hyde, Lewis, 217

idealism, 13, 15, 108–24, 177, 201, 212
Indian, see Native American

Johnson, Linck C., 49, 58, 60, 64, 207, 208, 209, 214, 215

Kant, Immanuel, 13

Lane, Charles, 84–85
leaf, 36–38, 42–43, 49–50, 146, 160–61, 185–91, 207, 213, 218–19
Lebaux, Richard, 206, 209
Lewis, R. W. B., 214
Locke, John, 13
Loring, Edward G., 170
Lyon, Melvin E., 213

Marx, Leo, 90, 211
materialism, 12–13
Matthiessen, F. O., 212
McCuskey, Dorothy, 206
McGregor, Robert Kuhn, 111, 212, 213, 217

McIntosh, James, 214, 215
Melville, Herman, 22, 180–81, 206, 218
Mexican War, 55, 211
Meyer, Michael, 211, 217
Milder, Robert, 187, 206, 208, 212, 213, 215, 216, 217, 219
Miller, Perry, 86, 211
Milton, John, 73–74
Minkins, Shadrach, 168
Moller, Mary Elkins, 210–11, 216
Myerson, Joel, 206, 208

Nash, Roderick Frazier, 215
Native American, 39, 46–47, 93–99, 212
natural life, 1–2, 40–43, 74–83, 127–30, 143–47, 155–61, 178–85
nature, see ecology
Neufeldt, Leonard N., 205, 206, 211, 216
New York Tribune, 51

O'Connor, Dick, 32–33, 206
Oelschlaeger, Fritz, 216
old naturalists, 182–85
Ossian, 39

Packer, Barbara, 40, 169, 207, 210, 211, 215, 217
Parker, Theodore, 54, 86, 126, 208
pastoralism, 77–99, 174, 211, 217
Paul, Sherman, 40–41, 58, 90, 207, 211, 212, 213, 214
Peabody, Elizabeth Palmer, 30, 51, 206
Peck, H. Daniel, 58, 114, 184, 206, 209, 212, 213, 218, 219
Petroski, Henry, 208, 214
Petrulionis, Sandra Harbert, 217
Plato, 112

Richardson, Robert D., Jr., 117, 123, 205, 206, 207, 208, 209, 210, 211, 212, 213, 214, 215, 217, 218, 219
Robinson, David M., 205, 210, 214, 216
Ronda, Bruce, 206
Roorda, Randall, 215
Rose, Anne C., 211
Rosenwald, Lawrence, 217
Ross, Donald, Jr., 209, 211, 214
Rossi, William, 149, 213, 217
Rowlandson, Mary, 46
Ryan, Barbara, 208

Sattelmeyer, Robert, 15, 38, 101, 126, 128, 205, 206, 207, 209, 210, 211, 212, 213, 214, 215, 219
Sayre, Robert F., 97, 212
Scharnhorst, Gary, 208
Scheese, Don, 180, 206, 218
Schneider, Richard J., 211, 216, 217
Schulz, Dieter, 212, 213
science, see Thoreau, scientific studies
self-culture, 18–28, 30, 157, 164–65, 178, 186, 205
Sessions, George, 215
Sewall, Ellen, 62–63, 209
Shanley, J. Lyndon, 100–01, 214
Shi, David, 214
Sims, Thomas, 168
slavery, 6, 101, 149–50, 166–75, 217
Smith, Harmon, 210, 211
Stevenson, Robert Louis, 20, 205
Strauch, Carl F., 210
Sundquist, Eric J., 210

Tallmadge, John, 215
Tauber, Alfred I., 210, 217
Teichgraeber, Richard F., III, 206, 210, 217
Thatcher, George, 132
Thoreau, Henry David: "border life," 157–61; farming, 88–89, 103, 130–32, 211; friendship, 3, 11–12, 32–33, 48–76, 141–43, 209; health, 33, 40–43, 49–50, 62–63, 119, 176–77, 206–07, 217; houses, 52, 101, 128; moonlight walks, 4–5, 140–47, 157, 160, 174, 215–16; New York sojourn, 50–52, 125, 127, 210; political thinking, 6–7, 148–75; poetic aspirations, 28, 32–40, 147, 207; scientific studies, 5–6, 18–19, 40–43, 101, 108–24, 147, 150, 176–203, 217, 218, 219; sexuality, 62–63, 79–81, 141–43, 216; teaching, 2–3, 12, 28–33, 206; vocational struggles, 18–19, 29–52, 78–79, 126–30
Thoreau, Henry David, works: "Autumnal Tints," 7–8, 185–92, 218–19; "Civil Disobedience," 7, 55, 77, 79, 126, 166–68, 216–17; *Dispersion of Seeds*, 5–6, 149, 178, 197–201, 217, 219; "The Fall of the Leaf," 36–38, 185, 218–19; "Inspiration" 35–36; "The Inward Morning," 209; Journal, 5–7, 9–11, 18–28, 34–35, 43, 49–50, 52, 59, 78–82, 101, 123, 140–51,

Thoreau, Henry David (continued)
162, 177–85, 193, 202–03, 206, 215, 216,
218; Kalendar, 7, 149, 185, 218;
"Ktaadn," 4, 47, 57, 77, 79, 126, 129–41,
144–45, 157, 174, 209, 214–15; "The Last
Days of John Brown," 175; "Life without Principle," 7–8, 161–66, 216;
"Moonlight," 150–51; "Natural History
of Massachusetts," 40–43, 48–49; "Resistance to Civil Government," see
"Civil Disobedience,"; "Slavery In Massachusetts," 6–7, 167–75; "The Succession of Forest Trees," 198, 200–01;
Walden, 3–4, 10, 23, 40, 42, 47, 59, 71,
76, 77–130, 140, 146, 148–51, 153, 161,
164, 166–69, 176–77, 186, 187, 189, 191,
197, 202, 213, 214, 217, 218; "A Walk to
Wachusett," 43–47, 207; "Walking," 5,
150–62, 192, 216; "Walking, or the
Wild" (lectures), 140, 150, 161–62, 216;
A Week on the Concord and Merrimack
Rivers, 1–3, 38, 39, 40, 47, 53–76, 123,
126–27, 130, 141, 189, 208, 209, 215;
"What Shall It Profit," (lecture) 151;
"The Wild," (lecture) 150; "Wild
Apples," 7–8, 189, 193–97, 219; Wild
Fruits, 5–6, 149, 178, 191–93, 201, 217,
219

Thoreau, John, 1–4, 32–33, 40–44, 48–77,
128, 138, 139, 203, 206–07
Tillman, James S., 211
transcendentalism, 3, 12–15, 29–30, 53–54,
58, 61–62, 64–65, 70, 74, 101, 116, 164,
186, 200, 205–06, 208, 209
Trowbridge, Augustus 214, 215

Unitarianism, 12, 30
Universalism, 12

Versluis, Arthur, 208
Very, Jones, 205–06
Virgil, 44, 45, 47
von Frank, Albert J., 209, 210, 217

Walls, Laura Dassow, 116, 149, 178, 198,
209, 212, 213, 218, 219
Warner, Michael, 216
West, Michael, 212, 213
Westling, Louise, 216
Whitman, Walt, 214
Witherell, Elizabeth, 34–35, 206, 207, 216,
218
Woodson, Thomas, 211
Wordsworth, William, 14, 89

Zwarg, Christina, 210